AF698859

Invisible Indians

LAKE ERIE
NEW YORK
OHIO
WEST VIRGINIA
MARYLAND
DELAWARE
NEW JERSEY
ERIE
CRAWFORD
MERCER
LAWRENCE
BEAVER
BUTLER
VENANGO
WARREN
FOREST
CLARION
ARMSTRONG
ALLEGHENY
WASHINGTON
GREENE
FAYETTE
WESTMORELAND
INDIANA
JEFFERSON
ELK
McKEAN
POTTER
CAMERON
CLEARFIELD
CAMBRIA
SOMERSET
BEDFORD
BLAIR
CENTRE
CLINTON
TIOGA
LYCOMING
HUNTINGDON
FULTON
FRANKLIN
MIFFLIN
JUNIATA
PERRY
CUMBERLAND
ADAMS
YORK
UNION
SNYDER
NORTHUMBERLAND
DAUPHIN
LEBANON
LANCASTER
BRADFORD
SULLIVAN
COLUMBIA
SCHUYLKILL
BERKS
CHESTER
SUSQUEHANNA
WYOMING
LACKAWANNA
LUZERNE
CARBON
LEHIGH
MONTGOMERY
BUCKS
WAYNE
PIKE
MONROE

INVISIBLE INDIANS

Native Americans in Pennsylvania

David J. Minderhout and Andrea T. Frantz

CAMBRIA PRESS
AMHERST, NEW YORK

Copyright 2008 David J. Minderhout and Andrea T. Frantz

All rights reserved
Printed in the United States of America

No part of this publication may be reproduced, stored in or introduced into a retrieval system, or transmitted, in any form, or by any means (electronic, mechanical, photocopying, recording, or otherwise), without the prior permission of the publisher.

Requests for permission should be directed to permissions@cambriapress.com, or mailed to: Cambria Press, 20 Northpointe Parkway, Suite 188, Amherst, New York 14228.

Cover image reproduced with the kind permission of James Baxter

Library of Congress Cataloging-in-Publication Data

Minderhout, David Jay, 1947-
Invisible Indians : Native Americans in Pennsylvania / David J. Minderhout and Andrea T. Frantz.
p. cm.
Includes bibliographical references and index.
ISBN 978-1-60497-511-6 (alk. paper)
1. Indians of North America—Pennsylvania—Government relations. 2. Indians of North America—Legal status, laws, etc.—Pennsylvania. 3. Indians of North America—Pennsylvania—Social conditions. 4. Pennsylvania—Ethnic relations. 5. Pennsylvania—Social conditions. I. Frantz, Andrea T. II. Title.

E78.P4M63 2008
323.1197048—dc22

2008005639

Illustrations by Sarah L. Nemeth

Table of Contents

List of Boxes

List of Illustrations

Acknowledgments

This book began as an undergraduate independent study project in September 2004 conducted by Andrea T. Frantz, who was then a junior at Bloomsburg University of Pennsylvania; David J. Minderhout was her supervising professor. She began her research by attending powwows in northeastern and southeastern Pennsylvania, where she distributed surveys to people claiming Native American ancestry at those events. It soon became apparent that there were a great many people in Pennsylvania claiming native ancestry, but public institutions refused to admit their existence. As the project grew, we expanded our research to other parts of the state, as well as tribal organizations, and we extended interviews with a sample of our informants.

The inspiration for this book came upon reading *More Than Black: Afro-Cubans in Tampa*, by Susan D. Greenbaum (2002). Greenbaum had interviewed members of the African-American/Cuban community in the Tampa area (especially Ybor City) who had been overlooked by city planners and municipal, state, and federal officials in the 1960s and 1970s as Tampa began to reinvent itself and urban renewal got underway.

Greenbaum's informants represented an invisible community in Tampa, just as the people we were interviewing were invisible to Pennsylvanians. A library search revealed that there was no text that described Native Americans in contemporary Pennsylvania, though a variety of historical works existed that talked about American Indians in the 17th and 18th centuries. When we asked our informants what they most would like to say to Pennsylvanians, the most common response was "We are still here." This book is intended to make that point.

As we conducted our research and began writing this book, we received some much-needed help. A small grant from Bloomsburg University's Kozloff Undergraduate Research Fund provided some initial financial help. Dr. Jim Dalton introduced us to the psychology literature on ethnic identity in the United States. Mr. Donald Repsher, historian for the Lenape Nation, provided us with advice and historical references. David Ramsey was a source of encouragement and support. Bethany Klein helped us transcribe our tape-recorded interviews, and Angela M. Jackson helped us prepare the final version of this manuscript. Sarah L. Nemeth provided us with the illustrations found within the text.

The cover illustration was donated by James Baxter. It represents a sculpture done by him of Mesing'w, the Lenape Keeper of the Game. We appreciate his generous support.

We especially wish to thank the many Native Americans who welcomed us into their homes and to their events. One of the people we interviewed told us, "But nobody seems to try to really understand the native people. I don't understand that because they're good people. I think they're great. They're a giving people, a sharing people." We certainly found that statement to be true. Without the cooperation of the people we interviewed, as well as the event organizers and the officers of native organizations, this book would not have been possible.Our interviews were conducted with the understanding that we would not share the identities of those who spoke with us, and, thus, we refer to those who spoke to us only in general terms (e.g., a Mohawk woman from Bradford County). The only exceptions to this practice were those who gave us explicit written consent to use their names or persons associated with specific organizations whose names are a matter of public record.

We also wish to thank the staff of Cambria Press for all their help and hard work.

Finally, we wish to thank Bonnie Minderhout and Joshua Ramsey for their patience and encouragement throughout this project.

Invisible Indians

INTRODUCTION

There are no Indians in Pennsylvania.

This was a phrase we heard repeated often as we began our research. If there were Native Americans in the state, public institutions certainly did not admit their existence. Pennsylvania is one of very few states that neither contain a reservation nor officially recognize any Native American group within its borders. This is ironic, because Pennsylvania was one of the first places where Europeans came in contact with Native Americans. Pennsylvania culture heroes like William Penn and Conrad Weiser are known in large part because of their interactions with native peoples. For a time during the 18th century, Pennsylvania was a sanctuary for Native Americans from all over colonial America, and Tuscaroras, Conoys, Nanticokes, and others migrated into the area. In time, however, the press of European settlement and the spread of smallpox both severely reduced the number of Native Americans and drove them westward. As far as contemporary textbooks go, the history of Native Americans in the state ends in the late 18th century.

This lack of official interest in Native Americans is reflected in the state's educational institutions. Pennsylvania is the only state without a university-level Native American studies center or program. Inquiries with museums and academic departments in the state were met with puzzlement: Time and again, we were told that no one knew any contemporary, living Native Americans. The four major anthropology graduate schools in the state—the Pennsylvania State University, the University of Pennsylvania, the University of Pittsburgh, and Temple University—listed no one as a specialist in contemporary Native Americans. Similarly, the authors of history books about Native Americans from the 17th and 18th centuries that we interviewed told us they did not know of any American Indians in the state now. This sentiment was echoed when we contacted the Delaware Nation in Oklahoma to ask them if they knew any Delawares or Lenapes still living in Pennsylvania. The tribal secretary replied, "As far as we know, there are no Lenape in Pennsylvania today" (personal communication, October 24, 2004).

Yet we knew that this could not be true. According to the U.S. Census, 18,348 people in Pennsylvania indicated they were Native Americans in 2000—an increase of 50% since 1990. Another 34,302 people indicated they had some Native American ancestry. Barely a weekend went by without a scheduled powwow or gathering somewhere in the state. There were occasional newspaper stories about school programs or patriotic celebrations featuring local Native Americans. Most of all, we knew people who claimed Native American ancestry—not many, to be sure, but a few nonetheless.

Therefore, in September 2004 we began attending powwows and tribal gatherings to learn more about the resident Native American population. To help us understand who these people were, we developed a survey with 22 questions (see Appendix A). The questions we asked were directed toward four primary goals:

1. How did the respondents see themselves—were they Native Americans, American Indians, Lenape, or some other ethnic group?

2. How familiar were they with their legal status—or lack thereof—within the state?
3. How did they feel about Native American issues nationwide, such as self-determination on reservations, casino gambling, or the use of Native American symbols as team mascots?
4. What did they see as the most important issues facing them in Pennsylvania today?

We set up tables at powwows and invited attendees to complete the survey. We also searched for Native Americans through the Internet and invited them to participate. As we met interested people, we asked them to distribute surveys to their friends. When possible, we sat down with people and asked them for more detail in regard to their responses. For the most part, the response to this effort was positive. Powwow organizers made an effort to give us a good location, one where attendees could not help but pass by our display. We used brightly colored posters and signs to attract attention to our effort. We also learned about the various Native American organizations in the state and received invitations to attend their council meetings. Most people were friendly and encouraging. Unfortunately, not all the surveys we received were usable. Some people indicated that while they were interested in American Indians and were sympathetic to their issues, they were not Native Americans themselves or were uncertain about their own backgrounds.

Eventually, we collected 281 usable surveys. One hundred and forty-nine women responded to the survey, along with 132 men. Fifty of the people responding were between the ages of 18 and 30, 80 people were aged 31–43, 95 people were aged 44–56, 49 were aged 57–69, and 6 people were aged 70–82. The respondents came from 49 of the 67 counties that make up the state of Pennsylvania. Twenty-five different tribal identities were claimed among those who chose to name a specific tribe. Lenape/Delaware was the most common identity claimed by the respondents, followed by Cherokee.

The surveys revealed a great deal. We found with regard to some issues that there was a great deal of variation in people's responses. For example, our respondents basically were evenly divided on the question of casino gambling. The use of team mascots invoked angry opposition in some people, indifference in others, and positive responses from some. Most people knew that Native Americans in Pennsylvania did not have reservations, state or federal recognition, or special hunting

Box 1. Pennsylvania counties represented in survey and interview samples.

Allegheny	Lancaster
Armstrong	Lebanon
Beaver	Lehigh
Bedford	Luzerne
Berks	Lycoming
Blair	Mercer
Bradford	Mifflin
Bucks	Monroe
Carbon	Montgomery
Centre	Montour
Chester	Northumberland
Clarion	Perry
Clearfield	Philadelphia
Clinton	Pike
Columbia	Schuylkill
Crawford	Snyder
Cumberland	Sullivan
Dauphin	Tioga
Delaware	Union
Erie	Venango
Forest	Warrington
Huntington	Wayne
Jefferson	Westmoreland
Juniata	Wyoming
Lackawanna	York

or fishing privileges. Census data had revealed that Native Americans earned an average of 74% of what other Pennsylvanians make and that they were four times more likely to be unemployed. But respondents did not list economic rehabilitation or jobs as their greatest needs. Rather, they felt that return of traditional lands, self-determination on reservations, and better representation in Washington, D.C. were more important issues. There were two issues on which almost everyone agreed: 98% of those that responded agreed that not enough was being taught in Pennsylvania's schools about Native Americans and much of what was taught was inaccurate.

Participants in the survey were encouraged to add written comments at the end of the questionnaire, and many did. Some took the time to fill out one or more pages with written commentary. These comments often expressed anger or frustration at being a Native American in the state. Samples include:

- Pennsylvania has got to be the worst in its treatment of native people. The state of Pennsylvania needs to recognize us. We are the only nationality that must prove we are who we say we are. That in itself is disgusting to me as a human being. I served as a Marine in 1970–73. I hold down a job, pay taxes, help put my kids through school, but yet because we have native ancestors, we are second class citizens to Pennsylvanians. We are not seen. To say we don't exist here is crazy. All I want from Pennsylvania is for them to recognize our tribe and make grants available to our tribe so we can build a cultural center. That's all I want. Nothing more!
- I would appreciate the Truth being told for once. I love my country. However, I am ashamed of this government and its lies. It has never honored one treaty, let alone that they still fail to acknowledge that they are the original and ultimate terrorists. When they could not kill enough natives in battle, they passed out blankets tainted with smallpox. White man's diseases and pollution killed more natives than battles ever did.

- We need to bring better awareness to all of mankind of the true Red Road (native spirituality). Not what is in the history books and movies. We have only one Mother Earth and one universe. We all need to walk in peace.
- Please teach your children only the Plains "Indians" lived in tipis! And by the way, "Indians" are from India. We are Native Americans. Thank you!
- Most info in schools is biased and from the colonial European point of view. Government agencies need to see native people as people, not as ethnic groups or a "number."
- Teach the true history of this country. Make student [*sic*] aware of the issues facing Native Americans in today's society. Teach that Native Americans are alive and not only in history books.

As our understanding of Native Americans in Pennsylvania grew, it became very apparent that they were active, interested people and intensely proud of their heritage. They knew that they were invisible to state institutions and agencies. When we introduced ourselves at council meetings, we often started by saying that we had been informed that the people meeting there did not exist. This was almost always met with smiles and rueful laughter—and then stories about how they had met with discrimination or surprise for the same reason. They expressed chagrin over stereotypes: "We don't live in tipis or say 'How!' or dress in buckskin in our everyday lives!" Then they wanted to know what we were planning to do about it.

This was a question about which we were greatly concerned. Vine Deloria's 1969 "Indian Manifesto," *Custer Died for Your Sins*, excoriated anthropologists for exploiting American Indians for their own academic benefit. We were determined to not be that kind of anthropologist. We liked the people we met, and we were impressed by their dedication on behalf of Native American rights, education, and state recognition. Many of the people we talked to lavishly thanked us for the efforts we were making: "Wanishi (thank you) for providing this survey;" "I am glad you guys are doing this;" or "You two are such a blessing to those of us who really care." This created a strong sense of obligation for us. We responded by creating displays and museum exhibits for the general public in an attempt to provide a more accurate picture of Pennsylvania's Native Americans, both in the past and today. We wrote grant proposals for projects to improve the content of the Pennsylvania K–12 curriculum or to initiate recruitment of native students into Pennsylvania's state-owned universities (to date, none of these proposals has been funded). We sponsored and organized a luncheon at Bloomsburg University of Pennsylvania in April 2006 to bring together Native American leaders and interested university faculty for the purpose of beginning a dialogue that we hoped would benefit all the participants. We created a newsletter to help the luncheon participants stay in touch and to inform university administrators about what was taking place.

However, it became apparent to us that our most valuable asset was the information we had collected from the Native Americans themselves. The surveys we had circulated were a good start, but surveys do not reveal much in-depth information. As a result, we began sitting down with individuals for protracted ethnographic interviews in the spring and summer of 2006. We had a standard set of questions we planned to ask (see Appendix B), but often we just listened as our informants told us their stories. When we began our initial research, we had been advised that Native Americans were hostile to interviewers and that they would not talk to us. We found just the opposite to be true. Our informants were eager to tell us what they knew. To be sure, there were a few who were reluctant to talk ("I'll be perfectly honest with you—I've been interviewed before and I've been misquoted;" "I don't usually talk to interviewers, but since [name withheld] introduced you, I guessed it was okay"). But most were willing to talk to us for as long as we had time to listen. Most interviews lasted at least 90 minutes, and during that time, we often asked only four or five questions. In a typical interview, we met with one or more informants (several were married couples) in their homes or in a restaurant. After obtaining informed consent, we asked each of them to fill out a brief form that included a request for their names, native affiliations, and other demographic data. The interviews were tape-recorded with the informants' permission. Toward the end of the summer of 2006, as gasoline prices rose to over $3 a gallon, we resorted to a few telephone interviews, especially with people who lived more than 3 hours away from our location. In those cases, these interviewees were sent informed consent forms, which they returned to us in the self-addressed stamped envelopes we provided. Telephone interviews were not tape recorded; rather, we took extensive notes as people spoke to us via a speaker phone.

The first people we interviewed were among the officers of the various organizations we had encountered in the state. We were determined to speak to a cross-section of the Native Americans in the state, and so we strove to not be overrepresented in any organization or any particular part of the state. We often ended the interview by asking who else they would recommend to us. By word of mouth, the knowledge of what we were doing often preceded us; as we called to set up interviews, we found that people already knew who we were. Eventually, we talked to 70 people—31 females and 39 males—between the ages of 22 and 90. The average age of the people to whom we talked was 53, and they came from 34 different counties. Again, the most common affiliations were Lenape and Cherokee, followed by Mohawks and Senecas. Altogether, 19 different tribal groups were represented (combining the survey and interview samples, 52 counties and 32 tribal groups were represented in our samples). While some were actively involved in Native American organizations, others were not. Many had been active in seeking state recognition or in educational efforts on behalf of Native Americans; others were individuals who were interested only in knowing their family trees. Almost all of them presented us with their documentation of native background—sometimes as we walked through the doorway. These included various historical documents, genealogical research, or family pictures. Many had two or more native groups in their backgrounds.

Only a few were "full bloods," that is, people of exclusively Native American heritage. Almost all of them had complicated family histories of intermarriage, and many, like most Americans, could trace their descent to several different ethnic lines ("Yeah, I'm Nanticoke and Lenape, but I'm also German, Italian and Irish"). Some of them had

Box 2. Native affiliations claimed.

Abenaki	Nez Perce
Apache	Omaha
Blackfoot	Onondaga
Cherokee	Pawnee
Chickasaw	Potawatomi
Chippewa/Ojibwe	Powhatan
Choctaw	Saponi
Coharie	Sauk/Fox
Lakota	Seminole
Lenape/Delaware	Seneca
Lumbee	Shawnee
Miccosukee	Susquehannock
Mohawk	Taino
Mohegan	Tohono O'odham
Nanticoke	Tuscarora
Navajo/Dene	Waccamaw

grown up knowing about their native heritage; others had discovered it only later in life. Many had parents or grandparents who had tried to hide their native background, and older informants, in particular, had often been told growing up to keep their backgrounds secret. Everyone we talked to embraced their heritage with enthusiasm now, and many of the homes we were invited into were filled with Native American objects and display items. Most wore Native American jewelry—some of their own design and manufacture. If they participated in dances or powwows, they wanted us to see their dance regalia and describe its significance to us. Some volunteered to change into their regalia so we could take pictures of them.

They came from all walks of life. Most had lived in Pennsylvania all their lives. Some had come to Pennsylvania as a child, or with a spouse, or to find work. None had lived in the state for less than 15 years. They were factory workers, nurses, teachers, secretaries, social workers, realtors, and office workers. They were college students and college professors. They also were auto mechanics, ministers, truck drivers, housewives, journalists, artists, and musicians. Some were disabled, and some were retired. Many were proud of their service in the armed forces. They lived in urban apartments, suburban homes, farm houses, or in one case, a log cabin in the woods. Forty-seven, or 67%, provided us with information about their annual incomes. Twenty-two earned less than $30,000 per year, 15 earned between $30,000 and $50,000 per year, and 10 earned more than $50,000 per year. And all of them had a story to tell in their own words:

- It's kind of funny because my Indian blood is from my dad's side. He was pretty much in denial, and I think he actually made a promise to his dad to never tell anyone he was an Indian. Because when I was very little, we went to visit his father's mother's family, up in Canada. And I'm like holding on to his coat saying, "Dad, these are Indians!" He's like "Sh-sh-sh, they're not Indians, they're your relatives." But they were visibly Indians.
- My grandmother was Seneca. She was born Susquehannock, going way back to the early 1700s, but then after the dissolution of the Susquehannocks, my grandmother's grandmother's grandma went to live with the Seneca people. She left the reservation [in New York State]. She couldn't stand the confines, and she left the reservation and met my grandfather in Pennsylvania here. He had Lenape background.
- I didn't know about it until I was about 9. Then my grandfather told me about my Lenape ancestry. My grandmother, who was still alive at that point, confirmed it. As far as my mother's side, the Indian ancestry, I didn't know anything about that until last year when my cousin's daughter decided she would do a genealogical study on that line of the family, and she found out that we have actually have some Powhatan in our background. So

I'm one person who might really be able to claim that they were descended from an Indian princess.

- I'm Cherokee through my mother's side. My great-grandfather is listed on the Dawes' Rolls as a Cherokee; he was a Neal. I wrote to Cherokee, North Carolina. For $100, they'll research a name for you, and they confirmed that I had Cherokee blood. We had always known it, but we didn't follow through with it until a few years ago.
- My great grandfather was the person who told us about our Lenape heritage. He didn't talk much about it. He spoke about his grandmother often and the fact that she was native and she had black, piercing eyes.
- I've known about being an Indian since I was little. My grandfather always called me his little Indian. Other people in the neighborhood thought we were black or Chinese because we had dark skin and slanted eyes. But we were Indian, though we didn't talk about it much outside the home.

In the following chapters, we share what Native Americans in Pennsylvania told us in conversations, interviews, and surveys collected over a 3-year period. All direct quotes used within this text which are not cited from published sources are derived from those conversations and/or interviews. The organization of the book follows the pattern that most of our discussions took. Insofar as is possible, we use our informants' own words to tell their stories and to highlight the issues most important to them. Accordingly, throughout the book we use a number of terms to refer to our informants including Native American, American Indian, and native person. As will be discussed more thoroughly in chapter 3, this apparent confusion is a reflection of our informants' use of the many different terms by which they identify themselves.

In chapter 1, we look at the history of American Indian-European relationships from the time of William Penn in the 17th century to the 21st century. The focus of this chapter is to look at the legal status of Native Americans in colonial America and the United States. That is, are native peoples autonomous, sovereign nations, or are they subject peoples to be administered by outside agencies? The process by which legal recognition is granted by the federal and state governments is reviewed. Since Native Americans in Pennsylvania do not have that recognition, their current situation is compared with similar native nations in the eastern United States who do have legal recognition; examples include the Lumbees of North Carolina, the Pequots of Connecticut, the Abenaki of Vermont, and the Nanticoke-Lenape Tribe of New Jersey.

In chapter 2, we give a brief overview of the history and traditional cultures of Native Americans in Pennsylvania with a special emphasis on the Lenape, Susquehannock, and Iroquois (or Haudenosaunee) people—those cultures that are most closely associated with Pennsylvania history. The sense of history among our informants is strong. We were told again and again that reclaiming native identity required careful research into the past. Many of our informants were especially proud of the authenticity of their dance regalia or the artifacts in their homes. It is not possible to thoroughly describe either the entire history of native-European interactions within the state since the 17th century or the cultures of all the native groups that have passed through the state or have settled here within the confines of this short text. Instead, we focus on the points that most interested or concerned the people with whom we talked. In particular, we take a look at early trade relations with Europeans, the Walking Purchase of 1737, the Treaties of Easton and the conflicts in the Wyoming Valley in the 18th century, the Trail of Tears, the Carlisle Indian Industrial School, and the flooding of the Cornplanter Tract in 1964—all events or institutions that either framed people's discussions with us or helped to explain how they saw themselves as Native Americans.

In chapter 3, we look at some of the prominent myths that shape non-native perceptions of Native Americans. Over and over again, we were told how hurt or angered our informants were when they were asked if they lived in tipis or why they did not look like American Indians in the movies or on television. "They expect us to go to Wal-Mart in buckskins with feathers in our hair," said one person to us. "Go into Kmart in regalia and they call security on you," said another. A number of the people with whom we talked urged us to set the record straight: "We're not what you see on TV." Many described the steps they had taken to try to dispel the stereotypes people had of them, but they felt their efforts were not reaching enough people.

Chapter 4 looks at the controversial issue of Native American identity: Who can legitimately claim Native American status and who cannot? This chapter examines the general history of Native American identity in the United States, such as the significance of blood quantum. It also looks at the issues of identity that most concerned our informants, all of whom wanted us to know that their identity as American Indians was authentic. The issue of "Wannabes," non-Indians who act like American Indians, is also addressed, and the range of opinions our informants expressed on this issue is detailed. Finally, chapter 4 looks at the difficulties of reclaiming native identity in Pennsylvania, an effort that has consequences for other issues such as gaining state recognition.

In chapter 5, we look at Native American spirituality. Almost every conversation we had eventually turned to Native American spiritual values; often, spirituality was what had motivated some people to assert their native heritage. We provide an overview of Native American spiritual values and review our informants' opinions on the similarities and dissimilarities between native beliefs and Christianity. These conversations almost always led to a discussion of the value that Native Americans place on preserving the natural environment. Chapter 5 looks at this issue, too, as well as the assertion of religious rights with regards to Native American prisoners and native patients in hospital care.

Chapter 6 looks at a number of other contentious issues facing Native Americans in Pennsylvania. Chief among these is the struggle for state recognition. Chapter 6 reviews the history of negotiations on this issue between Pennsylvania and various native groups, as well as the problems that stand in the way of recognition. One of the most prominent of these has been a concern that Native Americans want recognition in order to open casinos. Casino gambling has been a controversial issue in Pennsylvania for years, and there has been open opposition to Native American casinos by prominent Pennsylvania officials for some time. Chapter 6 examines whether this is a realistic concern.

In chapter 7, we look at the various Native American organizations within the state. Where possible, we outline their history and programs. A certain amount of animosity exists between these organizations, and we try to explain the reasons for the conflicts and their consequences. In addition to formal organizations like the Lenape Nation, we also look at groups such as the Native Nations Dance Ensemble and Totem Rhythms, which provide educational programs to the general public. Finally, we look at powwows and gatherings within the state and describe their purposes, as well as appropriate behavior for non-Indian visitors to them.

The overall approach we take in regard to this book is captured in the following statement by a Lenape man from Monroe County, Pennsylvania. In response to the question, "If you could tell non-Indians just one thing about Native Americans in Pennsylvania, what would it be?" he said,

> If you put Indian corn on your front door on Thanksgiving, we're coming to eat! Because that means you have too much to eat and everybody's welcome [*laughs*]. No, but seriously, I want to tell them that we have lived here. We have already lived here amongst you generation after generation. . . . We are not asking for anything special. We don't want anything, but something that is really helpful for the state of Pennsylvania. We want to celebrate the roots of the culture of Pennsylvania, which will help tourism. We want to celebrate the roots of Pennsylvania, which is our culture. That's not bad. We just want to be able to have people come and find the correct history instead of the things that have been taught—that there's nobody here. We're still here. I guess that what the main thing should be—that we're still here.

ILLUSTRATION 1. Pennsylvania counties represented in the research (shaded areas).

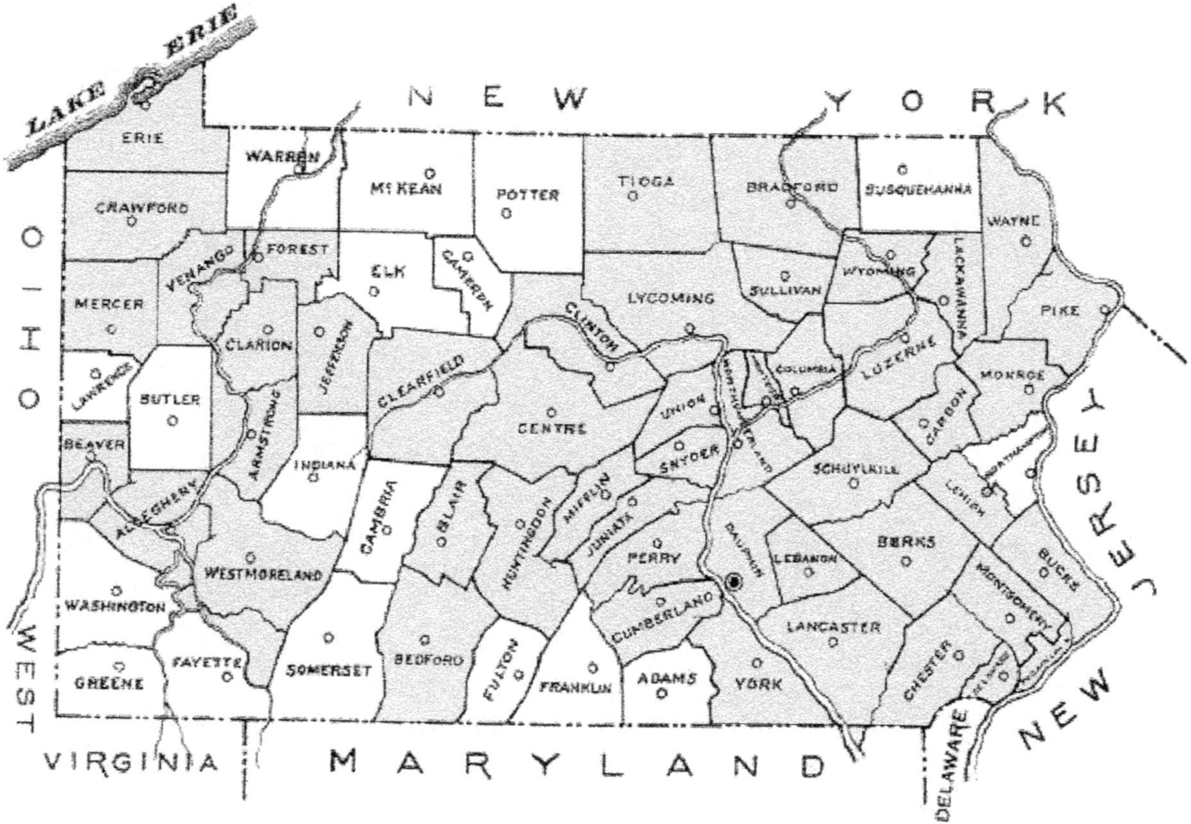

Chapter 1

Native Americans and the Law

A Native American was asked, "What did you call the United States before Europeans arrived?" He replied, "Ours."

—Native American joke

The Colonial Period

In 1681 William Penn wrote a letter to the native people of his new colonial possession, Pennsylvania ("Penn's Woods") from his home in England, assuring them of his benevolent intent and friendship toward them. He wrote,

> There is one great God and Power that hath made the world and all things therein, to whom you and I and all People owe their being and wellbeing, and to whom you and I must one Day give an account, for all that we do in this world: this great God hath written his law in our hearts, by which we are taught and commanded

> to love and help and do good to one another, and not to do harme [*sic*] and mischief one unto another; and the king of the Countrey [*sic*] where I live, hath given unto me a great Province therein, but I desire to enjoy it with your Love and Consent, that we may always live together as Neighbors and friends, else what would the great God say to us, who hath made us not to devoure [*sic*] and destroy one another but live Soberly and kindly together in the world. Now I would have you well to observe, that I am very Sensible of the unkindness and Injustice that hath been too much exercised towards you by the People of these Parts of the world, who have sought themselves, and to make great Advantages by you, rather then be examples of Justice and Goodness unto you, which I hear, hath been matter of trouble to you, caused great many Grudgeings [*sic*] and Animosities, sometimes to the shedding of blood, which hath made the great God angry. But I am not such a Man, as is well known in my own Country: I have great love and regard towards you, and I desire to Winn [*sic*] and gain your Love and friendship by a kind, just and peaceable life; and the People I send are of the same mind, and shall in all things behave themselves accordingly; and if in any thing any shall offend you or your People, you shall have a full and Speedy Satisfaction for the same by an equall [*sic*] number of honest men on both sides that by no means you may have no just Occasion of being offended against them; I shall come shortly to you my selfe [*sic*]. At what time we may more largely and freely confer and discourse of these matters; in the mean time, I have sent my Commissioners to treat with you about land and a firm league of peace. Lett [*sic*] me desire you to be kind to them and the People, and receive these Presents and Tokens which I have sent to you, as a Testimony of my Good will to you, and my resolution to live Justly, peaceably and friendly with you, I am your Friend. (Beatty, 1975, p. 271)

Penn did arrive in Pennsylvania in 1682, and while he spent only 4 years of his life in his colony, during the next 32 years until his death in 1718, Native Americans in Pennsylvania enjoyed a degree of autonomy and fair treatment that has never again been provided to them. As the letter of 1681 clearly states, Penn saw the native peoples of Pennsylvania as sovereign over their land and the social equals of Europeans. When he stated that he intended to govern with "your Love and Consent," he was stating a principle few others in the history of the Americas would ever agree to again: Native Americans had the right to govern themselves and dispose of their resources as they chose. With regard to their traditional lands, Penn showed that he intended to deal with the native Lenape people fairly. He emphasized that native lands must be purchased from the Lenape with their full consent. A famous painting by Benjamin West commemorates such a purchase in 1682 under an elm tree at Shackamaxon with the Lenape sachems Tamamend and Metamequam. Penn seems to have understood that the Lenape concept of property was different from his own and that of other Europeans. The Lenape did not believe that anyone was the sole and individual owner of a piece of property, but rather that boundaries were flexible and anyone had the right to use the resources on the land as they needed. Thus, Penn purchased the same piece of land from several Lenape more than once, and he permitted natives living on land he purchased to continue to live and use the land as they pleased until they removed themselves. Penn labeled his governing of Pennsylvania a "holy experiment," by which he meant a true democracy in which each person's rights were protected.

After Penn's death in 1718, his sons, John, Thomas, and Richard, inherited the colony. European settlement continued to increase, and the Lenape and other indigenous peoples in Pennsylvania began to feel the pressures of contact and conflict. The history of Native Americans in 18th-century Pennsylvania is one of continual relocation farther and farther west as a result of fraudulent treaties (see chapter 2 for a discussion of the Walking Purchase of 1737) and encroachment by settlers. Continuing conflicts between English and French interests meant that American Indians were whipsawed back and forth by those competing colonial concerns, culminating in the French and Indian War in 1755. Some found havens in Pennsylvania where they converted to Christianity and became settled farmers; others were the objects of raids and reprisals for hostile acts, both real and imagined. Though William Penn's vision of a Pennsylvania where Europeans and American Indians could live as neighbors and equals did not come to pass, one aspect of his legacy remained intact: Europeans saw native peoples as sovereign nations. And when Europeans wanted something from a native nation, such as alliance or land purchases, they approached the American Indians using the same kind of diplomacy that would have been used between European nations.

THE UNITED STATES

When the 13 colonies declared their independence, the newly emerging nation of the United States continued to deal with Native Americans as if they were sovereign powers with autonomy in the control of their own affairs. The U.S. Constitution states that "Congress shall have a Power…to regulate Commerce with foreign nations, and among the several States, and with the Indian Tribes" (art. I, § 8). This passage equates Native Americans with other self-governing political units. The 14th Amendment to the Constitution, adopted in 1868, reinforces this concept by noting that Native Americans were not regarded as U.S. citizens unless they paid taxes (§ 2). That is, Native Americans were like citizens of another country; in fact, Native Americans were not expressly granted U.S. citizenship until 1924.

Robert J. Miller (2006) argues that the authors of the Constitution believed that problems with Native Americans in the past originated when individuals or states acted on their own with regard to American Indians. Examples of this abound in Pennsylvania's colonial history. For example, it was the intervention of settlers from Connecticut that incited the "First Wyoming Massacre" of 1763. This occurred after the Commonwealth of Pennsylvania had legally ceded the Wyoming Valley to the Lenape. Similarly, it was the actions of the vigilante band called the Paxton Boys that led to the massacre of Susquehannocks in Lancaster County in 1763; in this case, community authorities had guaranteed the safety of those people. The Constitution's wording with regard to Native Americans was designed to ensure that only Congress had the right to deal with Native Americans—not states or individuals. While this assertion was subsequently disregarded, as will be discussed as follows, the Constitution seems to make clear that Native Americans were to be dealt with on a nation-to-nation basis.

In the late 18th and early 19th centuries, Native Americans living east of the Mississippi had enough power to constitute a significant threat to the new nation, and the government of the United States responded to this threat by negotiating treaties. In these treaties, Native Americans granted land rights to the United States—again, as if they were a foreign power. The U.S. Supreme Court ruled in 1905 that treaties were not a grant of rights by the U.S. government *to* Native Americans, but were rather a grant of rights to the United States *by* Native Americans.

Despite these constitutional and court guarantees, in the early 19th century, individual states began to act independently of the U.S. government and Congress in dealing with the Native American populations contained within their borders. The state of Georgia, in particular, acted to remove the Cherokees from their territory. Georgia annexed the lands belonging to the Cherokee in 1827, and in 1830 the Georgian delegation to Congress pushed through a bill which gave the U.S. president, rather than Congress, the authority to remove Native Americans from their ancestral lands.

This bill led to two court cases brought by the Cherokee Nation against the state of Georgia which were eventually decided by the U.S. Supreme Court. The first, *Cherokee Nation v. Georgia* in 1831, argued that Georgia did not have the constitutional right to intervene in a treaty relationship between the nation and the Congress. William Wirt, the U.S. attorney general of the Monroe and Adams administrations, argued for the Cherokee Nation that the Cherokees were a foreign nation over which a state had no jurisdiction. The Court ruled that it did not have the right to strike down laws enacted by Georgia, but at the same time asserted that the Cherokees were a "domestic dependent nation" under the guardianship of the United States. In a sense, the Court sidestepped the key issues in this case but left the possibility that it would support the Cherokees in their conflict with Georgia.

In 1832 a second case, *Worcester v. Georgia*, brought a stronger assertion of Native Americans' legal status. Samuel Worcester was a missionary from Vermont who had been assigned by the American Board of Commissioners for Foreign Missions to the Cherokee. Worcester became sympathetic to the Cherokees' situation and advised them on their political and legal rights. In response to Worcester's advocacy for the Cherokee people, Georgia passed a law forbidding any "white person" from living in the Cherokee Nation without the express permission of the state of Georgia. Worcester and 10 other missionaries were subsequently arrested by the state for living among the Cherokee, and in September 1831 they were tried and convicted and then sentenced to 4 years in prison at hard labor. The case was brought before the Supreme Court, which struck down the convictions as well as Georgia's laws that intervened in the affairs of the Cherokee Nation. Chief Justice John Marshall, writing for the majority of the court, wrote that the Cherokee and other American Indian nations were "distinct, independent political communities retaining their natural rights" (Williams, 1994, p. 313). Marshall rebuked Georgia for its actions and wrote that the Cherokee should be free from interference from the state on their legal territory.

This court case led to one of the famous phrases in American history, as President Andrew Jackson is said to have said: "John Marshall has made his decision. Now let him enforce it" (Loth, 1949, p. 365). In fact, Georgia ignored the court's decision, and the president refused to take action against the state. (Subsequent negotiations led to the eventual freeing of the missionaries.) Pressure from the state of Georgia would lead to the removal of the Cherokees from the state in the Trail of Tears in 1838 (see Burke, 1969, for a more thorough discussion of the Cherokee cases).

Nonetheless, between constitutional guarantees and Supreme Court decisions, it would appear that Native Americans in the 19th century had a distinct legal advantage. If they were "distinct, independent political communities," then they could continue to be seen as sovereign and autonomous. Unfortunately for Native Americans, the decisions made by Marshall and the Supreme Court did not go that far. When Marshall wrote in *Cherokee Nation v. Georgia* that the Cherokee existed under the guardianship of the United States, he was asserting an old principle of Western law: the doctrine of discovery. This doctrine gave the European nation that first contacted a non-European people the exclusive right to deal with those non-Europeans. A native nation could keep its land and its sovereignty, but only to the extent that it had to enter into legal arrangements with only one European nation. The first centuries of European-Indian contact can be seen at least in part as different European countries trying to assert their rights of discovery over one American Indian group or another (e.g., the struggles between the French and the English over trade rights or military alliances with various native groups in the Northeast). The U.S. government believed it inherited the right of discovery from England.

From the standpoint of the U.S. government, the initial significance of the doctrine of discovery was the ability to assert the rights of Congress over states or individuals in negotiations with native nations. In treaties signed between the United States and American Indian nations after 1832, Congress or its representatives acted as though it was dealing with a foreign nation. The end of the Civil War in 1865 gradually brought the U.S. government to a new set of ideas about native nations. As the United States expanded westward, asserting its right of Manifest Destiny, the American Indians of the Great Plains, the Southwest, and California began to look more like impediments to national progress rather than as foreign nations with sovereign rights. The Indian Wars of the 1870s, which play such a big part in American folklore to this day, brought sharply into contrast the intent of expansion on the part of the United States with the right to control of traditional lands by natives. Ethnocentrism had always played a role in how the United States looked at native peoples; natives were usually officially portrayed as unfortunate pagans without civilized virtues. Now, ethnocentrism became xenophobia: American Indians were bloodthirsty savages who terrorized peaceful settlers. The West needed to be cleared for settlement, and American Indians had to be defeated, pacified, and removed.

The U.S. government had always expressed an interest in "civilizing" Native Americans. Early treaties extended educational and welfare benefits to Native Americans based on the assumption that American Indians needed to lose their native identity for their own good. For the most part, American Indians ignored these provisions of treaties (see Box 3). By the 1870s, the United States was ready to more actively assert the need to "detribalize" American Indians and coerce them to assimilate into mainstream Euro-American cultures. To do this meant directly meddling in the lives of American Indians and dismissing any notions of native sovereignty. Clearly, however, the United States felt this was necessary.

In 1887 Congress passed the General Allotment Act, sometimes called the Dawes Act after Congressman Henry Dawes. The General Allotment Act divided up reservation land into 160-acre parcels; each of these parcels was to be assigned to a native head of household to be farmed or ranched. The basic idea behind the Act was to break up the communal lifestyle of native peoples by forcing people to live on their allotments with only their immediate families; members of extended families were often given allotments miles apart from each other. Congress felt that the Act would engender a respect for private property among natives and thus would begin to assimilate them into mainstream American life. In addition, if any reservation land was left over after the assignment of allotments, that land would then be available for lease to non-Indians.

The Act both defied the concept that Native Americans had the right to make decisions about their own land and impoverished them by giving them plots of land too small to be useful; on a 160-acre ranch in Montana, for example, there was enough pasture to support 10 cows. Subsequently, many American Indians had to depend on leasing their own allotments to non-Indians for their incomes. Today, much of the land on Western reservations is controlled by non-Indians. The Act effectively reduced 139 million acres of reservation land to 34 million acres (Carlson, 1994).

Another effort to undermine Native American culture and sovereignty was the creation of boarding schools for Native American children in the 1870s. In 1878 the Hampton Institute in Norfolk, Virginia was converted from a school for the children of ex-slaves to a boarding school for Native American children. In 1879 the most notorious of the boarding schools, the Carlisle Industrial School, was opened by a former U.S. army officer, Henry Pratt, in Carlisle, Pennsylvania (see chapter 2). The concept behind the boarding schools was, again, to detribalize and assimilate American Indians. Children arriving at the school had their clothing

Box 3. Benjamin Franklin on Native Americans.

In 1784 Benjamin Franklin wrote about an offer made to the Haudenosaunee in 1744 to send several of their young men to the College of William & Mary to be educated at colonial expense. Franklin records that after some consideration, the natives refused this offer, saying this:

> We know you esteem the kind of learning taught in these Colleges, and that the Maintenance of our young Men, while with you, would be very expensive to you. We are convinc'd, therefore, that you mean to do us Good by your Proposal; and we thank you heartily. But you, who are wise, must know that different nations have different Conceptions of things; and you will therefore not take it amiss, if our Ideas of this kind of Education happen not to be the same with yours. We have had some Experience of it; Several of our young People were formerly brought up at the Colleges of the Northern Provinces; they were instructed in all your Sciences; but, when they came back to us, they were bad Runners, ignorant of every means of living in the Woods, unable to bear either Cold or Hunger, knew neither how to build a Cabin, take a Deer, or kill an Enemy, spoke our Language imperfectly, were therefore neither fit for Hunters, Warriors, nor Counsellors [*sic*]; they were totally good for nothing. We are however not the less oblig'd by your kind Offer, tho' we decline accepting it; and to show our grateful Sense of it, if the Gentlemen of Virginia will send us a Dozen of their Sons, we will take great Care of their Education, instruct them in all we know, and make Men of them. (Madison Archives, 2007, pp. 1–2)

and possessions confiscated and burned. Once in the school, the children were forbidden to leave the school grounds, speak their languages, or practice their religious beliefs: They were to become English-speaking, Christian, working-class Americans. The concept of the boarding school quickly spread across the United States as an effective way to destroy native cultures. It was not until 1933 that official policy began to move away from boarding-school educations for native children.

When Native Americans protested actions such as the General Allotment Act or boarding schools, they were told that under the doctrine of discovery, the U.S. government viewed Native Americans as wards of the United States, that is, minors without legal standing before the courts or Congress. The Supreme Court's ruling that American Indians constituted "domestic dependent nations" under the protection of the United States meant that Congress had the right to determine what was best for them (Williams, 1994, p. 314). Thus, Congress and its agents, such as the Bureau of Indian Affairs (BIA), had the legal right to act on behalf of what were thought to be the best interests of native peoples.

THE 20TH CENTURY

In a sense, the 20th century was a roller-coaster ride for Native Americans living in the United States. In 1934 Congress passed the Indian Reorganization Act, which overrode the General Allotment Act of 1877 and gave Native Americans living on reservations the right to elect their own tribal governments and write their own tribal constitutions (leases of reservation land to non-Indians were not rescinded, however). For almost 2 decades, American Indians were given a measure of self-rule on reservation lands and were encouraged to revive their customs. However, in 1953 Congress passed a law that terminated 109 formerly recognized tribes. Reservation lands guaranteed to these tribes were now given over to the states to manage as they saw fit. Assimilationist policies once again defined U.S. policy toward Native Americans, who were now encouraged to leave reservations and migrate to cities. Federally funded "Indian Centers" were created to help with this transition.

In the 1960s the civil rights movement swept across the United States. Of course, the movement initially was created by and acted on behalf of African Americans, but by the late 1960s, other groups in the United States, such as women and the elderly, began demanding—and receiving—recognition of their claims of being members of populations that are discriminated against. For American Indians, the civil rights movement took the form of Red Power and the raising of American Indian consciousness. The latter was experienced in at least two ways.

On the one hand, Native Americans themselves began to reassert openly their cultural heritage and pride; in Pennsylvania, descendants of the Lenape and other native groups stopped hiding their existence and began reclaiming their roots. On the other hand, other Americans began to be more appreciative of and sympathetic toward the Native Americans living among them. A renaissance of sorts occurred for Native Americans; they were no longer the "bad guys" of Western myths, but people to be admired for their losses, their pride, and their native values (see Clifton, 1989; Cornel, 1988; V. Deloria, 1969; Nagel, 1995, 1998).

In response, Congress passed the Indian Self-Determination and Education Assistance Act of 1975, which transferred control of many federal programs to American Indians on reservations. The American Indian Religious Freedom Act of 1978 recognized the right of Native Americans to practice their religious beliefs with the same constitutional guarantees that other Americans had (though this seeming advance in rights was vitiated by the Supreme Court in 1988 when the Court ruled that the 1978 law was advisory only and did not apply to the states—see chapter 5). The Indian Tribal Government Tax Status Act of 1982 gave *recognized* American Indian groups the same federal tax benefits enjoyed by states and local governments. The extension of legal rights for Native Americans would continue into the 1990s with the Native American Graves and Repatriation Act (NAGRA) in 1990, which mandated the return of human remains and artifacts from museums to American Indian groups, and into the 21st century with the Religious Land Use and Prison Act (2000). The latter protected the right of Native Americans to use their land for religious purposes without interference and guaranteed the rights of Native American prison inmates to practice their traditional ceremonies.

In the last paragraph, an important qualifier arose—the "recognized" Native American nations. As attitudes changed toward Native Americans and the assimilationist policies of past decades seemed to relax, Native American groups began to assert their right to be officially recognized by the U.S. and state governments. There were two primary categories of Native Americans who actively sought recognition: (1) One was made up of the 109 nations that had had their legal status terminated in 1953 (see

Grobsmith & Ritter, 1992); and (2) the other was composed of groups like the Lenape of Pennsylvania, which had never been recognized previously by any governmental body in the United States. Recognition was seen to have many benefits, such as health and welfare benefits and the right to claim human remains under NAGRA (see chapter 6), but a primary consideration was one of identity. Groups like the Lenape wanted the rest of the United States to admit to their existence.

At the federal level, the U.S. government responded by creating (and periodically revising) a set of steps through which American Indian groups could petition for legal recognition. At the current time, native groups must direct their petitions through the Bureau of Acknowledgement and Research (BAR), a branch of the BIA. The current process for obtaining recognition was formalized in 1978. At its core are a set of seven criteria American Indian nations must meet to achieve recognition. They are:

1. To establish that they have been identified from historical times to the present on a substantially continuous basis as "American Indian" or "aboriginal"
2. To establish that a substantial portion of the group inhabits a specific area or lives in a community viewed as American Indian and distinct from other populations in the area, and that its members are descendants of an American Indian tribe that historically inhabited a specific area
3. To furnish a statement of fact, which establishes that the group has maintained political influence or other authority over its members as an autonomous entity throughout history until the present
4. To furnish a copy of the group's present governing document, or in the absence of such a written document, a statement describing in full the membership criteria and the procedures through which the group currently governs its affairs and its members
5. To furnish a list of all known current members of the group and a copy of each available former list of members based on the group's own defined membership criteria. The membership must consist of individuals who have established, using evidence

acceptable to the Secretary of the Interior, descendancy from a tribe that existed historically or from historical tribes that combined and functioned as a single autonomous entity

6. To establish that the membership of the group is composed principally of persons who are not members of any other North American Indian tribe
7. To establish that neither the group nor its members are the subject of congressional legislation which has expressly terminated or forbidden the Federal relationship

These criteria require considerable documentation on the part of the petitioning native group. The burden of proof falls on the American Indians. Documents are submitted to the BAR, which is a panel made up of a small number of anthropologists, historians, and genealogists. Bruce G. Miller (2003) writes that "the BAR decisions are peculiar in that they need provide no evidence to counter the evidence presented by petitioners; they merely need to conclude that evidence presented to fulfill various legal tests is inadequate" (p. 80). To avoid being seen as not presenting enough information, native petitioners have increased their documentation over the years so that current petitions are thousands of pages long. The large number of native groups petitioning for recognition combined with the increasing length of documentation and the small number of BAR members available (currently, there are eight members) to assess the evidence means that the process moves very slowly with rarely more than one group per year achieving its goal.

For a population like the Pennsylvania Lenape, the BAR establishes standards that they are unlikely to be able to meet. As will be discussed in chapter 4, there are many barriers to presenting adequate evidence of continuous existence of the Lenape people as an autonomous entity since William Penn's time. Too much time has passed, and the Lenape have been effectively removed from their traditional lands since the 1760s. But states may establish their own standards for granting official recognition to American Indians, and it will be state standards that the Lenape and other Pennsylvania-based Native Americans—as well as this book—will have to address.

NATIVE AMERICANS IN PENNSYLVANIA TODAY

There are essentially three different kinds of Native Americans living in Pennsylvania today. The first group contains people like the Lenape who have a claim to being the original indigenous population of the state at the time of European contact. The second group is made up of people descended from native groups that lived in neighboring states but who migrated into Pennsylvania in colonial times; examples include the Seneca, the Shawnees, and the Cherokees. The third group is made up of more recent immigrants—primarily people who were encouraged to leave reservations elsewhere in the 1950s and early 1960s and move into urban areas such as Pittsburgh and Philadelphia. Federal assistance to these "urban Indians" led to the creation of Indian Centers in Philadelphia, Harrisburg, and Pittsburgh in the 1950s, as well as to the formation of some of the first Native American advocacy/social groups in the state, such as the United American Indians of Delaware Valley, a Philadelphia-based organization that is currently defunct.

As noted in the introduction, there are no reservations in Pennsylvania. William Penn and his descendants made a point of purchasing land from the Lenape with the idea of obtaining clear and undisputed title to it. American Indians living on that property at the time of purchase were allowed to stay, and some Native Americans living in Pennsylvania today refer to those agreements as reservations. However, those were never viewed as land grants to the Lenape, but rather were viewed as a courtesy to existing populations. Penn made it clear that when the existing American Indians vacated the land, they could not return. Since the traditional Lenape way of life involved hunting wild animals and gathering wild plants, as well as practicing a shifting kind of agriculture called horticulture, Lenape communities moved locations periodically to till new fields or to find better hunting sites. Later grants to the Lenape in the mid-18th century in the Wyoming Valley were subsequently extinguished by warfare and the expulsion of the American Indians. Communities of Christian American Indians had been formed in colonial times, but these people, too, were eventually forced to flee because of hostilities between Europeans and American Indians. By the 20th century, the only thing that could be called a "reservation" in the state was the Cornplanter Tract in northwestern Pennsylvania. But, as described in chapter 2, the Cornplanter Tract was not truly a reservation, but rather a grant to an individual Seneca and his family; at any rate, the tract was flooded in 1966.

Native Americans survived in Pennsylvania by moving into remote areas of the state and staying hidden; as will be seen in chapter 4, there were plenty of reasons to maintain a low profile. In the process, they assimilated into the European communities around them, a development that included intermarriage. A woman of Lenape descent from Northampton County told us, for example, the following:

> One of the great strengths of the Lenape was that they assimilated. Many of the other tribes, there would be no way that could happen, and that's why they became extinct or went onto reservations. It may have kept a more pure blood line, but the Lenape who stayed here assimilated. According to the Lenape elders, Lenape women preferred the German farmers to the English. They could make a connection with the German farmers in the area because they were workers, they were farmers, they were more connected to the land.

She went on to say this:

> In the Northampton County area here, we've learned from the elders that people would leave their children with the German farmers before they fled to keep from getting killed. One was the daughter of George Rex [an 18th-century Lenape sachem]; she was left behind to be raised by the Frantz family. Many of the Frantz's around here don't know that they're related to a Lenape princess [*laughs*] if you want to use that word. It was done mainly to keep a connection to the land, which you know is sacred to a native.

Intermarriage was not restricted to the Lenape, of course, and Native Americans in Pennsylvania are usually people of "mixed blood," that is, descended from Native Americans and other ethnicities. This does not make Pennsylvania's American Indians less proud of their native heritages or less determined in their efforts to win state recognition. As a Shawnee man from Tioga County wrote in an e-mail,

> Yes, I am a "mixed blood," Shawnee and German. And yes, I do know my heritage quite well, both sides. How could I honor one without honoring the other? I have no shame for who I am. No one should have shame because they were born "mixed." But it is my native ancestry that I have embraced, and for many years. I am a dancer, a drummer, and a veteran warrior. I am proud to honor that part of me that is Shawnee regardless of what any "full blood" might think. I am Shawnee.

It is also the case that there is no unified political voice for Native Americans in Pennsylvania. Among the Lenape, for example, there are the Lenape Nation, the Eastern Delaware Nation (EDN), the Thunder Mountain Lenape, the United Traditionalist Lenape Nation, and others, all of whom see themselves as legitimate representatives of the Lenape people. These organizations often are in conflict, and some enmity seems to exist between individuals in the different groups. In addition, there are other organizations to which Pennsylvania's native people belong that are organized on a regional basis (e.g., the Native American Alliance of Bucks County), or by other affiliations (e.g., the Southeastern Cherokee Confederacy of Philadelphia). And there are many who are either wholly unaffiliated or belong to two or more different groups.

Therefore, at first glance, the task for the Pennsylvania Lenapes to gain any kind of official recognition, state or federal, may appear hopeless. They are not connected to a traditional land base, such as a reservation; they are clearly of mixed backgrounds; and they have no unifying political structure. Yet that has not prevented native groups of similar circumstances from gaining either state recognition elsewhere or federal recognition. Some comparisons are in order.

The Lumbees

The Lumbees are a state and federally recognized tribe in North Carolina (see Blu, 1980). Like the Lenape, the Lumbees have neither a reservation nor a unified political organization, and they are probably of mixed background. Blu reviews the several local theories about the origins of the Lumbee people, the most popular of which is that they are descendants of the "Lost Colony" of English settlers from the 17th century. The members of the Colony are said to have migrated from the coast into the heartland of North Carolina where they intermarried with the resident native people. Blu believes that their background is a complex blend of many different remnant native populations who fled from pressure of settlers into the swamplands of Robeson County, North Carolina. Throughout their recorded history, the Lumbees have been called many different things: mulattos, Cherokees, Croatans, Cheraws and Eastern Siouans. The name "Lumbee" was settled on in 1952 using the name of a river running through Robeson County. Blu writes that this is a question of great importance to the Lumbees:

> However uncertain and poorly documented they are, the origins of the Lumbee are vital to the Indians as validation of their Indianness and important to such government agencies as the Bureau of Indian Affairs (BIA) and the Office of Economic Opportunity (OEO) because benefits may have to be conferred on the basis of their aboriginal status. Knowing where they came from is also essential to many Indians' peace of mind because such knowledge ties them to a distinct past in a satisfyingly specific way rather than an unsettingly [*sic*] vague one. (p. 36)

North Carolina first officially recognized the Lumbees in 1887 when it established a segregated school system for them; at that time, they were known as Croatans. Congress recognized the Lumbees in 1956, though it denied the Lumbees the health and welfare benefits other recognized native nations had or have. Since that time, the Lumbees have lobbied Congress to extend them those benefits. A tribal government was not created until 2001.

In the absence of a reservation, a confirmed origin as a people, and an organized political organization, Blu (1980) says that Lumbee identity is built around three primary markers: (1) Pride in being Native American is seen as being one of their strengths: They take pride in their heritage. (2) The second marker is "meanness," by which is meant that Lumbees are willing to stand up for their heritage and their communities. Meanness also has the connotation of being touchy and easily angered. Lumbees say they don't back down from any threat and they are willing to fight for what's theirs. Finally, (3) the Lumbees see themselves as having a strong sense of community cohesiveness, even if historically they have not had a unified political voice (pp. 143–148). Blu says "If the Lumbee lack the traditional mechanisms for holding themselves together—formal organization, explicit membership criteria, distinctive cultural paraphernalia—then what does hold them together? My answer is…their shared ideas about themselves as a people" (p. 2).

The Mashantucket Pequots

The Pequots are native to Connecticut (see Hauptman & Wherry, 1988). They first came in contact with Europeans in the early 17th century when they were estimated to number approximately 8,000 people. As was the case elsewhere, the Pequots soon came into conflict with settlers encroaching or trying to seize their land. The Pequot War (1636–1638) was the first significant conflict between Europeans and the native peoples of New England. In this war, the Pequot were soundly defeated, which resulted in the loss of much of their land and most of their population.

Today, the Pequots are divided into two populations, the Paucatuck Pequots and the Mashantucket Pequots, which both have reservations in Connecticut. The Paucatucks, or Eastern Pequots, have a reservation near North Stonington; the Mashantucket, or Western Pequots, have reservation land within the town of Ledyard. Reservations were granted to the Mashantuckets in 1666 and the Paucatucks in 1683. The Mashantuckets have been a federally recognized tribe since 1983, while the Paucatucks have Connecticut state recognition; efforts to win federal recognition for the Paucatucks thus far have not succeeded.

Both reservations are small. The Mashantucket reservation was reduced in size over the decades, like many American Indian reservations, until it stood at less than an acre by the early 1970s. A successful lawsuit initiated in 1976 eventually expanded the Mashantuckets' land holdings to 1,250 acres. The Paucatuck reservation is 226 acres, though the exact boundaries remain in dispute. Pequot populations had diminished over the years; in 1907 the Mashantucket population was estimated to be only 25 people. In 1974 when the tribal government was reorganized, there were 55 people on the tribal rolls. In 2005 Mashantuckets claimed a tribal membership of 785 people, with 325 of those members living on the reservation.

Like the Lenape, Mashantuckets had intermarried with non-Indians and assimilated into non-Indian society. As can be seen, most had moved off the reservation. With the rise of American Indian consciousness and Red Power in the late 1960s and early 1970s, individuals with Mashantucket ancestry began returning to the reservation and asserting their ethnic pride and traditional rights. Initial interest was concentrated in restoring land that was lost in the 19th century in what was seen as an illegal land grab; the 1976 lawsuit was a result of this focus of community interest. After gaining back much of what was lost in the 19th century, the Mashantuckets began to look for a way to raise money to buy more land and to promote the development of their economy. Early efforts included opening a restaurant and establishing a sand and gravel business. In 1986 they opened a bingo parlor on the reservation, and in 1992, taking advantage of the 1988 Indian Gaming Regulatory Act, they began building a tribally-owned casino.

The casino, now known as the Foxwoods Resort Casino, is the largest in the world (at the time of this writing), and, with its proximity to New York City and Boston, it is enormously successful. A study conducted by the University of Connecticut in 2000 estimated that the casino has provided direct and indirect employment in the state for over 41,000 people, and it annually generates $1.2 billion dollars for the state economy.

Profits from the casino are shared among tribal members and are also used to purchase additional land and promote cultural events. In 1998 the Mashantuckets opened the Pequot Museum and Research Center on the reservation with funds generated from the casino. In December 2006 the Mashantuckets were given permission by the state of Pennsylvania to build a second Foxwoods Casino in Philadelphia.

The success of the Mashantucket Pequots is based on their reservation—one of the oldest, continuously occupied reservations in North America—and the economic clout they have gained through their casino income. The Lenape do not have a reservation in Pennsylvania, and as will be seen in chapter 6, they have expressed no interest in building a casino. As one of the informants, a Lenape man from York County, put it, "Everyone wants to be a Pequot."

The Abenaki

As of this writing, the Abenaki are the most recent Native American group within the United States to have achieved some degree of legal recognition, having been granted state recognition in Vermont in May 2006. At the time of European contact, the Abenaki occupied much of what is today Maine, Vermont, and New Hampshire. Like the Pequots, the Abenaki were caught up in the wars fought in the 17th century between European colonists and native peoples. Many Abenakis fled these conflicts to settle in Quebec, Canada, where they maintain two reservations today. The Abenaki have federal recognition in Canada, but the Abenakis still living in the United States have neither a reservation nor U.S. recognition.

The circumstances of the Abenaki in the United States are very similar to those of the Pennsylvania Lenape. Many of their people fled European encroachments on their traditional territories. Many of the Lenape settled in Canada and Oklahoma; the Abenaki fled to Canada. Neither has a reservation in the United States. Both are made up of assimilated populations that are nonetheless very proud of their native heritages. The Abenaki have started "reverse boarding schools" to teach their children about their past (see Lutz, 2006b); the Lenape, as will be seen in chapter 7, are supporting many projects to inform both their children and non-Indians about their native backgrounds. The primary difference to note here is that the Abenaki have received state recognition while the Pennsylvania Lenape have not.

According to Ullmann (2006), the Abenaki were blocked from state recognition in Vermont for many years due to the concern of state officials that recognition would lead to land claims and casinos. As will be seen in chapter 6, Pennsylvania state officials have raised the same concerns about Lenape efforts to win recognition. Ullmann writes the following:

> Proposals to recognize the tribe have been introduced in the Vermont legislature year after year in various resolutions and in bills that always stalled in committee. "Resolutions aren't enough," said Vermont State Senator Diane Snelling, who sponsored the bill. "I wanted it in the state law books." (p. 8)

In 1977 a previous governor had granted the Abenaki recognition by executive order, but his successor, Richard Snelling, Diane's father, had overturned that ruling. Senator Snelling wanted to set things right. The Pennsylvania Lenape have also been on the brink of recognition before, only to have their hopes dashed before recognition could become state law. In many ways, the Abenaki and the Lenape have had common experiences.

The Wampanoag

The Wampanoag are the original inhabitants of southeastern Massachusetts, including Cape Cod and Martha's Vineyard. It was the Wampanoag who greeted the Pilgrims in 1620. Squanto, a figure enshrined in American folklore for the help he gave the Pilgrims as they struggled with this new land, was a Wampanoag. An estimated 12,000 Wampanoag lived in Massachusetts at the time of contact (see Weinstein, 1989), but their numbers were then sharply reduced by smallpox. In 1675 a sachem of the Wampanoag, called King Phillip by Europeans, rallied the Native Americans of southern New England to drive out the Europeans, but after some initial successes by the Native Americans, the colonists were able to defeat Phillip's forces. While their numbers were considerably reduced, the remaining Wampanoag were not driven out of their ancestral territories.

As of this writing, the Wampanoag are divided into five regional autonomous groups. One of these, the Gay Head Wampanoag, has had federal recognition since 1987. The Gay Head Wampanoag number about 600 members who live on Martha's Vineyard. They do not have a reservation, but they do maintain ownership of several parcels of land on the island. The Mashpee Wampanoag number over 1,000 members, approximately 600 of whom live in the town of Mashpee. The Mashpee have Massachusetts state recognition and they have applied for federal recognition (without success). The other groups are represented in the Massachusetts State Commission on Indian Affairs. Like the Abenaki, the Gay Head and Mashpee Wampanoag support a variety of programs and activities that are designed to both promote their culture and inform others of their heritage.

The Pequots, Abenaki, Wampanoag, and Lenape all had similar traditional Eastern Woodland cultures. All spoke variants of the Algonquian language family, and all practiced a mixed economy of hunting, fishing, gathering wild plants, as well as horticulture growing corn, beans, and squash. All lived in small, autonomous local communities without a unifying or centralized political structure. Except for the Wampanoag, they were displaced or driven from their lands and forced to assimilate into colonial or American society to survive. All have experienced significant cultural revivals in the 20th century. All of these groups, plus the Lumbees of North Carolina, show how uneven the process of legal recognition can be. Some have reservations, some do not. Some have federal recognition, others have state recognition, and some segments of these groups have no recognition at all. Their past- and present-day circumstances all mirror those of Native Americans in Pennsylvania.

One final set of cultural comparisons needs to be made, and that is with Lenape/Delaware organizations outside of Pennsylvania. In this section, we will look at the Delaware Tribe of Oklahoma and the Nanticoke-Lenape Tribe of New Jersey.

The Delawares of Oklahoma

Early in the contact period, English traders and colonists in what is now Delaware, New Jersey, and eastern Pennsylvania began calling the Lenape people "Delawares" after the river on which many of them lived. Those Lenapes who migrated westward in the 18th century have continued to call themselves Delawares, while most organizations in New Jersey and Pennsylvania prefer the aboriginal name of Lenape—an exception is the Pennsylvania-based organization called the Eastern Delaware Nation. Those people who moved westward migrated from state to state. Some small communities still exist in Wisconsin and Kansas, but most of the Delawares eventually settled in what was originally known as "Indian Territory," now the State of Oklahoma (see Weslager, 1972, pp. 399–440, for a complete discussion of the complex process by which the Delawares came to live in Oklahoma). The Delawares in Kansas had entered into treaties with the U.S. government guaranteeing them reservation land and rights, but by the mid-19th century, it was apparent that the government could not or would not protect the Delawares' treaty rights from incursion by settlers. Instead, the federal government offered the Delawares land in Oklahoma. Unfortunately, the land offered to the Delawares had already been promised to the Cherokees, and the government was forced to negotiate a settlement whereby the Cherokees allowed the Delawares to live on their land. This settlement was reached in 1866, and in 1867 the Delawares began to relocate.

The agreement the government reached between the two nations had a profound effect on Delaware sovereignty, since it assigned the Delawares to the Cherokee Nation. Specifically, the settlement stated that "the children hereafter born of such Delawares so incorporated into the Cherokee Nation, shall in all respects be regarded as native Cherokees" (Weslager,

1972, p. 426). The Delawares, who apparently numbered only a few hundred persons, were considerably outnumbered by the approximately 14,000 Cherokees. Weslager reports that hostilities existed between the two groups; many Cherokees regarded the Delawares as interlopers on their land. Nevertheless, the Delawares applied for full membership in the Cherokee Nation and received that recognition from the federal government in 1890.

The 1890 recognition did not end the question of the Delawares' legal status in Oklahoma. The Delawares took the position that while they were part of the Cherokee Nation, they maintained a sort of separate status as a band within the Nation. In that regard, they believed they had the right to elect their officers and maintain their own band government—the 1890 recognition seemed to guarantee them that right. The Cherokees disagreed and petitioned the federal government to revoke its recognition of the Delawares. In 1979 the BIA agreed with the Cherokees' position and revoked federal recognition for the Delawares. The Delawares protested, and in 1996 they persuaded the BIA to reverse itself yet again. In 2002 the BIA's decision to reinstate the Delawares' recognition was upheld by the U.S. District Court.

From 2002 to 2004, the Delawares of Oklahoma existed as a separate nation with its own tribal government with a reported membership of approximately 10,500. During this time, the Delawares attempted to purchase an 11-acre property in Pennsylvania with the expressed intent of opening a casino. This action was opposed by both the local communities and the state of Pennsylvania. However, in 2004 the U.S. Court of Appeals reversed the decision of 2002 and returned the Delawares to the jurisdiction of the Cherokee Nation, citing the 1866 agreement. An American Indian Web site offers a comment stating, "It is ironic to note that the first American Indian Nation/Tribe to recognize the United States was no longer recognized by that government" (Indianz.Com, 2004, p. 4). Nonetheless, the Oklahoma Delawares continue to seek separate status and a reinstatement of federal recognition.

The Nanticoke Lenni-Lenape Tribe of New Jersey

As noted earlier, the Lenape people lived in what is today Delaware, New Jersey, and eastern Pennsylvania, but while there is no official recognition of the Lenape in either Delaware or Pennsylvania, they do have state recognition in New Jersey through the Nanticoke Lenni-Lenape Tribe. The Nanticokes received their name from Europeans; they lived along the Nanticoke River in Delaware (see Porter, 1987). While they are seen today as a distinct nation, they may have been indistinguishable from the Lenape in the past. Certainly, they experienced the same pressures of colonial settlement and diseases, and many of them migrated to the Wyoming Valley in northeastern Pennsylvania during the mid-18th century where they often lived in mixed communities of Lenape, Mohegans, and others. A town near Wilkes-Barre bears their name—Nanticoke. A community of approximately 1,000 Nanticokes still lives in Delaware, but they have no state-recognized status there. Porter writes that, like other eastern nations, the Nanticokes' native identity has been constantly challenged.

Lenapes living in New Jersey tell much the same story as their counterparts in Pennsylvania—that is, they were displaced from their homes early in the colonial era, and many of them moved westward, first to Pennsylvania and then to Ohio and beyond. However, not all of them left New Jersey. The Web site of the Nanticoke Lenni-Lenape Tribe reports the following:

> Some were able to continue to live in their homeland… . Those who remained survived through attempting to adapt to the dominant culture, becoming farmers and tradesmen. Many Nanticoke-Lenape Indians embraced Christianity while not forgetting or devaluing many ancient tribal ways. (Nanticoke Lenni-Lenape, 2007, p. 2)

Most resided in or around Bridgeton, New Jersey, which informally became known as "Indian Town."

In the 1970s, the Native Americans in New Jersey organized into a political structure: the Nanticoke Lenni-Lenape Indians of New Jersey. Like nascent Native American groups in Pennsylvania, their first step toward recognition was winning 501(c)(3) nonprofit status as a community benefit agency. From this base, they began working toward their goals: helping Native Americans in need, preserving and promoting their native heritage, and acquiring land for environmental preservation. In 1982 the Tribe received official recognition from the state of New Jersey. The Tribe also maintains a good relationship with Sweden, which in turn recognizes the sovereignty of the Tribe. The Swedes were among the first Europeans to engage in trade with Native Americans in Delaware, New Jersey, and Pennsylvania, and a treaty of friendship was signed between Sweden and the native peoples in the 17th century—a treaty that Sweden still honors. The Nanticoke-Lenape Tribe claims a membership of over 3,000 persons.

The Nanticoke-Lenape Tribe of New Jersey and the native peoples of Pennsylvania have much in common, including a common culture and history. Neither has a reservation, though each has purchased land for native purposes. In our research with Lenapes in southeastern Pennsylvania, we found many who had family or friendship ties with those in New Jersey, and several prominent members of Pennsylvanian Native American organizations actually live in Bridgeton, New Jersey. Both have encountered opposition from state officials who were concerned that they might use their status to create casinos. The Nanticoke-Lenape Tribe responded to this by a formal tribal proclamation that forbids the group's participation in casino gambling; Pennsylvania groups have not been able to take this step, but they have clearly expressed no interest in opening casinos.

The Nanticoke-Lenapes of New Jersey have found advantages in both their numbers and their unity. With 3,000 members, the New Jersey organization has a considerably larger organization than any in Pennsylvania, where the largest group (the Eastern Delaware Nation) lays claim to 600 members. The New Jersey organization is more concentrated in a single geographic location, while Pennsylvania's American Indians are spread thinly across the state. Also, the American Indians of New Jersey have been represented since the 1970s by a single political structure, while Pennsylvania's organizations have split and factionalized over time (see chapter 6). (An exception to this is the Unalachtigo band of the Nanticoke-Lenape Nation [NLN], which is unaffiliated with the NLN and advocates casino gambling.) Nonetheless, significant historical, cultural, and political parallels exist.

Conclusion

In general, the Native Americans of Pennsylvania have a great deal in common with Native Americans in the rest of the United States, and in particular, with native groups in the East. The Lenape were early victims of European colonization, and many were forced to move out of Pennsylvania altogether over a period of several generations in the 17th and 18th centuries. Those that remained behind assimilated into American life in order to survive, a process that both permitted their survival while threatening their claims to a native heritage. Nonetheless, Native Americans in Pennsylvania are convinced that they deserve the same consideration as other native groups like the Pequots or the Lumbees and especially their neighbors, the Nanticoke-Lenape Tribe of New Jersey.

In our research, we found that not only were Pennsylvania's Native Americans proud of their heritage, but also they were willing to negotiate with state and local governments on a cooperative basis, despite the long history of conflict, broken treaties, and conflicting policies. As a Seneca man from Sullivan County told us,

> People say, "Don't you hate the government?" Well, the government today isn't the government that did all the wrongs. And the government that did all the wrongs were actually people not from here. They were not from this land, but they were the ones who started the laws and decided where we could go and where we couldn't go. We can work with the government today.

A Nanticoke man expanded on this idea by saying the following:

> I had an elder tell me, "We had the land lost once, we're not going to do it again." But they're including all of America in that. You know, we want the right to practice religion and stuff—it doesn't mean we want to take over the country or anything like that. We *all* live here now.

ILLUSTRATION 2. Iroquois pot rim design.

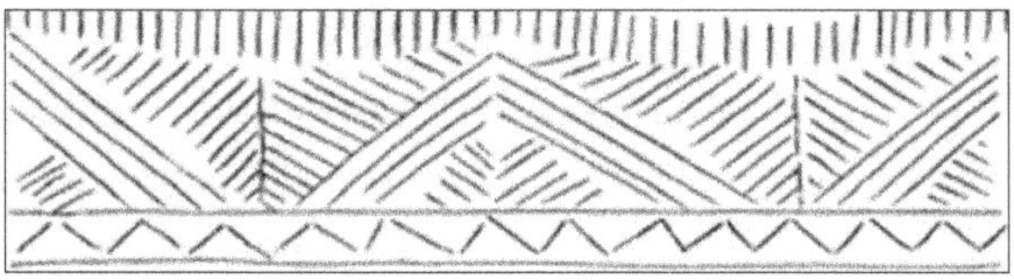

Chapter 2

The History of Native Americans in Pennsylvania

Introduction

This book is about Native Americans in Pennsylvania *today*, so a chapter that looks back to the 17th or 18th centuries may seem out of place. However, we doubt that Native Americans themselves would find this to be the case. Native Americans in Pennsylvania are proud of their heritage, and in large part, they define themselves by it. Past events such as the Walking Purchase of 1737 or what happened to Native American children at the Carlisle Industrial School from 1879 to 1918 are spoken of as if they occurred yesterday. Events such as these are used to explain lost identities or uncertain family histories (e.g., "it wasn't safe to call yourself an Indian") or a renewed sense of being Native American (e.g., "my grandmother was at Carlisle…"). Dancers at powwows compare regalia and place a particular dress or dance in history (e.g., "women wore dresses like these on the Trail of Tears"). Therefore, no discussion of Native Americans today would be complete without a sense of their history. To be a Native American is to recognize the native past and the injustices that occurred during contact with Europeans.

NATIVE AMERICANS IN PENNSYLVANIA

When Europeans first arrived in the Delaware River basin, they met the people known as the Lenape. The Lenape were located in the Delaware River Valley, an area that today encompasses Philadelphia and its surrounding counties in Pennsylvania, New Jersey, and northern Delaware. Along the Susquehanna, they encountered the people who are known to us today as the Susquehannocks. Two other populations of Native Americans populated western Pennsylvania at the time of contact, but both groups were gone before Europeans met them, and little is known about them. The Eries (Eriechronon) lived in northwestern Pennsylvania but were apparently wiped out by the Iroquois by 1655 in competition for hunting territory to provide pelts for trade to Europeans. In southwestern Pennsylvania, a culture known only from archaeological excavations, the Monongahela, lived. Richter (2005, pp. 30–32) suggests that they may have been victims of the smallpox epidemics that accompanied European contact.

The Iroquois (or the Haudenosaunee, "the People of the Longhouse"), were actually five related but different Native American groups living in what is now New York State. From east to west across the state, they were the Mohawks, the Oneida, the Onondaga, the Cayuga, and the Seneca. In their efforts to increase trade and assert their autonomy in the face of colonialism, the Iroquois became embroiled in events in Pennsylvania. In addition to their hostilities toward the Eries, the Iroquois also fought with the Susquehannocks. The Iroquois extended some measure of control over the Lenape. The Iroquois refusal to intervene on behalf of the Lenape over the Walking Purchase became a major reason many Lenapes began to migrate west out of Pennsylvania in the 18th century.

European settlement, trade, and warfare scattered Native Americans up and down the Eastern Seaboard and created migrations of people, many of whom settled briefly in Pennsylvania in the 18th century. Shawnees from Kentucky, Nanticokes and Conoys from Maryland, and Tuscaroras from the Carolinas are all examples of native groups that moved into Pennsylvania during this period. Some of them settled in the state and intermarried with both natives and Europeans. In the 1950s, in an effort to promote better economic opportunities and assimilationist policies for Native Americans, the U.S. government began encouraging Native Americans to leave reservations and to settle in cities. Many of them moved eastward to settle in places like Philadelphia and Pittsburgh. These "urban Indians" came from all over the United States. Some of the first Native American associations in Pennsylvania were built around these urban migrants (e.g., the United American Indians of the Delaware Valley).

From today's perspective, the past seems neat and tidy, especially compared to the rapid changes we see in our own lives. In this view, it is easy to believe that the world has always been as we see it now. Pennsylvania has always existed; the Lenape and the Susquehannocks always lived where and how they lived at the time of contact; and sharp cultural differences separated Lenapes, Susquehannocks, Mohawks, and others into distinct, bounded entities that seldom interacted or intersected. In this way, the Native American past seems like a series of dioramas in a museum. This glassed-in box contains all there is to know about the Lenape, this one the Susquehannocks, and so on. To many, Native Americans only existed in this past. Some of our informants commented on this:

> We did a show once with a group of Cub Scouts, and it was with a man that I worked with. He met me in the hall the next day. He said, "I had an awful time telling my son you were Indian." And I said, "Well, why?" "Well, Indian people don't wear wristwatches. You had a watch on." They don't see. They think Indian people are supposed to stay the same as we were 500 years ago. Their people, the Pilgrims, they've changed, but they don't see Indian people as changing at all.

The reality is that the Native American social landscape was fluid and always changing. Oral histories among Native Americans tell of waves of migration in—and out—of the Northeast. Villages were relocated periodically; even "permanent settlements" shifted every 15 to 20 years as resources in an area were depleted and housing deteriorated. Native Americans warred with each other, traded with each other, and intermarried with each other. Raiding parties often sought to obtain captives to either avenge a death or replace someone who had died. Englebrecht (2003, p. 162) writes that some Iroquois villages had as many non-Iroquois as Iroquois living in them. Alliances were made or set aside, and "traditional territories" expanded or contracted as circumstances intervened. A system of trails crisscrossed Pennsylvania and allowed the opportunity for Native Americans to travel great distances. A code of hospitality meant that Native Americans looked after strangers in need who were traveling these trails and that people, information, and goods could pass with relative ease between cultures we now think of as isolated by geography.

European contact added to this flux of cultures. Diseases devastated Native American communities and intensified the need for captives and intermarriage. Warfare escalated as Europeans used one Native American group to attack another; Native Americans also warred among themselves over trade rights with Europeans. Some Europeans admired natives, living among them and fairly dealing with them. Others hated natives and carried out attacks or designed policies against them. The availability of European-made trade goods led Native Americans to expand their territories or to travel great distances to obtain what they needed or wanted. As the pressures of European settlement increased, natives of different tribal backgrounds united, if only briefly, to defend their territory or to attack the Europeans. Villages of natives of mixed backgrounds became common. Thus, the distinctions among different groups that the modern world demands ("are you a Lenape or a Nanticoke?") may not have been as fixed in the past as we see them now.

This chapter is not intended to be a comprehensive description of the social lives and history of Native Americans in Pennsylvania. There are many texts available that give detailed information on the lives of the various native groups that lived in or passed through Pennsylvania. Examples include Weslager (1972), P. Wallace (1981), Kent (1984), Kraft (1986), Englebrecht (2003), and Richter (2005). Other texts deal with Native Americans in North America in a general manner, and these normally include a section on the cultures of the Northeast. Among these are Garbarino and Sasso (1994), Oswalt (1998), and Bonvillain (2001). What we present here is a thumbnail sketch of the principle groups indigenous to Pennsylvania—the Lenape and the Susquehannocks, as well as the Iroquois—whose influence on both native and European life in Pennsylvania was considerable. We will also present an overview of key historical events of the contact period, especially those such as the Walking Purchase, which had a profound effect on Native Americans.

One additional introductory note is necessary. In this book, we have used what we believe are the most commonly used names for the various groups indigenous to Pennsylvania and neighboring states, but different groups were often known—and are still known—by different names. Different Europeans called the same people by different names. Thus, the French called the Lenape "Loups." Some Europeans used the label "Seneca" to refer to all the members of the Iroquois Confederacy. It was a common European pattern to refer to a native group by the river along which they lived; thus, people of the same ethnicity who lived on different rivers were known by different names. The Lenape were called "Delawares" by many Europeans because of where many of them lived, and many Lenape still use or prefer that label. Kent (1984) points out that no one knows what the Susquehannocks called themselves; that was what the native interpreters traveling with John Smith in 1608 called them when he encountered them. The Susquehannocks that lived along the Conestoga River in Lancaster County came to be named for that waterway. In addition, names for various clans or tribal sections within a tribe came to be used as if they represented separate tribes. Thus, the label "Munsee" is used sometimes to refer to a tribal segment of the Lenape and sometimes as a name for a separate tribe that is seen as being related to the Lenape. The diverse array of labels for groups of what were probably the same people is a good symbol of the flexibility in native social lives and the absence of centralized authority, or a "national" identity, for these groups.

THE LENAPE

The Lenape, or Lenni Lenape (as already noted), lived in what is today Delaware, New Jersey, and Pennsylvania, from the Atlantic Coast to the Susquehanna River. According to their oral tradition, the Lenape migrated into this area from the western part of North America. The 18th-century Moravian missionary, David Zeisberger, who lived among the Lenape for 62 years, reported that they called themselves "Wabanaki," "the people living towards the rising sun." Weslager (1972, p. 80) suggests a less picturesque translation: "easterner." Most sources accept the Lenape tradition that they were the original settlers of the area in which Europeans found them. Indeed, the name Lenape translates as "the common people," with "common" having the connotation of "original." ("Lenni" is a derivation of "Lenape" and carries the same meaning; Lenni Lenape is, technically, redundant.) Both the Lenape and their neighbors referred to them as the "Grandfather People," to indicate their place as the original settlers—supposedly, neighboring groups honored them in this role. The Lenape belong to the Algonquian language family, a language family stretched over a huge geographical area from northern Canada to the southeastern United States. Other Algonquian speakers included the Shawnees, Mohegans, and Potomacs, as well as the Algonquin people of Ontario, Canada, for whom the language family was named. As pointed out earlier, the Lenape came to be called the Delaware by the Europeans, and today, both individuals and organizations often use this label rather than Lenape. Estimates of the Lenape population at contact range from 8,000 to 12,000, though Becker (1989) has a much more conservative estimate of 350–500 people.

Today, the Lenape are referred to as a "tribe," a term that suggests a great deal more political unity than was, in fact, the case. In reality, the Lenape lived in widely scattered villages that ranged from 50 to 100 people. Each village occupied a conventionally agreed-upon territory.

The Lenape were what anthropologists call "horticulturalists" (people who grow crops on small plots only using handheld tools). Fields were cleared by removing the bark from the base of trees and building a fire there; large dead trees were left standing. For the Lenape, as for all the native peoples of the Northeast at contact, the chief crops were corn or maize, beans, and squash. Often referred to as the Three Sisters, these crops were grown in the same field, with the seeds of all three plants placed in a hill. The seeds germinate at about the same time and grow in a complementary manner. The beans vine around the growing corn stalks for support, and the squash vines spread across the ground acting as a ground cover. Recent research indicates the great potential productivity of this system (Wolkomir, 1995). In addition, sunflowers, purslane, and a number of other plant foods were cultivated, and some wild plant foods such as strawberries, crabapple trees, or nut trees were encouraged to grow or were perhaps deliberately planted. Corn, beans, and squash were eaten either fresh or dried, and they were stored in underground pits for winter consumption. Corn was either roasted or ground to be used as mush. Food was either placed directly in a fire or boiled in pottery containers. (Becker [1989] disagrees; based on his archaeological research, he believes that the Lenape did not practice horticulture until after contact with Europeans.)

In addition to collecting wild plant foods, the Lenape also hunted and fished. Deer and a variety of other animals were hunted with bow and arrow, trapped with snares, or driven into enclosures. Animals provided meat, pelts or skins for clothing, and grease or oil for cooking. A gender division of labor occurred: Men hunted and cleared the fields for planting, and women tended the fields and collected wild plants. In the course of a year, the Lenape moved to take advantage of the availability of different resources. Often, men were away from the village hunting. In the winter, particularly, men built lean-to shelters or used rock overhangs for protection in their hunting territories.

A village was made up of several scattered family dwellings called "wigwams." Most commonly, these structures were made out of saplings bent into a hemispherical shape, which was then covered in elm bark.

Wigwams were used mostly for sleeping or getting out of inclement weather; otherwise, most activities took place outdoors. A wigwam usually housed a single married couple and their dependents.

The basis of social organization was kinship, and villages were largely collections of kinsmen rather than centrally organized political units. Kinship was organized through matrilineal descent. That is, descent and inheritance were traced through the mother's side of the family—this will be discussed in more detail in the next chapter. As is the case with matrilineal societies generally, Lenape women had respect and status. Many sources point out that many European women who were taken as captives by native people in the colonial era would refuse to be rescued to go back to colonial society. In a kin-based society like the Lenape, all aspects of social life revolved around the kin group. Decisions about the village were made collectively by kin groups. Matrilocal residence dominated residence patterns; that is, a new husband moved into the community of his wife. Several villages in the same region were usually linked by kinship ties. People married outside their kin group (clan), which often required searching for an eligible spouse in a village some distance from one's own.

Personal life was built around the combined ideals of individual choice and community responsibility. Our modern informants often emphasize the values of tolerance and respecting the "paths" of others. As one informant told us,

> There are people out there dictating to other people what things are done. It's not the native way. The native way is that everyone has a path. If I hear you talk about something on your path that I like, I should ask permission to carry that on my path. If I say something he likes, he should ask permission to carry it on his path.

At the same time, individuals were responsible for fulfilling their economic and social responsibilities to their spouses and families, as well as being responsible for the maintenance of the environment and the community. ("Our reason to be here…wasn't the feathers or the beadwork or the drumming, our purpose is to be caretakers. Being caretakers of this earth and caretakers of each other," said a Lenape woman.) Hospitality was an important expectation, and sharing was mandatory. Generally, no one went hungry unless everyone was hungry.

Weslager (1972) had this to say about the Lenape lifestyle:

> The [Lenape's] simple tools, weapons, utensils and clothing met their economic needs; their religious life gave them spiritual fulfillment; and they lived in peace with the unhurried life of their little villages, where they were taught to share with each other, lacking the competition present in European society. According to their own standards, the [Lenape] satisfied their living requirements through an attunement to their environment; they were content because they had few unfilled wants. (p. 73)

Weslager goes on to say that the Lenape's inexperience with warfare and their vulnerable village locations along navigable streams and rivers would leave them unprepared for the period of European contact.

In their book about Native American culture, Garbarino and Sasso (1994) add this rather sad paragraph:

> The Leni Lenape...once were a very important and respected tribe. Many other Algonkian tribes called members of the Lenape tribe "grandfather," a title of honor; the Shawnee and Mahican believed that they were descended from Lenape. In the early 18th century the Iroquois assumed control over the Lenape, then both Iroquois and white pressure pushed the Lenape out of their traditional lands. They settled in Ohio and Indiana and eventually lost all cohesiveness, some groups ending up in Arkansas, Texas, Kansas and Oklahoma. (p. 301)

The Susquehannocks

By comparison to the Lenape, relatively little is known about the people called the Susquehannocks. No one knows what they called themselves. In 1608 John Smith met a party of 60 warriors as he sailed up the Susquehanna River; his native interpreters called these warriors Susquehannocks. The Lenape called them Minquas, a name that translates as "treacherous," a reflection of the raids Susquehannocks made on the Lenape in the 17th century. The French called them Andaste or Gandastogues ("people of the blackened ridge pole"). The latter name was later transcribed as Conestoga, which is what English settlers called them. Smith claimed that there were six Susquehannock towns along the river, but by 1625 their only known community was at present-day Washington Boro. Demographers estimate that there may have been as many as 5,000 to 7,000 Susquehannocks in 1608, but smallpox and warfare rapidly reduced their numbers to around 300 by the year 1700.

The Susquehannocks spoke an Iroquoian language, related to the languages of the Iroquois in New York State and the Hurons of Ontario. The language survives only as small lists of vocabulary items written down in the mid-18th and early 19th centuries. Like their neighbors to the north, the Susquehannocks lived in large palisaded towns. Unlike the loosely affiliated Lenapes, the Susquehannocks maintained a centrally controlled political system. According to Kent (1984, p. 37), in 1647 there may have been as many as 4,000 people living in the single Susquehannock town. Decision making and the arbitration of disputes in a community of that size would have required some kind of centralized authority, unlike a Lenape village of 50 to 100 people where kin elders and informal sanctions (like gossip) could keep the peace.

The Susquehannocks were also unlike the Lenape in that they were a warrior society. Smith was impressed by their size, arms, and demeanor, and the natives who accompanied him seemed to fear them. Their palisaded forts were solid, well-placed, and well-guarded. They defeated the Mohawks in 1651. An attack by the Senecas on the Susquehannock town in 1663 was easily repulsed. Maryland entered into a treaty with the Susquehannocks in 1661 to defend Maryland's trade interests against the Seneca. The Lenape were victims of Susquehannock expansions into their territory after 1633.

Two things led to the ultimate defeat of the Susquehannocks: (1) the aforementioned smallpox epidemics that accompanied contact with Europeans, and (2) the loss of their allies. The Susquehannocks had allied with the Hurons in Ontario to contain the Iroquois and to gain control of the fur trade with Europeans. But the Iroquois defeated the

Hurons in the 1630s, removing them as a threat; they would then turn their attention to the Susquehannocks. Maryland, as noted, had entered into a treaty with the Susquehannocks against the Seneca in 1651, but in 1674 Maryland unexpectedly severed their ties with the Susquehannocks and made peace with the Senecas. The Susquehannocks abandoned their Washington Boro site in 1675 and moved to a site on Piscataway Creek, below present-day Washington, D.C. There they were surprised by a force made up of Virginia and Maryland militiamen and were soundly defeated. P. Wallace (1981) wrote: "The survivors scattered; eventually most of them were adopted by the Iroquois; others returned to the lower Susquehanna, where they were joined at Conestoga by a group of their former enemies, the Senecas" (p. 104).

The Susquehannock community in Conestoga survived until 1763 when they fell prey to the Paxton Boys, a vigilante group fired with hatred of all American Indians brought on by Pontiac's Rebellion (1763) and the French and Indian War. On December 14, 1763, the Paxton Boys murdered six unarmed Susquehannocks at Conestoga. Fourteen others, mostly old men, women, and children, fled to Lancaster where they were placed under the protection of the local authorities. Thirteen days later, the Paxton Boys marched into Lancaster, invaded the "safe" house in which the Susquehannocks were being given refuge, and killed them all. Most historical accounts conclude that the last of the Susquehannocks died that day, but as seen, P. Wallace reports that some of them had been absorbed into the Iroquois, most likely the Senecas.

One of our informants put it this way:

> This area, too—the Susquehannocks were all through this area, and the white history books will tell you that there's no Susquehannocks alive, they were all massacred—the Paxton Boys—and yet, many people have Susquehannock blood. They hid. They hid with people they knew would protect them, and, no, they don't exist as a cohesive tribe, but there's a good number of them pretending they're Senecas. They will say, "We're Susquehannock" until something goes down on the Seneca Reservation, and then, "Oh, we're Seneca."

Almost nothing is known about the daily lives of the Susquehannocks. Because of their militancy, Europeans did not live among them as they did with the Lenape, and Susquehannocks numbers were reduced quickly by warfare and disease. Garbarino and Sasso (1994) said the following:

> All Iroquoian speakers had a subsistence similar to the Algonkian. Their foods were cultivated crops, game, and wild plants. Farming and wild-plant gathering were women's tasks, while men took care of fishing, hunting and warfare. Material culture too was much like the Algonkian in weapons, tools, and utensils. (p. 303)

Archaeology in known Susquehanna sites confirms this conclusion. Therefore, most researchers assume that the daily lives of the Lenape, the Susquehannocks, and the Iroquois were very similar. This would have made trade and assimilation into one another's communities relatively easy. Where the Susquehannocks differed from the Lenape was in the structure of their communities; Susquehannocks lived much like the Iroquois in this regard.

THE IROQUOIS

While the Iroquois did not reside in what would become Pennsylvania at the time of European contact, they subsequently became very influential in the lives of both the indigenous peoples and the Europeans in Pennsylvania in the 17th and 18th centuries. While "Iroquois" is the name by which these people are known today, the word itself is a label applied to these people by others. Most sources believe that the word "Iroquois" is an Algonquian word meaning something like "slayer." Englebrecht (2003, p. 137) suggests that the word might have been Basque, but with a very similar meaning. The Iroquois referred to themselves as the Haudenosaunee or "People of the Long House." The Iroquois lived in large palisaded villages like the Susquehannocks, but unlike the Lenape wigwams (i.e., "single family dwellings," to use today's language), the Iroquois (and the Susquehannocks) lived in longhouses. The term "longhouse" is very descriptive. They were structures 50 to 100 feet long (and sometimes much longer) that housed an extended family. The basic construction was like a wigwam—poles bent in a curved shape, covered with bark. (Englebrecht argues that they were much more substantial structures, i.e., that the walls were supported by tall, vertical poles set deep in the ground, covered by a domed roof.) Doors covered with hides were located at either end (and sometimes in the middle in very large structures). Individual nuclear families lived in separate compartments on the sides of the longhouse; they shared a firepit in the middle with the family on the opposite side. The sides were lined with platforms for sleeping and storage. Like the Lenape, the Iroquois practiced matrilineal descent and matrilocal residence, so basically, the longhouse was inhabited by a large number of women related through a common female ancestor along with their husbands and children. Women owned property and were the cultivators; men hunted, fished, and engaged in war. Extended families were organized into matrilineal clans headed by the senior women of those kinship units.

Iroquois towns were set on hilltops and were surrounded by three rows of palisaded logs, set deep into the ground. Occasionally, a ditch surrounded the outer walls. The gates leading into each of the walls were narrow and offset to make them easily defensible. Watchtowers and firing stations made it easy to guard the walls and defend them. The walls of the longhouses faced the gates so that any visitor or invader making it through the gates was confronted by longhouse walls, rather than a corridor leading easily into the community. Sources suggest that 300 to 600 people lived in each village. The area outside the walls was cleared to provide fields for cultivating corn, beans, squash, and other crops and to help make an invading force conspicuous. Despite the solidity of these communities, they were moved every 10 to 20 years. Horticulturalists did not typically replenish the soil they cultivated with fertilizers, so eventually the fields became less productive. Also, these wooden and bark-covered structures eventually deteriorated, and it was apparently easier to move to another location rather than rebuild. Moving a village was a gradual process, as a great deal of work was necessary to clear new fields and build the fortress walls. Englebrecht (2003, p. 102) says that one historical source reports there were eight Mohawk villages, but he suspects that there were really only four, with another four in the process of being built.

As noted earlier, the Iroquois were not really one tribe, but rather five related tribes across New York State and bordering regions of Canada. From east to west geographically, they were the Mohawks, the Oneidas, the Onondagas, the Cayugas, and the Senecas. These five tribes visualized themselves as a longhouse stretched across their territory. The Mohawks were the Keepers of the Eastern Door, and the Senecas were the Keepers of the Western Door. The Onondagas occupied the central region and became the Keepers of the Council Fire. The five tribes were confederated into the Five Nations, or the League of the Iroquois (later, the Iroquoian-speaking Tuscaroras migrated into the region from North Carolina and were added as a sixth nation in 1722). Sources do not agree on when the League was formed. Some say that the League is very old, stretching back into the early prehistory of the Northeast; others believe it was formed at the time of European contact as a response to pressure to competition over trade and to European settlement. The most widely accepted version suggests that the League was the idea of a 16th-century Mohawk visionary named Deganawidah. Deganawidah was concerned that the five tribes weakened themselves by fighting among themselves; he saw the tribes as vulnerable to the Hurons to their north. He persuaded another Mohawk named Hiawatha to join him in persuading the five tribes to form an alliance. The alliance that emerged from this never entirely did away with hostilities among the five tribes, but it did produce a mechanism by which to adjudicate disputes among the different tribes and to fight their common enemies, the Hurons.

The original League was made up of 50 members of a council appointed by tribal councils with the approval of the women who headed up the matrilineal clans. The League debated matters that affected all member tribes, as well as disputes between different tribes. Issues that affected only one tribe were dealt with by that tribe. League decisions had to be unanimous, and considerable debate often occurred before consensus was reached. Within each tribe, the women who led the clans selected a male who represented the clan at a tribal council; the women had the right to recall a representative they felt was unsatisfactory. Today, the League still exists and consists of 50 members. It meets periodically in the Onondaga territory because of their central location; one of the Onondaga representatives serves as chair of the League.

The Iroquois League probably served as an important role model for the emerging U.S. government after independence. Weatherford (1989) notes that the Founding Fathers had few examples in democracy or federalism within their own political traditions. Certainly, England in the late 18th century was no democracy. In 1744 an Iroquois representative, Canassatego, complained to the colonial government that the Iroquois found it difficult to deal with 13 separate colonies, each with its own administration. The original independent government was formed under the Articles of Confederation, which made each of the 13 states separate and sovereign, but this arrangement quickly became unworkable. Benjamin Franklin, who had been appointed Indian commissioner by the colony of Pennsylvania in the 1750s, had suggested to the Albany Congress in 1754 that the colonies follow the lead of the Iroquois and adopt a central government for national issues while allowing colonies local control over their own matters. Thomas Jefferson was also very aware of the Iroquois' form of government, as his writings make clear. Many of the constitutional compromises we regard today as due to the cleverness of people like Franklin and Jefferson had already been in use by the Iroquois for decades.

The Iroquois became an effective force in the politics and trade in New York, Pennsylvania, Ontario, and other neighboring areas. The total population of the original Five Nations at contact has been estimated at only 10,000, but because of their unity, the Iroquois exerted an influence far beyond their numbers. When they needed to fight, they did so, and the forces they could muster as a League were large enough and organized enough to be a substantial threat to their neighbors.

When fighting would not work, they were able diplomats, offering concessions and friendship to an array of European governments. In Pennsylvania, they tried to buffer themselves from European incursions by supporting the rights of the Lenape and other native groups in the Wyoming Valley after the Treaty of Easton was signed in 1757. As a solution to the "Indian problem" in Pennsylvania, the colonial government through its agents, Conrad Weiser and James Logan, had signed a treaty with the League in 1731; this treaty granted the Iroquois authority over all the native people of Pennsylvania and gave them the responsibility of keeping the peace. When Weiser was sent by the colonial authorities into central Pennsylvania to deal with native problems in 1731, he met with Shikellamy, a representative of the League at present-day Sunbury, at the confluence of the west and north branches of the Susquehanna River. Shikellamy had come from New York as a resident emissary to speak for all the native peoples of Pennsylvania. Most sources refer to the League as a great power to be reckoned with, a sort of native imperial state, dominating native affairs in the Northeast in the 17th and 18th centuries until the French and Indian War. By contrast, Jennings (1993, pp. 216, 295) disagrees, noting that attempts to extend Iroquois domination westward failed and that the Iroquois also failed to take advantage of the French and Indian War because they could not decide on which side to offer their support. At any rate, after the war, the victorious British severely limited the Iroquois' powers in New York State; with the independence of the former 13 colonies, the new U.S. government dealt harshly with people they saw as British sympathizers.

European Contact

In this section, we will highlight some of the more significant events that shaped the relationships between Europeans and the native peoples of Pennsylvania. Again, this is not intended to be a comprehensive description of the entire history of Lenape-European or Iroquois-European relations.

Trade

In the early 17th century, Dutch traders began to interact with the Lenape on the Delaware River. After Henry Hudson's voyage to North America in 1609 and his report that this new land had an abundance of fur-bearing animals, Dutch captains began to bring European goods to the new continent to trade for those furs. Trade dominated European-native relations for the next several decades. Native Americans at contact had a stone tool/ceramic vessel technology. They quickly appreciated the advantages of metal tools over stone ones, and they were happy to trade what was commonplace to them—pelts—for European goods. Englebrecht (2003) notes that glass beads and mirrors were more to the Iroquois than pretty trinkets:

> While Europeans may have thought these items of little economic value, native peoples wished to acquire them because they were similar to existing symbolically charged substances… . Today we view seventeenth-century…oxidized metal in museum display cases, and to most visitors these objects are dull and uninteresting. But when new, polished metal, crystals, and glass reflect the light of the sun or fire. To traditional Iroquois, all objects possessed animate power or orenda, but these reflective substances must have been seen as possessing orenda in abundance. (p. 135)

Native Americans quickly became addicted to European trade goods, and just as quickly abandoned their own traditional crafts. Metal cooking pots replaced pottery or were cut up to produce projectile points; a musket with shot and powder became essential for hunting; and Dutch clay pipes replaced ones made from local stone. Traditional Native Americans living above the Rio Grande were the only people who never distilled alcohol or brewed beer, so the introduction of whiskey was a great favorite, and subsequently, many natives became alcoholics. The early history of Pennsylvania is one of the Quaker leadership—often with the support of Native American leaders—trying to prohibit the sale of alcohol to natives, while traders, aware of market demand, used every subterfuge to get alcohol into the hands of American Indians eager to trade for it. In their eagerness for European goods, Native Americans were willing to trade away whatever they had. When beaver hats were the rage in Europe, Native Americans wiped out beaver populations in the Northeast; the eastern species of beaver was driven into extinction this way. When beaver pelts no longer were in demand, Native Americans turned to other wildlife—especially deer—for hides to trade. Hostilities among Native Americans increased as groups competed for hunting grounds or control of important trade routes; the Eries were destroyed by the Iroquois when the Iroquois needed to hunt beaver in Erie territory. As dependency for European goods increased, Native Americans found themselves easily manipulated by Europeans. If Europeans wanted something—land, trade routes, allies, and so forth—all they had to do was withhold those goods that had become essential to Native American life in the Northeast.

William Penn

In 1665 England took possession of the mid-Atlantic region, winning it away from the Dutch. In 1681 Charles II of England granted William Penn the right to claim land in Pennsylvania ("Penn's Woods"). Penn regarded his new grant as a "holy experiment"; he was determined to make Pennsylvania a democracy in which religious tolerance and civic freedoms would be upheld. Penn wanted to extend his ideals of benevolence and tolerance to Native Americans, as well. In 1681 before coming to America, Penn wrote a letter to the indigenous people and insisted that it be read by his agents in his new territory. In it, he wrote the following: "The king of the countrey [*sic*] where I live, hath given unto me a great Province, but I desire to enjoy it with your Love and Consent that we may always live together as Neighbors and Friends." When Pennsylvania first passed into English hands, it became crown land, the possession of the king; Native Americans were not recognized as having any rights to their traditional territories at all. Penn insisted that the Native Americans were the legal owners of the land and needed to be dealt with fairly. A hallmark of Penn's American Indian policy was the idea that if Europeans were to own land in Pennsylvania, they would have to purchase titles to the land from the native inhabitants. In a famous meeting in 1682 with the Lenapes Tamamend and Metamequam, Penn extended his friendship to the Lenapes and purchased land from them. In subsequent years, Penn purchased several additional pieces of property from Lenape groups. Eventually, Penn purchased most of what would become Philadelphia and the surrounding counties. Native American villages that existed on these purchases were allowed to remain; they were reserved for the original inhabitants—the first "reservations" in America. However, if the natives left their villages, all ownership rights went to Europeans.

Most accounts of the contact period emphasize the differences between Native Americans and Europeans with regard to property. To Native Americans, property was not private; it did not belong to individuals, and no individuals could dispose of it. Property was communally owned, and all members of the community had the right to use it. This included both the land on which villages were situated and the surrounding land for planting and hunting. Many misunderstandings occurred in European-native contact as deals were made with individual American Indians "allowing" Europeans to claim land that the individual had no right to sell or give away. Penn seems to have understood that. He dealt with village elders as agents of their people, and in his letters, he shows his belief that he had conveyed the concept of permanent ownership to native leaders. When misunderstandings arose, Penn was willing to purchase the same piece of land again to make certain that European ownership was not in doubt.

Penn also established laws in his new colony that dealt with native groups as sovereign nations and which offered the same treatment and rights to both natives and Europeans. There has been much speculation as to what would have happened to native-European relations had Penn been in residence for a longer period of time in Pennsylvania. However, his time in his new colony was relatively brief—two visits totaling 4 years of residence. In his absence, his agents were not as scrupulous as he, and Penn's influence was undermined by legal and financial problems in England. After 1712, when he suffered a stroke, he was also in poor health. He died in 1718, and ownership of Penn's Woods was inherited by his sons.

THE WALKING PURCHASE

After Penn's death, his three sons, John, Thomas, and Richard, assumed control of Pennsylvania. The sons were much less conciliatory toward native peoples than their father, and as more and more Europeans flowed into the colony, the pressures for land steadily increased. In 1735 James Logan, acting on behalf of the Penns, met with some Lenapes and presented them with what was said to be a copy of a deed signed in 1686. Allegedly an agreement between William Penn and the Lenape, this deed gave Penn the right to all Lenape lands that fell within a day and a half's walk from the borders of the properties the Penns currently held. This deed had supposedly been discovered by Thomas Penn in England; the original was missing, the copy was unsigned, and no official record has ever been found of the original transaction. Nevertheless, Logan informed the Lenape that the Penns regarded the document as binding and that they meant to enforce its terms.

Weakened by conflicts with the Iroquois and disease introduced by Europeans, the Lenape agreed to the provisions of the deed, believing that the Europeans would take a leisurely walk along the Delaware River. Instead, the Penns hired three fast runners and had a straight path into Lenape lands cleared. One of these runners managed to penetrate 55 miles into the countryside. This represented an area of 1,200 square miles, an area about the size of Rhode Island. Incensed by this duplicity, the Lenape turned to the Iroquois for support, since the Iroquois had been granted authority over American Indian affairs in Pennsylvania in 1731. The Iroquois refused to intervene, however, claiming that the Lenape, as a conquered people, had no right to negotiate or sell land rights at all. Sipe (1927) quotes Canassatego, the head of an Iroquois delegation, as saying to the Lenape the following:

> But how came you to take upon yourselves to sell land at all? We conquered you; we made women of you; you know you are women, and can no more sell land than women. Nor is it fit that you should have the power of selling land, since you would abuse it. The land that you claim is gone through your guts. (p. 172)

The Walking Purchase infuriated the Lenape, and our informants of Lenape descent still speak resentfully of it. But faced with the intransigence of both Europeans and the Iroquois, the Lenape felt they had little choice but to relocate farther west.

The Wyoming Valley/The Lenape Turn to War

In 1742 the Iroquois ordered the Lenape out of the Delaware River area and into the Wyoming Valley, where present-day Wilkes-Barre is located. The Wyoming Valley was a fertile, protected area, and it was to become the locus of conflict between the Native Americans and Europeans in the middle part of the 18th century. Shawnees had settled there as early as 1701, and some Lenape were already in the area after 1727. When the Nanticokes migrated into Pennsylvania in the 1740s, the Iroquois gave them permission to settle there. In all of these moves, the Iroquois, who were not numerous enough themselves to populate the valley, hoped to create a buffer zone between themselves and Europeans. Among the natives who settled in the area in 1754 was a converted Lenape named Teedyuscung; he led a small band of Lenapes and Mohegans into the valley. In 1756 Pennsylvania recognized Teedyuscung as the "king" of the Lenapes and other tribes in the Wyoming Valley and proclaimed peace between themselves and the American Indians.

The Iroquois repeatedly told the English colonial authorities in Pennsylvania how important the Wyoming Valley was to them. Shikellamy's son, John, told Conrad Weiser in 1755 that the Iroquois would kill any European who settled there. In 1753 the Susquehanna Company had been formed in Connecticut with the express purpose of acquiring land for settlement in the Wyoming Valley. Members of the company began to survey and map the land, and in 1754 they allegedly purchased the valley from the Onondaga. The Iroquois vigorously protested this treaty as a fraud. The Iroquois argued that the company had gotten a few Onondagas drunk and then tricked them into signing documents they did not understand. In 1762 the company began to cut a road into the valley, and the first settlers arrived. Teedyuscung ordered them off; he was ignored. In April of that year, Teedyuscung was burned to death in his cabin. P. Wallace (1981) suggests that the fire may have been accidental, but for the American Indians, "it must have been the last straw" (p. 158). When Connecticut families began to settle, Teedyuscung's son, Captain Bull, rose up and killed or captured all the European settlers in the valley. This is now referred to in Pennsylvania history as the First Wyoming Massacre (the second occurred in 1778, when British forces and their native allies raided the valley and killed large numbers of settlers).

Pushed to the point of violence, the Lenape became feared warriors. But as Weslager (1972) pointed out,

> Neither the social organization nor the economy of the [Lenape] could sustain lengthy warfare as practiced in more complex European societies. The Indians had no specialized class of soldiers; their warriors were also the laborers who cleared the fields for the women to cultivate, pursued the game, and engaged in ot her activities necessary to feed, clothe and house their families. Outnumbered by the superior and well-armed British troops, lacking powder and lead for their guns, their wives and children in jeopardy, their homes and fields in danger of destruction, the [Lenape] had no alternative except to admit defeat and lay down their arms. (p. 249)

The colonial militia and vigilante groups like the Paxton Boys did all they could to kill the American Indians; Pennsylvania paid a bounty on American Indian scalps. On November 14, 1764, the Lenapes and the Shawnees surrendered to Col. Henry Bouquet at Coshocton.

In 1768 the Iroquois joined the Lenape in defeat. At the Treaty of Fort Stanwix, they handed over to Pennsylvania all claims they had to land in the state. This effectively ended any protection the League might have provided to the remaining Lenape. The treaty ceded all American Indian lands west to the Ohio River; beyond the Ohio was still American Indian territory. European settlers almost immediately began to pour over the Alleghenies to take possession of land on the Monongahela River. Many Lenape, Shawnees, and others took this opportunity to relocate to Ohio. Not all, however, chose to leave. As one of our informants said,

> But a good amount of people stayed behind and assimilated and grew up in the back woods and grew up in the back area along the rivers and streams—stayed behind… . It's not that odd of a deal. There's still places you can go up there and never be seen again. And that's a lot of what our people did, you know.

The Trail of Tears

In 1838 another event occurred that still reverberates through Native American communities. This was the Trail of Tears, the forced relocation of approximately 13,000 Cherokees from their homes in the east to what would become Oklahoma. Earlier relocations had involved the Chickasaws, Creeks, and Seminoles; the phrase "Trail of Tears" is sometimes used for all of these actions. The 1838 removal was a result of the treaty of New Echota, which was signed between the state of Georgia and a handful of Cherokees, none of whom had official standing among the Cherokee people. In fact, in 1835 the Cherokee leadership had previously rejected an offer by the U.S. government under the Indian Removal Act of 1830 to relocate west of the Mississippi, regardless of the offer of $4.5 million as compensation at that time. Despite thousands of protests over the suspect legality of the Treaty of New Echota, President Martin Van Buren chose to send 700 federal troops under the command of General Winfield Scott to enforce the treaty. The Cherokees were rounded up from their homes and communities in Georgia, Alabama, Tennessee, and Kentucky with what they could carry, and they were forced to walk to Oklahoma. An estimated 4,000 Native Americans died along the way; as Jennings (1993) said, "[These were] casualties that few armies have had to endure in combat" (p. 333). Most died from disease in camps during the journey.

In North Carolina, approximately 400 Cherokees living on private land in the Smoky Mountains were not included in the move; these became the Eastern Band Cherokees of today. Lenapes, Shawnees, and others also were caught up in the dragnet of federal expulsion. Several of our informants spoke of having relatives who either were part of the Trail of Tears or were able to hide and escape it. Since a significant number of our informants claim Cherokee descent, it is not surprising that Pennsylvanian Native Americans feel so strongly about the Trail. Cherokees have migrated into Pennsylvania since the mid-18th century. In general, the Native Americans we met felt that the Trail of Tears was one of the worst offenses experienced by American Indians at the hands of the U.S. government. Given the intensity of their feelings, we were surprised that so little attention is paid to the Trail in the majority of texts about Native American culture and history. Nevertheless, Congress designated the Trail of Tears National Historic Trail in 1987, and a monument to those who died on the Trail now stands in New Echota.

The Carlisle Indian School

From the beginning, treaties signed between the U.S. government and various Native American groups have included promises that the government would provide Native Americans with educational opportunities. As a result, schools were set up on a voluntary basis for Native American children in various locations around the United States. While some were successful, most Native American families did not see the point of sending their children to a government school; they had their own socialization practices to transmit their own cultures.

By the 1870s, the Board of Indian Commissioners, the predecessor to today's BIA, became alarmed that Native American children were not attending government schools in large numbers. Congress and the board were convinced that it was in the best interest of Native Americans to become assimilated into mainstream American society as quickly as possible. Native Americans were to be "civilized" or "detribalized," according to the language of the time. To achieve this end, the board created boarding schools for Native American children. These boarding schools were deliberately set far away from reservations so that Native American children could be removed from the influence of their parents. The first school was established at the Hampton Institute in Virginia in 1878. This had previously existed to give the children of ex-slaves an education. The second was the Carlisle Indian Industrial Training School in Carlisle, Pennsylvania, on an abandoned military post. The Carlisle school opened for Native American children in 1879 (see Witmer, 1992).

While many other boarding schools were created across the United States in the 1880s and 1890s, the Carlisle Industrial School remains the most notorious of these institutions among Native Americans, and especially among our informants. The founder of the Carlisle School, Richard Pratt, is widely quoted as having said of his mission in opening the school, "Kill the Indian to Save the Man" (Witmer, 1992, p. 24). This phrase ranks in infamy among Native Americans along with General Sheridan's famous 1870 phrase, "The only good Indian is a dead Indian" (Mieder, 1993, p. 38). For his time, Pratt was seen by non-Indians as a liberal reformer acting in the best interests of native people. He was determined that Native Americans could be "civilized" if they could be removed from all native contact and customs. Upon arrival at the school, Native American children had their clothing and possessions confiscated and burned, their hair was cut, and they were clothed in the working-class dress of the period. They were forbidden to either speak their native languages or worship their native religions. Christianity and English were mandatory. The same standards were adopted by boarding schools everywhere. For example, in 1887 the commissioner of American Indian affairs wrote, "Instruction of Indians in the vernacular is not only of no use to them, but is detrimental to the cause of education and civilization and will not be permitted in any Indian school over which the government has any control" (as cited in Spicer, 1962, p. 439). Children were deliberately mixed by background to make using native languages more difficult, and teachers refused to learn or use the native languages and were generally antagonistic toward native customs.

At Carlisle, children lived in dormitories and stayed on the school grounds throughout the school year. In the summer, they were boarded in private non-Indian homes. Contact with their parents and other family was extremely restricted—most children were not even allowed to attend the funerals of their parents. Until the school closed in 1918 (the demands of World War I required that Carlisle become a military installation again), around 10,000 Native American children had been enrolled at the school. The largest single number—1,776—were from the Iroquois; nearly 4,400 were from east of the Mississippi. One hundred and eighty-six children are buried on the grounds. Many others stayed in Pennsylvania after leaving the school. One of our informants, an Abenaki man, recalled a family connection he has with the school:

> I had some free time on my hands and started doing research, and I actually found out that my grandparents had gone to Carlisle. The story is my grandfather turned 18 while he was there, and he went back and kidnapped my grandmother. She was 5 years younger than him… . They decided they had one foot in the white world and one foot in the native world, and they decided to live outside the reservation because there was more here than there was out there.

Several sources emphasize a few positive aspects to the boarding-school experience for Native American children. McBeth (1984) says that boarding schools gave Native Americans the tools they needed to fight back against mainstream society. Having mastered English, some boarding-school graduates became the leaders of Native American communities in the first half of the 20th century. Robert Yellowtail—the leader of the Montana Crow for much of the 20th century, a boarding school graduate, and a self-educated lawyer—was fond of saying, "Without an education, you are the white man's victim; with an education, you are his equal" (Hoxie, 1986, p. 839). Richter (2005, p. 77) points out that while the best a child could achieve at Carlisle was the equivalent of a 10th-grade vocational education, that was still better than most non-Indians achieved in the same era. Richter also suggests that for eastern American Indians who already spoke English and were somewhat assimilated into mainstream society, Carlisle was a consciousness-raising experience that helped to make them aware of their background.

Nevertheless, today Carlisle is remembered by Native Americans as a form of cultural genocide. One Lenape informant said the following:

> My grandfather hated who he was because according to my family story, when he was a kid, he was taken to Carlisle. He was taken away from his family for 5 years. He wasn't on a reservation. He wasn't the member of a tribe. He wasn't anything—nobody in his family was proclaiming him to be an Indian, but somebody found out about it and somebody came and took him away from his parents and put him in a boarding school. He wasn't out West; he wasn't Cheyenne; he wasn't Lakota. He was living in New Jersey. So when he grew up, completely angry about who he was, he was very much an alcoholic and very much abusive to his family and he hated everything about his life and his world.

Home of a military war college, Carlisle is a place of pilgrimage for today's Pennsylvanian Native Americans, though access to the grounds has been severely restricted since the September 11, 2001, terrorist attacks.

As we were interviewing Native Americans, we were shown a painting made by a woman of Lenape background, Jean Moyer. It is a picture of one of the Native American girls who died and is buried at Carlisle, a Lakota girl named Lucy Pretty Eagle. The painting shows Lucy from behind, wearing the 19th century working-class costume that was standard dress for girls at the school. She is staring into a mirror, where she is reflected as a Lakota girl living on the Great Plains. We contacted Moyer to learn the history of the painting. She told us that she visited the cemetery at Carlisle and meditated on what she might paint to capture the anguish of the children held there. She said that Lucy appeared to her in a vision and directed her to paint the scene she did. The painting is a powerful image that symbolizes both the purpose of the school and the feelings the school engenders among Native Americans.

THE CORNPLANTER TRACT/KINZUA DAM

One final event needs to be mentioned to show the impact of history on Native Americans in Pennsylvania. In 1791 the U.S. government granted one acre of land in northwestern Pennsylvania to a Seneca chief named Cornplanter (*Kaiiontwa'ko*—"By What One Plants"). This was a reward for diplomatic services performed by Cornplanter during the American Revolution. Cornplanter originally had been a leader in the fight against European settlement; he had participated in the Second Wyoming Massacre in 1778. He also had been an outspoken critic of the Treaty of Fort Stanwix of 1783, arguing that the concessions made by the Iroquois were not being adequately compensated. Nonetheless, he came to accept the authority of the U.S. government and helped negotiate an end to hostilities between the Shawnees and the new government in Ohio.

Technically, the Cornplanter Tract was never a reservation; rather, it was a land grant to one particular Seneca. Nonetheless, approximately 400 Senecas came to settle with Cornplanter by 1798. Among them was Cornplanter's brother, Handsome Lake, who would later become the founder of a revitalizing Iroquois religious vision at the turn of the 19th century. Cornplanter died in 1836 and was buried on the tract.

As we surveyed Native Americans in the initial part of our research, we asked this question: "Were there ever reservations in Pennsylvania?" There were 281 responses to this question, and 114 (41%) replied "yes." A number of respondents commented on this question, noting that Cornplanter's Tract had been a reservation. When the survey asked "Are there any reservations in Pennsylvania today?" only 31 (11%) said that there were, but one commented "Yes, but the Kinzua Dam is covering it."

In the 1950s the U.S. government, in agreement with the state governments of Pennsylvania and New York, began work on the Kinzua Dam on the upper Allegheny River. The government planners saw multiple advantages to this project: flood control, recreational opportunities on the lake that the dam would create behind it, and hydroelectric power. The reservoir that the dam would produce would cover 9,000 acres, inundating both the Cornplanter Tract and the Seneca reservation in neighboring New York State. This was a direct violation of the Canandaigua Treaty of 1794, which granted the New York reservation to the Seneca. Approximately 200 people were still living on the tract, and the tract contained a number of historic buildings and a cemetery. Native American groups from all over the country protested the building of the Kinzua Dam, and they were joined by a number of prominent non-Indian supporters. Regardless of the objections, the dam was built and completed in 1966. The cemetery was relocated to higher ground and the Senecas eventually received $15 million in compensation for their loss, but resentment over the dam runs deep among Pennsylvanian Native Americans. As Richter (2005) writes, "Perhaps no single event in the state's history—not even the Conestoga Massacre—so eloquently symbolizes the tragic history of American Indians' Pennsylvania" (p. 88).

Conclusion

Today, nearly 400 years have passed since the first Lenape saw a European sailing ship on the Delaware River. During that time, successive governments—colonial, state, federal, and so forth—have presented Native Americans in Pennsylvania with a very clear message: We don't want you here. Through trade, treaties, war, disease, and forced relocation, a very thorough effort was made not only to severely reduce the numbers of Native Americans living in the state but also to destroy their cultures. But Native Americans have endured and are ready to reassert their cultural heritage in the state.

ILLUSTRATION 3. Eastern woodlands pot.

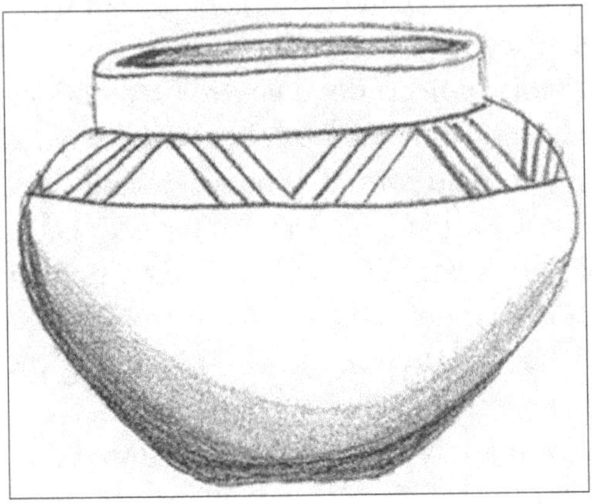

Chapter 3

Stereotypes and Myths

The Indians knew nothing of firearms until they saw them in the hands of the white men. Like the ancient barbarians of other countries, they made use of the primitive bow and arrow, spear, tomahawk, knife and club. Swine, sheep, cows and horses were unknown until brought across the ocean by white men. America, in turn, gave tobacco to the Old World The warrior lolled in his wigwam or tepee, smoking his pipe, while his squaw scratched the earth and raised maize and a few vegetables. Now and then the head of the household wandered into the woods to hunt for game, or to fish in the streams. His delight, however, was in going on the "war-path," and in slaying those of his own race, who belonged to another tribe. Through the gloomy depths of the forest, where only his trained eye could trace the prints of the moccasin, he tracked his enemy, braving storm, heat, cold, fatigue, starvation, and every kind of hardship, for the chance of stealing upon the sleeper, or catching him off his guard. Burying his knife in his breast, or driving his deadly arrow into the heart of his enemy, he wrenched the scalp from his crown, and with a shout of triumph, headed back to his own people, with the shocking proof of his bravery.

—Edward S. Ellis, *True Stories About Indians*, 1905

INTRODUCTION

President John F. Kennedy wrote in 1963, "The American Indian is the least understood and most misunderstood of all Americans" (1963, p. 1). Vine Deloria wrote that "Indians are probably invisible because of the tremendous amount of misinformation about them" (1969, p. 12). For decades, Americans have read stories of the daring exploits of white heroes such as Kit Carson or George Armstrong Custer as they fought and killed "savage" Indians. With the advent of Hollywood, Americans became familiar with the Western movie, as Tom Mix, John Wayne, or a host of other noble white cowboys protected wagon trains or settlers against the threat of slaughter at the hands of American Indians. The 1950s brought television into American homes and along with it, the television Western with characters such as the Lone Ranger and his faithful American Indian friend, Tonto; Roy Rogers; and many others. Children grew up playing "cowboys and Indians," games in which, almost invariably, the American Indians were the "bad guys;" it was hard to find someone to play the part of the American Indian, who, of course, had to be killed. The 1960s brought the Red Consciousness movement and an assertion by many Native Americans that they were the victims of a systematic war of extermination by Europeans. But school texts continued to tell stories of white men bringing "civilization" to red men (Loewen, 1995). While there was an increased sensitivity to Native American issues, Americans as a whole continued to think of Native Americans as adorned in eagle-feather headdresses, hunting bison, or living in tipis on the Great Plains.

Some of our informants told us how they were affected by these stereotypes. One Mohawk woman told us, "And then, of course, tv came in and it was Western movies and I would see how the native people were on there, you know. I didn't tell nobody [I was an Indian], even when I was that young. I never went out and said, 'Yeah, I'm an Indian' at school. I never said that. I knew who I was and I just left it at that. And when I would see these things on tv, I'd say, 'Oh, my God, I'm glad I didn't say that because they're really mean, these Indians. Nasty and hurtful.' " Another Mohawk woman said that when she was young, she thought boarding schools for Native American children were a good thing because "For some reason, when you're growing up hearing about Indians, but not knowing you are one, and you hear that kids were taken away and sent to school and trained to be white people. Somehow I thought that was okay. I thought, 'Oh, of course, because they were savage Indians.' And sometimes when I looked at those letters [from the Carlisle school to her grandfather], I got the feeling that Indians must not have cared about their kids, if they just let people take them away."

Others talked about how they were affected by the stereotypes. One Cherokee woman told us how her employer for years greeted her in the morning with a raised hand and "How!" She said she talked to him and asked him not to do it because it offended her, but he wouldn't stop. A Lenape man said that his coworkers routinely called him "Chief" and asked if he lived in a tipi. A Lakota man said, "Where I work, there is a large misconception with what an Indian is, and this is something I have to deal with every day. They can't figure out why, if I'm an Indian, how come I don't live in a tipi? Well, I haven't been able to get a buffalo with the proper hide and the proper skins because we don't have them walking in our yard anymore [*laughs*]." A man from Centre County said, "When I tell someone I'm an Indian, they're either afraid of me, because they think we're savages, or they think I'm some kind of New Age earth guru. You'd think by now people would know us better."

In this chapter, we hope to dispel some of the more common myths and improper stereotypes about Native Americans by replacing them with more accurate conceptions of what Native Americans were or are like.

"Indians" and India

One of the enduring myths about Native Americans is that Christopher Columbus called them "Indians" because he thought he had landed in India when he "discovered America" in 1492. A great many American myths surround this voyage. Among them are that Columbus was the first to prove the world was round (scholars and sailors had thought this for centuries) and that his was the first European voyage to this hemisphere (it is now thought the continent had been visited hundreds of times by Norse adventurers, European fishing vessels, etc.). Columbus may well have mistaken an island in the Bahamas for India, but there is no evidence that he called the native peoples—probably Arawaks—"Indians." Rather, Spanish priests began calling the natives of these Caribbean islands "*los niños de Dios*"—"the children of God"—because of what the priests perceived as a childlike innocence and trust among the natives. This quickly became shortened to "*Indios*," the name by which indigenous peoples throughout Latin America are still known today.

In this book, we have used a variety of terms, including "Native American," "American Indian," "native peoples," "indigenous peoples," and occasionally, "Indian." This apparent confusion or indecision is purposeful. Especially in regard to the following text, it is reflected in the responses of the people we surveyed or interviewed. To maintain accuracy of the terms used by interviewees, all direct quotes and discussions regarding the survey maintain the use of each interviewee's preferred term.

The Lakota journalist, Tim Giago, advocates avoiding the use of a generic term like "Native American" and using a tribal designation instead. But many of the people we spoke with in Pennsylvania have a diverse array of backgrounds, both native and nonnative. We met people who claimed descent from three or more different Native American groups. Others felt that their European background was just as important to note as their native one: "The St. Regis Mohawks—they're the red-headed Indians because they were always kidnapping Irish people. And then the people wouldn't leave! Tarvil, Cook and Gray—those were the three names that come down through my family. Cook was a Scot; Gray was black, and Tarvil was English. The two Tarvil boys got kidnapped, and they turned them into good Mohawks! They gave them land and wives." Native Americans also intermarried with African Americans; several of the people we interviewed were phenotypically African American, even though they emphasized their Native American ancestry.

In our survey, we asked Native Americans living in Pennsylvania what they preferred to be called. The survey offered four choices: "Native American," "Indian," "Tribal Affiliation," and "Other." Respondents were allowed to choose more than one option, and they were encouraged to elaborate on their answers. While the most popular choice was "Native American" (146 of 281 responses, or 52%), many other labels were selected. Twenty-five preferred to be called "Indian." One hundred and eleven (40%) identified themselves by a tribal name or names. Forty different tribal affiliations were claimed, with Cherokee the most common (29), followed by Lenape (23). Many combinations were noted. Twenty-four identified themselves as "Native Americans" with a tribal affiliation. Twenty-one noted two or more tribes in their backgrounds; one person claimed four: Apache, Creek, Chippewa, and Omaha. Twenty-two also listed some non-Indian background, with 12 writing either "Caucasian" or "white." Other volunteered choices were "indigenous," "American Indian," and "native." One listed "human being" as the option. As can be seen, choosing a Native American heritage in Pennsylvania is a complicated business.

The 70 people we interviewed were all asked specifically what their tribal affiliation was as one of the first questions asked. In this case, the most common response was Lenape (13 of 70, or 19%), followed by Cherokee (12), Mohawk (6), and Seneca (5). A total of 16 tribal affiliations were claimed, and again, there were several complex mixes: Sauk and Fox, for example, or Cherokee-Lenape-Shawnee. As we conversed with people, we used the term "Native American" as our label of choice, and almost all of our informants echoed our choice. We noticed, however, as the conversation continued and grew more relaxed, people abandoned "Native American" and were more likely to call themselves "Indian;" they also referred generally to themselves as "the native people."

A few of our informants objected to "Native American" as too politically correct or as a creation of the Red Consciousness movement of the 1960s and 1970s. A number told us that it was people living east of the Mississippi who called themselves "Native Americans"; western people called themselves "Indians." One informant, a local historian, told us that the term "Native American" was very old and that 17th century accounts distinguished between Native Americans (or sometimes just "Americans") and colonists. Some insisted that "Native American" was a misnomer, since anyone born in the Americas could call themselves that. For example, a Lenape-Seneca woman who does school programs said "When we go to schools, I first of all ask the kids, 'Who's Native American here?' And you'll see one or two raise their hands. So I say, 'Who was born in the U.S.?' Ninety-nine percent raise their hands. 'Well, aren't you Native American, too? Aren't you a native of this country?' I'm against political correctness. Once you become an American, your history is American, then. We're American! Your history doesn't start in 1776. Your history doesn't start in 1492. Your history starts when America started. So I tell the children that our history is your history, too." On similar grounds, a few of our informants preferred "First American" over "Native American."

Another perspective was provided by the American Indian activist Russell Means: "I prefer the term American Indian…the American Indian is the only ethnic group in the United States with the American *before* [italics in original] the ethnicity… . We were enslaved as American Indians. We were colonized as American Indians and we will gain our freedom as American Indians. Then we can call ourselves any damn thing we choose" (Navajo Central, 2007, p. 1).

The complex issue is discussed in greater detail in chapter 4. But calling Native Americans "Indians" is not because of Christopher Columbus.

RED INDIANS

Native Americans have been called "red" people since the 16th century. By the 18th century, the idea that Native Americans were red skinned was so well-established in the minds of "white" Europeans that Linnaeus (1758/2005) used it as an identifying feature of "*Homo sapiens Americanus*," in his at-the-time new binomial classification system for all living species. Europeans were white, he wrote, while Asians were yellow, Africans black, and Americans (note his label for American Indians) were red. Each of these color designations carried with them personality features in Linnaeus' 18th-century way of looking at things. "Red" Americans were "choleric" or angry, compared with "cheerful" whites, "melancholy" Asians, and "sluggish" blacks. Looking back on European colonialism, we might say that "angry" or "melancholy" might have been an appropriate reaction to being displaced by Europeans. Linnaeus went on in his taxonomic description of American Indians to note that they were "upright. Hair black, straight, thick; nostrils wide; face harsh; beard scanty; obstinate, content free. Paints himself with fine red lines. Ruled by habit" (Europeans were ruled by law, Asians by belief, and Africans by caprice or impulse) (1758/2005, p. 157). While these obviously racist and ethnocentric labels are embarrassing to us today, we can see how early the designation of Native Americans as "redskins" actually was.

Linnaeus' remark that Americans were painted with fine, red lines comes close to historical truth. When Columbus arrived in the Caribbean at the end of the 15th century, he found two major populations of indigenous peoples there: the Arawaks, who lived in what are now called the Greater Antilles (Jamaica, Cuba, Puerto Rico, and Hispaniola), and the Caribs, who controlled the Lesser Antilles. The Spanish claimed control of the entire Caribbean area and began labeling native peoples in a way that would become standard throughout the Americas. The Arawaks were "good" Indians because they initially welcomed Europeans and were cooperative in early colonization efforts. The Caribs were "bad" Indians because they fought with the Spanish invaders (and the Arawaks). As a result, there is some historical knowledge of daily life among the Arawaks and almost nothing on the Caribs, except for their customs and abilities in war. The Spanish wrote that before they went into battle, the Caribs dyed themselves red with berries; these "red-skinned" warriors thus became the protypical "red Indians." In fact, ultimately, it made no difference to the Spanish who was good and who was bad; Native Americans were removed from almost all of the Caribbean by the late 16th century (Watts, 1987).

Many of the Native Americans we talked with in Pennsylvania pointed out that the general idea of what they are supposed to look like has been too influenced by the American Indians we have seen in the movies—that is, the native peoples of the Great Plains, such as the Lakota, Cheyenne, or Crows. These people of the plains did appear reddish because of their constant exposure to the sun; they also characteristically had (and often still do today) the high cheekbones most associate with Native Americans. But as one of our informants told us, "[They] were people of the forests. [They] didn't live out in the sun and so [their] skins were light." This remark echoes the comments of the Moravian missionary David Zeisberger who wrote that the Lenape were light-skinned; some were lighter in complexion than Europeans (as cited in P. Wallace, 1981, p. 21). For even those Native Americans of the Great Plains, centuries of intermarriage have led to many being very light-skinned today. A Tuscarora woman told us, "So they look at someone like me who has light skin, light colored hair, and they say you surely are not an Indian." Others told us that a problem they have in asserting their native identity is that they don't fit the stereotype of what "Indians" are "supposed" to look like.

"Indians" Don't Pay Taxes

When we asked a Choctaw woman living in Centre County what bothered her most about stereotypes people have about "Indians," she replied, "I get so tired of people thinking that because I'm an Indian, I don't pay taxes. Please tell people that this is not true." And it is not. Native Americans pay federal income tax like everyone else. Native Americans living in Pennsylvania are also subject to state and local income taxes, sales tax, and property taxes (if they own property). Indians who live on reservations do not pay state or local income or property taxes because they fall under federal jurisdiction, but should they leave the reservation to work or to buy things, they pay the same state and local taxes everyone else does. But since there are no reservations in Pennsylvania, this is not a consideration for Native Americans in this state.

Native Americans have the lowest average incomes of any identifiable American population. According to the U.S. Census, in 2005, the average American household earned US$46,326, but the average Native American household income was US$33,627—72% of the average American incomes overall. The Census also reported that 25% of Native Americans lived below the federal poverty line, which was defined as US$19,971 for a family of four or US$9973 for a single individual. The numbers for Pennsylvania alone are quite similar: Native Americans in Pennsylvania earn about 74% of the average income of Pennsylvanians as a whole, and they are four times as likely to be unemployed. Because of their overall low incomes, Native Americans may not pay much in taxes compared to a middle-class family, but they are certainly subject to taxation.

Eagle-Feather Headdresses and Tipis

Another stereotype that dominates non-Indians' views of Native Americans is that Native Americans wear eagle-feather headdresses and live in tipis. This stereotype also comes to us from the portrayal of the people of the Great Plains in movies. Some Lakota warriors (as well as other American Indians of the Great Plains) wore eagle-feather headdresses. These headdresses were a symbol of bravery for the warriors who wore them. Nevertheless, an eagle-feather headdress was certainly not everyday wear; they were worn in battle or for ceremonial occasions. As for tipis, American Indians of the Great Plains did live in these structures—an ingenious accommodation to their nomadic, horseback culture and the materials available to them.

Western movies have fixed both ideas in the minds of the general public. Native Americans in the Northeast are not the only native peoples who have become associated with headdresses and tipis; Navajos, Seminoles, and others are also expected to live up to this image. A good example is Chief Osceola, the mascot image of the Seminoles, Florida State University's football team. Seminoles are the indigenous people of Florida, but Chief Osceola, as he is seen on the sidelines of FSU football games, wears an eagle-feather headdress and rides a horse—a

Plains Indian image. We heard more complaints from the people we interviewed about being associated with tipis than with any other stereotyped issue. We have also directly experienced this stereotype in our work. We were approached by a local children's museum to construct an Eastern-Woodlands dwelling as part of an exhibit they were doing on the kinds of homes people from different cultures live in. The staff assured us that they could help us build a tipi. To their credit, they quickly adjusted when we offered to build an Iroquois longhouse instead. As part of the exhibit, we put together a poster illustrating the many different kinds of homes Native Americans lived in, including tipis on the Great Plains.

As seen in chapter 2, the native people of Pennsylvania and surrounding areas built structures of saplings covered with bark. These could have been either the single-family wigwam of the Lenape or the longhouses favored by the Iroquois and the Susquehannocks. Native Americans in the Northeast did not wear eagle-feather headdresses. Usually, both men and women wore their hair long; sometimes their hair was braided, and sometimes it hung free. Grease was sometimes applied to it to make the hair shine. Some men plucked the hair from their heads using clam shells as tweezers. They would leave a central row of hair called a roach or, more popularly, a Mohawk. Sometimes they would add deer hair to their roaches to make them appear taller. A man might attach an eagle feather to his roach, if he chose to do so, but there was no tradition of eagle feather headdresses in the Northeast.

Tribes and Chiefs

Another persistent stereotype associated with Native Americans is that they lived in political structures called tribes with powerful political leaders called chiefs. There is no question but that is how Europeans perceived (or misperceived) them at contact. It is also the case that many Native Americans today accept the concepts of tribe and chief as part of their heritage. As anthropologists, we believe that both concepts are generally misunderstood.

We believe that "tribe" is one of the more misunderstood and abused ideas Americans have about non-Western cultures. We see two problems with the concept of a tribe overall. The first is that the word carries ethnocentric and racial overtones. Dark-skinned people are historically seen as living in tribes; white people have ethnicity. Conflicts in Africa are called "tribal"; in Northern Ireland, similar behavior is called a "religious dispute." Hollywood has shaped Americans' perceptions here, too, from Westerns to Tarzan movies.

The second problem is more technical. Anthropologists usually describe traditional political systems using four different terms: "bands," "tribes," "chiefdoms," and "states" (see Service, 1962). The differences among them are, first of all, ones of population size. A band is made up of 25 to 35 people; a state can be made up of millions. As societies become larger, there is a greater need for centralized authority to make decisions and settle disputes. Bands and tribes lack centralized authority; their numbers are small enough that decisions can be reached through face-to-face discussion among the people involved. Chiefdoms and states have centralized authority. Chiefdoms are smaller than states, and the chief is usually a hereditary ruler. States are larger, with leaders usually chosen by some means other than kinship.

Anthropologists have a clear idea of how a band and a chiefdom are put together. Bands are usually associated with foragers or hunter-gatherers—people who rely on what they find in the wild environment for their survival. Foragers do not domesticate animals (an exception was the dog) or deliberately cultivate crops. They live in small, nomadic groups of 25 to 35 people, moving as required within a shared territory. The traditional Arctic Inuit are a good example of a band, as are the pygmy hunters of the Central-African rain forests. A chiefdom has a settled population of several hundred to several thousand people who depend on agriculture for their survival. Their agricultural productivity is great enough to produce large surpluses of food, which make it possible to support the chief and his court. The chief collects and stores the surpluses through some redistributive principle like taxation; in addition to feeding the chief and his retainers, these stored surpluses may be used to feed the farmers and their families during hard times. The traditional Polynesian societies, such as the Hawaiians, are examples of chiefdoms.

Anthropologists usually associate the concept of a tribe with people who are pastoralists (people who depend on herds of domestic animals for their survival) or are small-scale horticulturalists (people who do some agriculture with hand-held tools, while also hunting and gathering wild foods). Beyond that, a tribe is hard to define—or even to see. On a day-to-day basis, a tribe looks like a band. The Lenape would have been a good example of this—a small number of people living together in a semipermanent community without centralized leadership. To the extent that a distinction can be made between bands and tribes, the distinction has to be that a tribe has a sense of common ethnicity and perhaps purpose. Each foraging band is autonomous and self-sufficient; they see no need or desire to come together into larger congregations of people. A tribe has the potential, at least, to form into a larger political entity for some purpose. Thus, on the Great Plains, people like the Lakota or Crow lived in small groups much like bands most of the year, but when desirable, such as for a coordinated bison hunt or a religious ceremony, they could come together in larger groups. General Custer and his troops blundered into one of these larger groupings of Lakota and Cheyenne in 1876 at the Battle of the Little Big Horn.

Morton Fried, in his 1967 book, *The Evolution of Political Society: An Essay in Political Anthropology*, raises the possibility that tribes did not exist before European colonialism. The argument here is that native peoples around the world came to realize that they needed to organize themselves better if they were going to be able to put up an adequate defense against well-organized and well-armed European troops or militias. This idea is reinforced by the European presumption that all humans lived in centrally organized societies; after all, what do we presume the Martian will say to us when we meet it on the street? A look at European-Native American interactions in the 17th and 18th centuries makes it clear that when Europeans were meeting with Native Americans, Europeans presumed they were dealing with sovereign and absolute rulers. The 18th century Lenape, Teedyuscung, was a good example of this process. Europeans were happy to anoint him "King" of the Lenapes in 1756, but he seemed equally pleased to assume that title for himself (see Weslager, 1972, p. 229).

The concept of "chief" is inexorably bound up with that of "tribe." As noted previously, Europeans thought of chiefs as true leaders with both authority and power over their people. The native peoples of the Northeast certainly had people in whom they vested authority; the Algonquian word for these people is variously transcribed as "sachem" or "sagamore." These people had important responsibilities, but limited power. When we asked one of the chiefs of a Pennsylvania Native American organization how he came to be chosen chief, his response was the following:

> Probably because I didn't want the job. And I think there's some truth to that. I didn't have any ambitions, as far as personal ambitions. I think [the person who chose me] felt that I would serve the people, so he chose me.

Weslager writes the following:

> Although the [Lenape] chiefs were considered [political] leaders, they hunted, fished, lived in wigwams, and raised their families like other villagers. The chiefs did not have servants, possessed no more "wealth" than their native associates, and exercised a very limited authority. Some Europeans called the village or band chiefs "kings," which was an exaggeration, because there was no comparison between the functions of a [Lenape] chief and the king of a European state who wielded vast powers. Even though the position of the chief entailed both executive and ceremonial responsibilities, a strong democratic spirit governed the conduct and that of their people in what was an economic as well as political democracy. (1972, pp. 62–63)

One of our informants described the role of a chief as being "a caretaker, someone who looks after the people and makes sure everyone had enough to eat and clothes to wear and shelter." Garbarino and Sasso write that "leaders served only with the people's consent and were guided by a council of respected elders" (1994, p. 302).

The traditional role of an Algonquian sachem, according to the *Encyclopedia of North American Indians*, was to oversee the distribution of land, judge disputes, receive guests, and carry out certain rituals. This source concludes that the role of a sachem was hereditary and that both men and women could be sachems (Hoxie, 1996, pp. 563–564). Weslager says that there seems to be evidence for the inheritance of title among the Lenape, but there is no mention of female sachems among them (1972, p. 63). It is clear that sachems, such as Tamamend who met with William Penn in 1682, were well-respected sometimes by both natives and Europeans. In keeping with the kinds of leaders seen in tribal societies in other parts of the world, these Lenape sachems seem to have led more by example and persuasion than by force. The European perception that these native "kings" had absolute power over their subjects is based on their own political realities and not on those of Native Americans.

An example of the limited power of a chief can be seen in Native American warfare. Native Americans did not conduct war as Europeans did; that is, as coordinated large-scale battles directed by officers. Rather, Native American warfare more often took the form of raids and ambushes. The purpose of combat was usually to take captives or to carry out revenge for a death of a friend or kinsman. In his novel, *Little Big Man*, Thomas Berger, writing of Plains warfare, captures the concept nicely: "A white man gets no pleasure out of war itself; he won't fight at all if without it he can *get his way*. He is after your spirit, not the body…[Indians] had no interest in power as we know it" (1964, p. 101).

Native Americans in the Northeast usually appointed a war chief, whose responsibility it was to recruit warriors and make plans for an impending conflict. Sachems were not war chiefs; if a sachem chose to go to war, he held no rank higher than any other warrior. War chiefs were chosen based on past exploits and reputation. The converse of the sachem, the war chief had no authority outside of preparing for war—and very little within a conflict itself, by European standards. As

Weslager notes, an American Indian society was a democracy. Individuals were allowed to go their own way, as long as doing so did not harm themselves or others. There was no mandate to participate in war; if a man felt that it was more important to hunt to provide for his family instead of going to war, he was free to make that choice and no shame was attached to it. When a conflict occurred, there was very little coordination of efforts; a war chief could suggest strategy, but individuals were allowed to do as they pleased, including withdrawing from the field when they chose to do so. Samuel de Champlain complained about this in an attack he witnessed by the Hurons on the Onondagas in 1615; instead of pressing their advantage in victory, the Hurons chose to go home (as cited in Englebrecht, 2003, p. 147).

As noted in the last chapter, Native Americans were excellent warriors, but they were not professional soldiers. Their numbers were relatively few, and they had many other responsibilities in terms of hunting, fishing, clearing fields, and generally providing security for their families and communities. They could not afford to take many losses in battle, and they did not wish to be away from their homes for a protracted campaign.

The exception to what has been said in this section would seem to be the Iroquois. Their confederacy seems to have elevated the position of chief (the term "sachem" is also sometimes used for the Iroquois) to levels not known among the Lenape and other native peoples in the Northeast. However, as already seen, Iroquois chiefs could be removed by the women in their clans. The position of an Iroquois chief was not hereditary, but was based on merit. All Iroquois could attend League meetings, but if they wished to express an opinion, they had to do so through their chiefs. In war, the Iroquois followed the same pattern as previously described.

Given all of these problems of misunderstanding, the international community has begun to abandon the concept of "tribe," replacing it with "nation." According to the United Nations Human Rights Subcommittee, a nation refers to a "self-identifying people, often united by a common language, religion and political consensus, who occupy all or part of an ancestral territory" (as cited in Nietschmann, 1984, p. 2). Many Native

Americans now prefer to call themselves nations to avoid the problems caused by the term "tribe." A possible substitute for "chief" might be "national spokesperson." The concept of a spokesperson comes closer to describing the role of a sachem than the Hollywood-influenced term, "chief." However, the leaders of the various Native American organizations in Pennsylvania today prefer to be called "chiefs."

MATRILINEAL KINSHIP

The Lenape, the Susquehannocks, and the Iroquois all practiced matrilineal kinship or descent. In matrilineal kinship, descent through the generations is traced through the mother's side of the family. Inheritance rights, titles, and property all pass through the women's side. Matrilocal residence meant that a newly married man moved in with his wife's family or community. Matrilineal kinship was found among a great many Native American nations. The two nations with the largest populations today—the Cherokees and the Navajos—both practice matrilineal descent, as do many other well-known native groups such as the Hopi and the Crows. Worldwide, about 15% of the world's cultures feature this kind of descent system, and Knack (2004, p. 55) claims that holds true for the native nations of North America as well.

Other common options for organizing kinship and inheritance are patrilineal descent and bilateral or bilineal descent. Patrilineal descent is the most common way cultures organize kin, with about 44% of the world's cultures following this pattern; the Shawnees practiced patrilineal descent. In patrilineal descent, inheritance rights and family relationships are defined on the father's side of the family. Bilineal descent is found in approximately 30% of the world's cultures; this is the pattern followed by American mainstream culture as well as most of western Europe. In bilineal descent, a person sees himself or herself as equally related to both his or her mother's and father's sides, and inheritance can follow both lines. Kinship terminology reflects these differences directly. In the U.S., generally, we call both the father's brother and the mother's brother by the same term: "uncle." Since our legal relationship to each is the same, an equivalent term is used. But in patrilineal and matrilineal descent, different terms are used for the father's brother and the mother's brother—and for other kin as well. In matrilineal kinship, a person's mother's brother is a very different kind of person, in terms of rights and obligations, than the father's brother; thus, different terms apply to them.

In general, a society with patrilineal kinship is a more difficult social system for women than a matrilineal society. In most patrilineal societies historically, women have few, if any, rights. By contrast, women have a great deal more freedom and respect in matrilineal societies. In his cross-cultural study of women in preindustrial societies, Whyte (1978, pp. 132–133) noted that in matrilineal societies, women are more likely to own property, have more authority within the household, have fewer restrictions on their movements, and have more value placed on their lives. Since the 19th century, anthropologists have wondered why some societies are patrilineal and others are matrilineal. Gallons of ink have been spilled over this question. But after years of speculation and quantitative analysis, only one correlation seems to hold generally true: A society is more likely to be matrilineal if men are away from the home community for long periods of time. The anthropologist Marvin Harris (1988: 341) noted that when men engage in war, hunting, or trade which result in long-distance expeditions lasting several months, then those societies are more likely to be matrilineal. Harris argued that organizing a society this way made sense. In a patrilineal society, women move in with their husbands' families. As a result, when the men are gone, maintenance of their property rests with women who do not own that property and have little reason to cooperate among themselves. But in a matrilineal/matrilocal society, the women own the property and belong to a close-knit kin group, which allows them to work together in a cooperative fashion.

When anthropologists talk generally about matrilineal/matrilocal societies, they almost always use the example of the Iroquois to illustrate the concept. Both the Iroquois and the Lenape reflect the conditions under which matrilineality is advantageous. The men in both societies were often away hunting; Lenape men often had winter deer hunting camps far away from the main village. The Iroquois men also engaged in long-distance warfare, traveling hundreds of miles on occasions to do battle with, for example, the Hurons. Prehistoric trade is harder to document, but the presence of European goods in archaeological sites in western Pennsylvania and New York State long before actual contact with Europeans suggests that trade networks did exist. Certainly, after contact, Iroquois and Lenape men traveled great distances to both hunt fur-bearing animals for trade and engage in trade with Europeans. The many diplomatic contacts between Europeans and natives also suggest that men could comfortably leave their homes to travel to Philadelphia or Albany for a meeting.

However, many of our informants confused matrilineal descent with matriarchal control. We were often told that prehistoric native societies were matriarchal. As an example, one man refused to fill out our questionnaire at a powwow unless he had the permission of his clan mother to do so: "Indian men couldn't do anything without the clan mothers' approval, you know." The term "matriarchy" means "rule by women," and few, if any, traditional societies met that definition. Ember and Ember, who for years have studied matrilineal societies and the conditions under which they are found, say the following:

> In a matrilineal system, however, although the line of descent passes through females, females rarely exercise authority in their kin groups. Usually men do. Thus the lines of authority and descent do not converge. Anthropologists do not completely understand why this is so, but it is an ethnographic fact. (2002, p. 373)

Generally, in matrilineal societies, authority is ultimately exercised by men related matrilineally. Usually the mother's brother or the maternal uncle is the chief authority figure. In matrilineal societies, men inherit positions or statuses from other men, just as in patrilineal or bilineal societies; the difference is that within matrilineal societies, men inherit not from their fathers, but from their mothers' brothers.

The Lenape seemed to fit this model better than the Iroquois. They practiced matrilineal descent with matrilocal residence. Women and men chose to marry one another, and married couples lived in nuclear family households. The gender division of labor was complementary: Men cleared the fields, and women cultivated the crops (Caffrey, 2000). Men hunted and fished; women prepared the food and skins for clothing. Women seem to have been held in great respect among the Lenape. Decisions were made by general consensus, and sharing and hospitality were critical values. But sachems were men, and as noted earlier, the position of a sachem seems to have been hereditary, rather than an appointed office.

The Iroquois, by contrast, seemed to have invested greater authority in women than almost any other traditional society. The longhouse built around matrilineal extended families would seem to have been the basis of female authority among the Iroquois. A man marrying into a longhouse would have found himself in a long-standing social structure in which large numbers of kinswomen interacted and cooperated daily; a husband would have been a true outsider in this structure. As already mentioned, these female kin groups chose Iroquois chiefs based on merit and could remove them from office if they were displeased with them. The League council which met at Onondaga was made up entirely of men, but within the council there were also a number of honorary positions called "Pine Tree Chiefs." These were people who were honored for distinguishing themselves in some way, and a Pine Tree Chief could be a woman, though most were young male warriors who had won their honors in battle. Pine Tree Chiefs did not have a vote in the council, but they were allowed to speak and could try to sway council opinions. Obviously, Iroquois women were very influential in their communities—much more so than was generally the case in traditional societies.

Schlegel (1977), in writing about the Hopi, offers an additional perspective on matrilineality which may help us see the Iroquois more clearly. She notes that while patrilineal societies emphasize the importance of males and downplay the social significance of women, matrilineal cultures tend to view both women and men as people of value.

Matrilineal societies give different tasks to men and women, but view both women's and men's roles as socially important. Among the Hopi, for example, women owned property and cultivated domestic crops, while men engaged in the critical religious rituals believed to bring rain and fertility to the high desert areas in which they lived. She suggests that in matrilineal societies, women gain their authority and respect through control of the domestic household and the fields, while men gain authority and respect by their accomplishments on what might be called the national level. Thus, while patrilineal societies rejoice at the birth of boys, but are disappointed at the birth of a girl, matrilineal societies celebrate the birth of any child: Every person has an important role to play.

Thus, Iroquois women were important because of their roles as cultivators and organizers of the extended family, while Iroquois men gained significance through participation in national councils, hunting, and war. War was an important activity for the Iroquois because it gave men the opportunity to prove themselves. War also either acted to defend Iroquois territory or expand it at the expense of their neighbors. Warriors enriched their families when they returned with captives or booty. Thus, both men and women were socially important. Iroquois society may best be seen not as a matriarchy but as a partnership between men and women.

One indicator of the status of women in native society is the stories of European women taken captive in raids. Hollywood has made this appear as if this would have been the worst possible thing that could have happened to a European woman, but in fact, historical sources show that some of these women refused "rescue" when it occurred (see Loewen, 1995; P. Wallace, 1981). There are even stories of European women escaping from rescue so they could return to their native homes. In general, women were treated better in native society than in European or colonial society.

A man from Sullivan County of mixed native background told us the following:

> Women are very powerful. Women were the real leaders. The women didn't look for recognition, and they're not braggarts,

> two-faced, liars or cheats. A man might be standing out front, but she'll be whispering in his ear, telling him what to do. What greater gift could creator give us than women, to give us children. They're very powerful and especially at certain times of the year or certain times of the month when their have their moon. That's a very powerful time.

After contact with Europeans, there appears to have been a shift in Native American society toward greater authority being given to men. This may have been because what we know from the historic period was filtered through European eyes, but it also may have been because of the greater importance that trade, diplomacy, and war began to play in Native American life. On the one hand, European authorities were not about to negotiate with native women; on the other hand, the constant pressure of European settlement made warriors critical to the defense and survival of their communities. Natives themselves seemed to have learned early that Europeans saw women very differently than they themselves saw women. When the Iroquois denounced the Lenape as "women" at the time of the Walking Purchase in 1737, they were clearly reflecting European values. This may have been for diplomatic reasons or for its effect on the Europeans present, since the Iroquois certainly were not treating their own women with the contempt they were putting into labeling the Lenape. The Lenape would also use European values at a later date when they decided to take up arms against the Europeans; the phrase used at the time was "taking off our petticoats." Something similar happened to matrilineal societies all over the world at the time of European encroachment. European colonial authorities almost always ignored the traditional values placed on women in matrilineal societies. In their colonial policies, Europeans ignored women and gave clear preference to native males.

One final word on this subject involves the use of the word "squaw" as a term for a native woman. The word "squaw" is one of the many Algonquian words that speakers of English borrowed; other examples include skunk, moccasin, papoose, and tomahawk. Most often, the Algonquian nations from which these words were borrowed were from

New England tribes such as the Abenaki, rather than the Lenape. As with some of these other words, the Algonquian word, once borrowed, was used by Europeans to apply to Native Americans of every native nation. Native Americans themselves universally speak of pecans, squash, and cougars, though these are all words of Algonquian origin.

There is a certain amount of controversy over what the word "squaw" originally meant. One popular etymology found in books and Internet sites is that "squaw" is actually a word of French origin and that it was an obscene reference to a woman's genitals. Native Americans themselves will assert that this is not true, and historians seem to agree. Rather, historians report that "squaw" was the Narragansett word for "woman." No obscene or pejorative connotations are implied. However, as can be seen in the passage with which this chapter begins, the word "squaw" has become stereotyped in general American usage to refer to any American Indian woman, but especially one who is a drudge or a domestic laborer of no status. While there were traditional societies all over the world that viewed women in this way, this was not generally true of Native Americans and especially not of the Lenape or the Iroquois. But there is no question that the word "squaw" has negative connotations for most Americans, and in our three years of meeting and working with Native Americans in Pennsylvania, we have never met anyone who used the word in even a joking manner.

CIVILIZATION

As Europeans conquered Native Americans and took their land from them, Europeans often justified their actions as "civilizing" the natives. As Loewen (1995, pp. 101–102) points out, primary- and secondary-school textbooks still contrast "civilized" Europeans with "primitive" American Indians. Europeans singled out the Seminoles, Cherokees, Creeks, Choctaws, and Chickasaws as the Five Civilized Tribes because their indigenous cultures were the ones most like European village life. Boarding schools for Native American children which attempted to destroy native cultures did so "in the name of civilization."

To an anthropologist, this use of the term "civilized" is misplaced. In anthropology, the word "civilization" is usually used in conjunction with the word "urban." The word "civilization" is derived from the Latin word "*civitas*" or "city." Anthropologists thus refer to a civilization as an urban-based society. Since it takes a large-scale society based on intensive agriculture to support a city, civilization also generally implies a hierarchically ordered society with social stratification, full-time leaders, a bureaucracy, monumental public works, and often, a written language. Anthropologists do not intend to make a value judgment when they refer to a civilization; rather, they are pointing to the existence of urban life and all that goes with it.

Of course, in general use, the word "civilized" has come to mean a great deal more than the existence of cities. To civilize has come to mean to bring to a technically advanced and rationally ordered state of cultural development. To be civilized implies a refinement of thought, manners, and taste—value judgments all.

For Native Americans, their presumed lack of civilization was used against them from the advent of European contact. Spanish priests approved of the "childlike innocence" of the American Indians of the Caribbean, but Spanish conquistadores saw them only as primitive people to be used as labor or to be annihilated. Native Americans in parts of Mesoamerica did live in cities—some of which, like the Aztec capital of Tenochtitlan, were larger and better maintained than European cities—but that did not protect them from European colonial domination. The Cherokee sachem, Sequoyah, invented a writing system appropriate to his language in the early 19th century, but that did not protect the Cherokee people from the Trail of Tears.

The point to be made here is that to be civilized or uncivilized ultimately depends on one's point of view. It is an ethnocentric judgment which usually overlooks the virtues a society possesses. The Lenape and the Iroquois at contact were reasonably well-fed, well-clothed, and housed. They looked after each other without sacrificing personal choice or ambition. Men and women had satisfying social lives in which both genders had a say. By comparison with the European societies of their time, they practiced democracy and made decisions by consensus. Their religious ideologies were rich and complex; their religion explained their lives and gave them comfort. When they came in contact with Europeans, they were willing to adopt European technology and ideas which they found useful; many became Christians, for example. They initially agreed to share or cede land to Europeans and enthusiastically entered into trade relationships with them. They fought among themselves and with Europeans, but often in their own defense. In short, theirs was a satisfactory existence which was, in some ways, better than what the average person in London or Paris—or colonial America—lived.

PAN-INDIANISM

Pan-Indianism can be described as the adoption of a common set of customs or traditions by Native Americans across the country, regardless of their nation. Whether they like it or not, Native Americans in this country are exposed to the same myths, stereotypes, and media images everyone else is. For example, when we told one Native American man in northeastern Pennsylvania about how a woman had been offended when her employer greeted her each day with "How!" he laughed and said, "You know what two Indians on the reservation say to each other when they meet? How!" But he quickly added, "In that situation, it's a joke, you see. We turn the white man's stereotypes into jokes among ourselves." Shively (1992) describes how she showed the classic John Wayne/John Ford Western, *The Searchers*, to an audience of Native Americans on a reservation. She asked them what they thought of the film. To her surprise, all of them said they liked it, that John Wayne was one of their favorite actors, and that Westerns were their favorite genre of films. (To be fair, when Shively showed the same film to an audience of young Native Americans who were students at a West Coast university, they reacted differently; they preferred the American Indian characters to the John Wayne character.) While both groups thought the portrayal of American Indians in the film was inaccurate, they still thought the film was entertaining.

The respected Native American historian, Vine Deloria, predicted in 1981 that there would be a trend among Native Americans toward Pan-Indianism. He felt it was expedient for some of the same reasons that the Iroquois felt inconvenienced by having to deal with 13 separate colonies: It is easier to deal with Native Americans as a united people than with hundreds of separate nations. Hultkrantz (1987), in his book on Native American religions, says that "most young Indians" believe in a Pan-Indian religion—one set of beliefs common to all nations. Fair, in her study of Native American Web sites (2000), found that if a Web site was targeted to an audience greater than a specific nation, it tended to portray American Indians in buckskins and eagle feather headdresses. (If the Web site was for a specific nation only, people were shown in everyday dress.) Fair quotes a Mattaponi man wearing a Lakota-style war bonnet as saying, "Your women copy their hats from Paris because they like them. We Indians use the styles of other tribes because we like them, too" (2000, p. 210).

We found that Native Americans in Pennsylvania had adopted a number of customs that have become Pan-Indian. Our informants wore Navajo and Pueblo jewelry, hung dream catchers on their walls, and surrounded themselves with pictures of bison and Plains Indians in eagle-feather headdresses. Plains Indian–style vision quests have become popular. P. Wallace (1981, p. 63) claims the Lenape had a vision-quest experience for young men in which they fasted and invited guardian spirits to claim them. By contrast, Englebrecht (2003) says the Iroquois used tobacco smoked in clay or stone pipes to communicate with the spirit world. Today, the vision quest seems to be well-entrenched as a custom among Native Americans in Pennsylvania. Men and women of all ages participate in them, and while the deprivations experienced now are not as extreme as in traditional Plains cultures, there is still an emphasis on isolation and sacrifice as a way of becoming closer to the spirit world or to nature. We also met a number of Pennsylvanian Indians who had participated in Plains Indian Sun Dances, which are also designed to give visions to the dancers; more about the Sun Dance is discussed in chapter 5.

Another example of Pan-Indianism among Pennsylvanian Native Americans is the use of the Plains "peace pipe" in rituals. As noted previously, the peoples of the Northeast made pipes and smoked tobacco as a way of seeing into the supernatural world, but the pipes they made had short stems—perhaps only 3 or 4 inches long. When Europeans arrived, one of the trade goods in great demand were long-stemmed clay pipes; often these are called Dutch pipes because the Dutch originally introduced them into the region. One of the most reliable markers of culture contact with Europeans in the archaeological record is the presence of Dutch pipes in burials or broken ones in waste pits. Today, ceremonies in the Northeast are accompanied by the use of the long-stemmed Plains pipe—typically beautifully made pieces which are carefully handled and used as part of purification rites. Another widely adopted custom is the use of sage as part of "smudging" or purification rituals. Native Americans in the Northeast did smudging, but typically used native cedar bark (*Juniperus virginiana*); sage (*Salvia apiana*, or "white sage") was typically used by Plains/Southwest natives. Some still use cedar bark, but sage has become the purifying element of choice for most in the Northeast.

Pan-Indianism is a source of controversy among Native Americans in Pennsylvania. While some embrace customs from native cultures from across the continent, others feel strongly that they must follow strictly the traditions of the Northeast. We met many Native Americans who took great pride in the authenticity of, for example, their dance regalia. These people tended to emphasize historical research as the way to reclaim native heritage; correspondingly, they were highly critical of people who didn't maintain their historical authenticity. One told us, "We wouldn't have an issue with any organization if they were doing factual things. It's when they're living up to the stereotype, the fantasies, the old books that they've read." Another said the following:

> I think that's one of the issues I have with the Pan-Indianism that you talked about earlier. There are a lot of people who have sweat

> ceremonies, vision quests, claim to be chiefs, claim to be clan mothers, claim to be some kind of spiritual leader—a lot of them in Pennsylvania. They're on their own little ego romanticized trips, and that's probably what upsets me the most about a lot of the things that go on.

Others were more forgiving of Pan-Indianism or blending modern and historic customs. One thing we heard again and again was this: The most important thing was what you were in your heart. For example, a person of Nanticoke ancestry told us,

> I'm more interested in what you have in your heart. It's like having to prove you're Italian in order to become Catholic. I think that's bull. The creator doesn't care what color your skin is or if you're mixed or full blood or any of that.

Another Native American said the following:

> I think people need to learn these things. They need to know these things, but when I see a young man out [in the dance arena] with a bustle on and he's got a CD as the center of that bustle, that's that kid! Leave him alone! He's saying, "My music is so important I have to take it into the dance area." I really think it's good to learn the history and know what your tribal regalia was like. But there's not anything available to us today—unless we start from scratch in the woods—that we can wear that's absolutely authentic. And I don't think there are that many people who are that dedicated. Even the most dedicated researchers—and that gets to be a hostile issue sometimes—some people don't like reenactors. I think they're fine. They're keeping our history together and teaching us things sometimes. Let them do their thing!

A Lenape woman said, "They say we have to follow the traditions. But which one? Do I dress in buckskins from before contact or in a cloth skirt from post-contact? Is traditional 1650 or 1750—or last week?"

Others emphasized the flexibility of Native American culture. A Lenape man told us, "But if someone comes up and says, 'Look, I don't know, but I want to learn.' Huh—teach him! Don't go away; teach him.... Our ancestors always judged people based on their hearts and minds." An Abenaki man said this about a friend of his who participates in the Sun Dance, a religious ritual that originated in the Plains:

> A lot of people question X going out there [to the Sun Dance]. Why do you as an Eastern Indian, why are you going out there? That's choice. That's the individual path I talked about.... They want you there. They want you to see what's going on.

A Mohawk woman took us to the wigwam she made in a field behind her house. The wigwam is made of poles and bark tied together with rawhide, as would have been past practice, but she has clear Plexiglas® covering the smoke hole in the roof. "I don't worry about that," she said. "My ancestors would have used it too, if it had come over on the boat then." Wigwams are not a Mohawk traditional style of house, but it's what she felt she needed to do. "I come out here when I need to get away by myself to just think."

A Mohawk woman who built her own Lenape-style wigwam for her personal use is a good example of what is going on in Pennsylvania today. This woman also was proud of her Scottish ancestry. Her grandmother was born on a reservation in New York State and spent several years at the Carlisle Industrial School. Her mother married a man from Pennsylvania and lived much of her life in the state before moving back to the reservation in New York. As a young woman, her mother did her best to hide her native ancestry, believing that it was not safe to talk about it; now in her 70s, she embraces her heritage. Our informant, who was 56 years of age at the time of our interview, said she did not learn that she was Native American until she was in her 30s. After learning of her heritage, she began to carry a Mohawk tribal card and regularly visited kin on the reservation. But she lived in Pennsylvania. She was a musician and an artist. She played the fiddle in a Scottish band, but she emphasized that the Mohawks were great fiddlers, too, and she liked to play the fiddle with her native kin when she was in New York. She made buckskin clothing and tanned her own hides using native techniques.

Her farmhouse home was filled with native artifacts—some were of her own making, while other pieces were handed down through the family. She was proud of and faithful to her traditions—all of them.

In the next chapter, we will discuss what it means to be a Native American in Pennsylvania in the 21st century. Questions such as which traditions to follow or which customs to emulate are critical ones in shaping a person's self-identity as a Native American. As will be seen in chapter 4, there are many ways to define oneself as a native person. However, suffice it to say that being American Indian is not being like the people portrayed in movies, cartoons, or 19th-century novels. As one Lenape told us,

> A co-worker of mine asked "Do you live in a tipi?" I said, "Yes. My tipi has four walls, rooms, doors, windows…" "That sounds like a house," he said. "Exactly," I said, "I'm an Indian. I live in a house."

Chapter 4

Personal Identity

> Naming and self-identity are two of the major issues within Native American Indian populations.
>
> —Jeffrey Mio (2003, p. 130)

> But my grandmother would always talk to me and say, "Don't forget you're an Indian. Don't forget you're an Indian. That's who you are. You're Lenape." So I grew up that way.
>
> —Lenape man, Monroe County, Pennsylvania

Introduction

Throughout our research in Pennsylvania, we found that conversations almost always turned to questions of identity: Who are you and how do you know that you're a Native American? In particular, the interviews we conducted with Native Americans in the state almost always began with some assertion of native identity. "I'm Waccamaw; I married a Mandan," began one woman from western Pennsylvania. A woman from southeastern Pennsylvania said the following:

> I was raised here in Lancaster County. One of those RD [rural delivery] things on a farm where we had no indoor facilities. My grandmother lived with us. Now my grandmother was born on a reservation. She was born on Cornplanter's reservation, which no longer exists. There are no reservations in Pennsylvania anymore. Matter of fact, according to one of our ex-governors, there are no Indians in Pennsylvania anymore [*laughs*].

People were anxious to show us family genealogies, census records, or family pictures ("Doesn't she look like an Indian?"). People who weren't entirely certain of their native heritage were often apologetic and offered reasons why they were uncertain. One man from Clinton County said the following:

> As far as my family goes, my grandmother's the only one left with knowledge of it on my father's side. To this day, to try and get information out of my grandmother is like pulling teeth. She doesn't want to talk about it. It's kind of the old thing where way back, if you were African-American, but you wanted to cover it, you said you were white. And the same with my family—they didn't want to show that heritage or they tried to get away from it because you were treated pretty much like an African-American at that time.

He concluded, however, by saying, "I know I'm Mohawk…I really don't care what people think. They can think of me however they want. It really doesn't make any difference to me."

In the rapidly changing world of the 21st century, the question of personal or cultural identity has become a critical one for many people—not just Native Americans. Historically, personal identity was ascribed at birth. If you were born into a Navajo family, you were a Navajo; if you were born into an Irish family, you were Irish. Who you were was integrated into everything you did or knew. You lived in a community where people were much like you and knew you very well. There was no question of "forgetting" you were Lenape; you lived and breathed your identity every day.

The rise of the modern state and European colonialism challenged traditional identities. Colonization ignored traditional identities and lumped together people into assigned national identities. To the European colonizer, the ethnic differences among native peoples were of little consequence; rather, they were all Africans or American Indians or whatever. To the leaders of new nations, traditional cultural identity was a threat. Leaders tried to break down traditional allegiances and realign personal identity to a state defined not so much by behaviors and traditional custom as by national boundaries. Assimilation became the goal of most states, and the myth of the melting pot dominated national policies. It was important to the state that people think of themselves first as Americans or French or Nigerians. Local affiliations were antiquated and a barrier to progress. The boarding school experience for Native Americans was a prime example of this way of thinking: Native Americans needed to be "detribalized" for their own good and for the good of "civilization."

In the second half of the 20th century, globalization emerged as another challenge to cultural identity. This economic model challenges the sovereignty of states, proposing instead a global economic network in which each state produces goods to trade to every other state. Workers need to be mobile in order to move where economic opportunities take them. Thus, migration has become one of the most important social and political issues of the last half century. When the U.S. government terminated 109 native nations in 1953, it was done in the hopes of forcing natives to leave their reservations and relocate to urban areas where economic opportunities might be better. As people world-wide migrated, personal identity was no longer tied to traditional culture or to national boundaries; as Gupta and Ferguson noted in 1992, identity was no longer a direct consequence of the space in which you lived. Leaving Puerto Rico to live in New York, for example, did not mean shedding Puerto-Rican identity; it might even reinforce it and make it stronger. The same was often true for the Lakotas, Navajos, and others who came to live in Philadelphia and Pittsburgh. Increasingly, identity, ethnicity, and even culture have become self-defined rather than a fact of birth. You are what you want to be.

Social-science research shows that having a positive sense of identity is important for many reasons. Trimble, Helms, and Root, writing about social and psychological perspectives on ethnic identity, say, "Self-identification and self-declarations are powerful phenomena that strongly influence personality, one's sense of belonging, one's quality of life, and one's sense of connectedness with others who share similar identities" (2003, p. 268). A strong sense of self-identity has been shown to be especially important to teenagers and to minorities. Studies done with Native Americans nationwide find that those with a strong sense of native identity are less likely to suffer from severe depression, less likely to feel anxious, and less likely to abuse alcohol and illegal drugs. Our informants certainly agree. One Lenape man told us the following:

> That's how it was growing up. When you're that way and you can't find where you're supposed to be, there's a piece of that whole history and culture that's missing. Then your family starts tearing apart and you're not connected to the Earth and you're not connected to your culture and you're not connected to your history and the seams of your family start to rip—it becomes chaos. And through my teen years and through my 20s and early 30s, there was nothing but chaos. There was alcoholism, a lot of different drugs, because I didn't fit in. I didn't fit in anywhere. I'm a mixed blood. I'm not raised on a reservation. I'm not with my people.

It is important to note that there is no universally accepted criterion that defines a person as Native American. Oswalt writes,

> in the history of United States Indian law, a uniform definition of an Indian has not existed. In general, however, if a person is considered an Indian by other individuals in the community, he or she is legally an Indian. (1998, p. 5)

In discussing DNA evidence for Native American ancestry, Shelton and Marks state, "The most obvious problem is that being Native American is a question of politics and culture, not biology: one is Native American if one is recognized by a tribe as being a member" (2001, p. 1). As a result, different native nations around the country have established different standards for defining Native American ethnicity. Usually, some combination of residency and degree of relatedness ("blood") is required. In Pennsylvania, however, where there are neither reservations nor legally recognized nations, there is no one body or organization that can establish standards for native identity.

Thus, on the one hand, research shows the importance of having a strong sense of personal or cultural identity; this is especially true for Native Americans. On the other hand, there is no standard that everyone agrees on to establish native identity. It would seem, therefore, that Pennsylvanians who wish to claim native identity could do so without any repercussions. But this is not the case. Those who claim native ancestry do not agree among themselves about who is a Native American and who is not. We found that a fair amount of animosity exists among the various native organizations within the state as to who was legitimately native—and who, therefore by extension, had the right to speak for other natives within the state. A consistent theme in our interviews was, "I'm a Native American, but X is only a Wannabe Indian." Any effort to unify Native Americans within the state comes up against this barrier. All of these uncertainties about identity are occurring against a background of a state legal system that refuses to admit the existence of Native Americans in Pennsylvania. In this chapter, we look at the problems in claiming native identity in Pennsylvania and the importance of doing so for the Native Americans who live here.

Native Identity in Pennsylvania

As we spoke to Native Americans around the state, we saw certain consistent themes emerge with regards to personal and cultural identity. The first was the great importance our informants placed on claiming Native American identity for their own personal satisfaction or redemption. Redemption may seem a strong word, but several of our informants told us that their identity pulled them through hard times or saved them from addiction or self-loathing. A Cherokee man from Clearfield County said the following:

> I had a rough life. I spent five years in youth corrections; 13 in adult corrections. What kept me going was my identity as an

> Indian. Rather than surrendering to the anger and violence in prison, I remembered the compassion of the elders. Now I work with youth. Young people find a home in our beliefs.

A Lakota woman from Westmoreland County said this:

> Until the late 60s, it wasn't a good thing to be an Indian. We didn't talk about it. We tried to pass as white. I felt I was a round peg trying to fit into a square hole. I didn't fit. As a teenager, I was very confused. I drowned myself in alcohol and drugs. I was miserable as a Native American. When I was 24, the Wounded Knee protest happened. AIM [American Indian Movement] made it okay to be an Indian…I discovered there were others like me; I wasn't the only one. I followed the Red Road to sober me up. I have been sober for 23 years.

We received many testimonials about the importance of native identity for the individuals we interviewed. A Shawnee man from Tioga County told us the following:

> But [my Indian heritage] was a connection that needed to be made. The other side of me is German, and growing up I studied all I could about the Germans—my heritage on that side…Now I wanted to know about the rest of me. It's like a puzzle, and you only have so many pieces before the puzzle is complete. And if you're missing a few pieces of the puzzle, well then, it's never the same. It can't be finished. So I got really involved with the Native American lineage. It swallowed me. Not because I wanted it to, but most importantly, it was supposed to. A very spiritual connection.

A woman in Sullivan County said,

> The transfer of culture is becoming more and more important to people, I think—that it's not to be done the way my mother taught me, but so I can say to my kids, "We do this because…" It's a way of helping them understand who they are. Their total heritage. We self-identify as Native Americans because that's where we feel comfortable.

Feeling comfortable with their native heritage was something many of our informants expressed. A frequently expressed idea was that people had felt uncertain about themselves until they encountered native culture. One man in Wyoming County remembered the first time he went to a powwow:

> The first powwow I ever went to, I was invited down to the drums. Hearing the drums beating…I couldn't tell you what songs they were singing. All I know is I couldn't get to them fast enough. I knew I wanted to be a part of it. And it's been twelve years, and I still can't get there fast enough. The changes in my life and lifestyle—the question to be asked is "Am I better for it? Yes!"

A man from Lycoming County said something similar:

> There's something, I don't know how to say it—you take somebody to a powwow, I'll give you two sides. You take the white man to the powwow, and he's bored because all the drum does is go boom-boom, boom-boom. But you take the Indian there and he finds the heart beat. Can you understand what I'm trying to say? I think that's what he was looking for. We're few and far between. If you sit down and play the drum, you can pretty much tell an Indian from a white man real quick because we have the step, we can pick it up, we can listen to it, while everyone else will walk away from it.

Others talked about how dissatisfied they were with mainstream Christian denominations, until they discovered Native American spirituality. The wife of the man from Lycoming County told us the following:

> When we were growing up, we were raised as very, very strict Baptists. I used to drag my feet about going to church because I didn't fit in. The first time X took us up to the Council House, it's like, this is home. I belong here.

A man from Clinton County expressed a similar sentiment:

> I was raised a Baptist. My mother was a Baptist. I was raised a strict Baptist. I really didn't—even though I believe in a higher power or

> a higher being—I didn't believe in their views. I didn't agree with what all they said and what all they did. I tried Catholic churches, Methodist churches, and everything, but I really never found a place where I felt at home. With the native religion, being more of an earthly religion, it felt right. It felt more at heart with me.

As will be seen in chapter 5, many of the Native Americans with whom we spoke found their strongest personal connection with native culture through native religious beliefs.

The second theme we saw consistently involved anger or frustration at being held to a higher standard of proof for personal identity than is true for other Americans. Many felt it was a form of discrimination that they were expected to prove their claims. A Lenape woman from York County said,

> Would you walk up to an African American person and say to them, "So, how much African-American are you?" No! You wouldn't do that to an [*sic*] Hispanic person, you wouldn't do that to an Asian person. You would only do that with a Native American…You know, if someone walks in and tells the government they're Hispanic, they're not going to argue with them. They're not going to ask you to prove it. They're not going to say "How much Hispanic are you?" They'll take your word you're Hispanic.

A Lakota woman lawyer told us "An African-American once asked me how much Indian blood I had. I turned to him and said, 'How would you like it if I asked that of you?' He agreed that it would make him angry."

A Cherokee man from Pittsburgh said,

> We're the only race of people that has to identify ourselves to the federal government. No one else has to. We consider this a form of genocide. Native Americans had our own Holocaust, long before the Jewish people, but unfortunately our Holocaust is not as popular as the Jewish Holocaust.

A Seneca man from Tioga County echoed these complaints:

> They don't ask people who are black [how much blood they have]. They don't ask Asians. If you come from Italy, they don't

say how much Italian blood do you have? If you're German or English or French, because they're lighter skinned people, they don't ask them anything. It hurts sometimes.

Blood Quantum

The concept of blood or the blood quantum was one that our informants referred to many times. Blood quantum refers to how many parents, grandparents, or other direct relatives a person has of native descent. Native Americans have intermarried with people of other ethnicities since the earliest contacts. Derogatory terms like "half-breed" have been a part of American life since the 17th century, and the amount of Native American ancestral heritage a person had has often been used to classify them or discriminate against them. The colony of Virginia decreed in 1705 that any "negro, mulatto or Indian" was to be denied civil rights within the colony. This denial was extended by defining a mulatto as "the child of an Indian, and the child, grandchild or great grandchild of a negro." (Forbes, 2000, p. 1). Other colonies rapidly followed Virginia's example. Forbes notes the following:

> Alabama's code stated that "all negroes, mulattos, Indians and all persons of mixed blood, to the third generation inclusive, though one ancestor of each generation may have been a white person, whether bond or free, shall be taken, and deemed incapable in law to be witnesses…except for or against each other." North Carolina possessed a code which prohibited marriages between white persons and "an Indian, Negro, Mustee, or Mulatto…or any person of Mixed Blood to the Third Generation." (p. 1)

The Dawes Act, also called the General Allotment Act of 1877, took land held communally by Native Americans on reservations and broke it up into smaller parcels which were then assigned to individual Native American families. The intent of the Dawes Act was to "civilize" Native Americans by instilling in them values held by other Americans, such as the concept of private property. Individuals were assigned plots of land based on tribal membership, and tribal membership was determined by the percentage of blood individuals contained. In the 20th century, as the number of Native Americans steadily grew, individual reservations began to wrestle with who was eligible to live on a reservation—and thus, also eligible for federal benefits. Most fell back on the blood quantum measure to decide who was a legitimate tribal member and who was not. However, no uniform standard was set. The Utes require five eighths blood for reservation membership, the Choctaws require one half, and the Fox and Pequot require one sixteenth. The Eastern Band Cherokees require one thirty-second, but the Oklahoma Cherokees require only that a person's ancestor be listed on the 1906 Dawes Roll. The most common standard across the United States is one quarter. As can be seen, the use of blood quantum is an arbitrary standard.

While measuring blood quantum percentages may be a handy classification device for a government or tribal bureaucracy, doing so inevitably leads to more questions. Some of our informants felt that using blood as a way of defining Native American status would ultimately lead to Native Americans being legislated out of existence. A Saponi woman in York said the following:

> I think that a lot of people have Indian background, but I don't think you are totally Indian anymore. But a lot of people do. Once my grandkids marry, their kids are not gonna be Indian. The bloodline's gone. It's a struggle today. I know the Cherokees, they go to one-eighth bloodline. A lotta tribes go to ¼ blood. So, four generations, it's gone. You can't go back six, seven generations and say you're Indian anymore. The government likes that. It's less Indian people around.

A Cherokee man from Pittsburgh said,

> Europeans used the percentage system. To us, it's a form of genocide, and that's what the U.S. government has done. The U.S. government sets the standards. The reservation itself does not look at percentages. The BIA does. And if they feel you don't meet the set standards of their blood quantum, then you will not be entitled

> to any land claims or any of the rights that go along with that. And that's their form of eliminating us.

We think there is a real ambivalence toward measuring blood quantum among the Native Americans we have met. On the one hand, many of the people we spoke to readily identified themselves as one fourth or one eighth or some other percentage Native American. There was also a strong tendency to correlate how native you were based on your percentage of native blood. On the other hand, there was a strong resentment against having blood quantum used by others to classify native status. We heard consistently that the use of blood quantum was meaningless except as a device to discriminate against individuals or as a bureaucratic hurdle. The widespread perception that other ethnicities in the United States did not have to prove their heritage or how much Latino or African American blood they had added strongly to the sense of unfair treatment.

Wannabes

The third theme that emerged in our research had to do with the issue of "wannabes." The term "wannabe" has been adopted by both natives and many nonnatives to refer to people who do not have any native ancestry but who want to be like Indians. The more charitable comments we heard about wannabes had to do with people who admired Native Americans and their values and who wanted to share some of the native lifestyle. The more negative comments had to do with people who pretended to be natives for economic gain or who were not serious about their interests in native cultures. "Playing at being Indians" was a phrase we frequently heard. Given the difficulties in determining native ancestry in Pennsylvania, an easy way to discredit someone else is to call that individual a wannabe. Disagreement over who is a legitimate American Indian and who is not consistently undermines efforts to create unity among native organizations in the state.

Philip Deloria in his 1998 book, *Playing Indian*, notes that there have been people of European ancestry who have "played at being Indian" since at least the early 18th century. Many genuinely admired Native American cultures and felt they could help preserve those cultures by attending powwows, collecting native artifacts, and wearing American Indian dress. The counterculture movement of the 1960s and the New-Age movement that emerged from it embraced what was seen as the moral strengths of Native American culture: a reverence for the land, respect for nature, and an emphasis on communal living. Deloria notes that as many Americans began to feel alienated from a consumption-oriented industrial society, Native Americans—at least in the form of the mythical Native Americans most Americans had been exposed to—seemed to present a fulfilling alternative.

Nationwide, Native Americans express little but disgust with wannabes. The prominent Native American activist, Ward Churchill, wrote the following in *Indians Are us? Culture and Genocide in Native North America*:

> Native American societies can and *do* suffer the socioculturally debilitating effects of spiritual trivialization and appropriation at the hands of the massive larger Euro-immigrant population which has come to dominate literally every other aspect of our existence. As Margo Thunderbird, an activist of the Shinnecock Nation has put it, "They came for our land, for what grew or could be grown on it, for the resources in it, and for our clean air and pure water. They stole these things from us, and in the taking they also stole our free ways and the best of our leaders, killed in battle or assassinated. And now, after all that, they've come for the very last of our possessions; now they want our pride, our history, our spiritual traditions. The lies and thefts just never end." (1994, p. 216; ironically, Churchill has been accused of being a wannabe by other native activists—see Harjo, 2006, p. 2)

In an Internet posting, members of the Lakota Nation urge zero tolerance for any non-Lakota who mimics or adopts Lakota beliefs or ways. In 1995 Vine Deloria wrote about people who are wannabe American Indians, saying the following:

> They are discontented with their society, their government, their religion, and everything around them and nothing is more

> appealing than to cast aside all inhibitions and stride back into the wilderness, or at least a wilderness theme park, seeking the nobility of the wily savage who once physically fought civilization and now, symbolically, at least, is prepared to do it again. (1995, p. 2)

Most of the people we spoke with in Pennsylvania did not feel so strongly about wannabes, though there were some who did, like the Abenaki man who told us, "The biggest problem we have in Pennsylvania are the wannabes." More often, asking about wannabes elicited a confusion of emotions and ideas among our informants. Some expressed amazement that anyone would want to be an Indian: "I don't know why anyone would wannabe an Indian. It's a hard life. There are fewer opportunities if you're native. There's discrimination against you all the time. Nothing is easy for an Indian." Some felt that wannabes didn't appreciate all Native Americans have gone through:

> Someone once said that, you know, with the wannabes, they want to be like you...But, no, they want to be dressed like me, they want the status that I have; they want to be recognized like me; but they want to go from Point A to point B on the Metro train, without going through the adventures and the divine intervention that has brought teachers into my journey and brought me to this point.

The Saponi woman from York said, "They [wannabes] don't know the hardships we faced growing up. It wasn't always pretty. I don't understand it. It's tough to be an Indian." She went on to say, "I can't say that they're not who they say they are. I just know what I've seen in the last 30 years in Pennsylvania. You meet people and they're not Indian and the next time they are. That's hard for me."

Several felt that nonnatives aspired to be wannabes because they were unhappy with their lives as they were. A Lenape man from Bucks County said, "Wannabes need a sense of direction—that's why they're doing it. They wannabe something better than they are." But, he added, "They should follow their own dream and leave Native American people alone." A Seneca woman from Allegheny County said the following:

> I think a lot of people have lost touch with their roots. They're seeking something that they think is fun, and they're not truly seeking out their own culture, and, you know, television movies have romanticized our lives. And they think they can get that back by pretending to be something they're not.

A man of mixed native background from Sullivan County said,

> I know a lot of people that come to our powwows, and they wannabe an Indian because I think they truly like our beliefs. I think they like the religion. They can be part of something they feel comfortable with.

This man thought that being Native American was like adopting a new religion:

> I think it's in your heart. I think it's a religion just like anything else. I think it's a spiritual way. I know a lot of people who don't even have any blood in them whatsoever, but they are truly of the Earth Religion.

There were two positive comments many of our informants made about wannabes. The first was that wannabes were acceptable if they were sincere in their desire to be like natives and if they were willing to do the work necessary to be authentic in their dress, beliefs, and so forth. A Lenape man from York County said the following:

> If someone walks up to me and says, "I'm white, I have no native blood, but I like the native culture," but they wanna learn. So, fine, follow me around. I have no problem teaching somebody like that. They're being honest up front, saying I'm not native. Or if "I'm native, but I don't know what I'm doing." As long as they're teachable, I have no problems teaching somebody.

This man also emphasized that "our ancestors always judged people based on their hearts and minds."

A Mohawk woman from Tioga County said,

> My cousin, Julia, I mentioned this to her once. We were out driving and talking. "What do you think, Julia, about people who are called Wannabes?" She said "I personally don't know, so I asked an elder the same question and he said to me, 'Well, let's put it this way. If they want so much to live and be like a native person, then let them be, as long as they do what's right. Don't do it for the sake of making money out of it, but because you either admire the native people, you admire the way they live and the way they are as people. That's okay. Accept them for that.' He said all you gotta do is watch them. Just watch them and see that they do right. That they do right in the name of the native people. I don't care how you live your life, but if you want to live like the native people lived, fine, but respect how they lived and their ideals."

However, the Mohawk woman went on to say,

> But nobody seems to try and really understand the native people. I don't understand that because they're good people. I think they're great. They're a giving people, a sharing people. They'll give you anything, their shirt off their backs if you need it.

Another comment heard less frequently was that wannabes had played an important role in turning around popular opinions about Native Americans. The Navajo woman from Lancaster County said,

> With the Wannabes, we joke about them, but the reality of it is, we need them. Natives like myself who live in a community that is not my people—I need them because they are from this community, and they open doors where I have a hard time getting in because of prejudiced people. So, the positive—I need them…I'd like to help them out. I personally believe if those people didn't wannabe, we wouldn't be as popular as we are.

Philip Deloria echoes this sentiment. He argues that what he calls "white Indian hobbyists" helped both to popularize Native American cultures and encourage American Indians to reassert their own cultures, which were in danger of being assimilated:

> The Indian who sang and drummed at the weekend powwow might return to an urban factory job on Monday, making him close cultural kin to the white worker who changed into Indian clothes on Friday night for a weekend of singing and dancing. (1998, p. 142)

He says that as the cultural boundaries between American Indians and non-Indians began to blur and breakdown, the non-Indian interest in native cultures helped to revive American Indians' distinctiveness.

However, there were plenty of criticisms of wannabes, as well. Two criticisms most frequently stood out. The first was that some wannabes were making money out of acting like natives—or hoping to make money. The Waccamaw woman who ran an American Indian center in Allegheny County said, "I get calls all the time. 'I think I'm an Indian. What money can I get?'" A Cherokee woman from Lebanon County said, "I have no problems with Wannabes but so many of them do it just to make money—to sell their crafts as being Native American, for example. That's wrong." We found something like this when we contacted the 11 students at Bloomsburg University who had indicated they were Native Americans on their application forms. Several told us they checked that box thinking they might get more financial aid if they were seen as Native Americans; however, none of these students had any evidence that they had Native American heritage.

The other common criticism was that wannabes misrepresented Native Americans to the general public. The Navajo woman said the following:

> The downside to [wannabes] is when you go to a function and the community is asked to pay a fee—I think they deserve to see Native peoples in their native dress speaking their native language and sharing a learning experience with that paying public. My concern with Wannabes on that issue, they see their neighborhood people dressed in gauze, K-Mart skirts, inappropriately dressed, kids running around as if they're from the cave man era. Men running around inappropriately dressed with everything hanging out. [The public] leaves thinking that's the way we live. It isn't.

Several emphasized that wannabes sometimes try to dictate to Native Americans what native culture is supposed to be like. A woman from Westmoreland County said,

> Wannabes have a perception of what we should be, and they have reinvented us. I'm getting angry. You are who you are. It's bad medicine to be what you're not. Wannabes are making a mistake; there will be a price. I met this woman at a small powwow. She was the head dancer, and she said she was a Native American, but I could see she wasn't. I was dancing in my own way. I was respectful; I honored the Drum. She said "You can't dance like that." Well, I dance a very old style. It was taught to me by the elders when I was a child. This little group had made up their own dance. I was so ashamed for them. They claimed it was Lenape, but I could see it wasn't. I left and didn't go back. They have reinvented us. Some of us are being disrespected by Wannabes. I stay clear of Wannabe powwows now. We're born to it. It's a game for them. It makes me angry, and they just don't get it.

The Abenaki man said,

> There are some people out there that are Wannabes that have learned a lot. I'm not saying they don't have the knowledge, but they're dictating to other people what things are done. It's not the native way. The native way is that everyone has a path…But Wannabes say, "I read this in a book. This is the way it's supposed to be."

The Cherokee man from Allegheny County expanded on this by saying,

> No offense, but the books about Indians are written by white people who don't know what they're talking about. But Wannabes read those books and think they know what to do. And then they try to tell me what it is to be an Indian!

Several of our informants summed up their feelings about wannabes or people with very little native heritage by saying that these people need to be proud of their entire background—not just their native side, real or imagined. A Cherokee woman from Butler County said the following:

> The biggest problem I see is, if you think about it, most of the population has a native ancestor somewhere in their background. I have a problem with them using it for the wrong reasons. If they want to learn about their culture, if they want to improve their lives, I have no problem with it. I think it's great because it doesn't matter what nationality you are—be proud of who you are—enjoy the history that you have, and honor the ceremonies, your customs and traditions, but don't try to be something you're not.

In describing the Pittsburgh American Indian Center, the director said, "Don't come here just to be Indian. You come here to learn about you as a total being—if you're German or whatever. You should know your total heritage."

The director also added,

> People say "I'm really sympathetic" and the next thing you know, they're an Indian. Who am I to judge? But you [wannabes] can go off the hill and change back into what you were. We can't. They're more Indian than we are. They can afford the clothes, the jewelry. We can't. But I just leave it alone. Sooner or later, they'll get tired of playing at it.

The Old People Didn't Want Us to Know We Were Indian

The confusion and controversies in Pennsylvania about who is an American Indian and who is not might lead an outside observer to wonder why Native Americans here are not more sure of their past. Most people in the United States have some idea of their background, even if they have no personal interest in genealogy or family trees. By name, they can identify themselves as Latino or Irish or Italian or some other background. The more recently their families migrated to this country, the clearer their sense of their ethnic past probably is. We as the authors can serve as examples of this search for identity. One of the authors (Minderhout) has Dutch, German, Irish, and English background. Being interested in family genealogy, he researched his family tree and traced his family in the United States back to the early 1800s—but after that, the information reached a dead-end. This was true despite the fact that some of his ancestors were 19th-century ministers or politicians, and as literate people, they kept records of their families, with births, marriages, and deaths carefully documented. The other author (Frantz) has German and Italian background. Her family has been in the United States for a shorter amount of time; thus, there are reliable links to at least her Italian kin. Even so, after a couple of generations back, her family ties are unknown. (And as our informants have stressed, our current status does not depend on our ancestry; if we say we're Swedish, no one is likely to challenge us.)

But Native Americans in Pennsylvania have to trace their families back farther in time, especially if they believe they are descended from the indigenous nations of Pennsylvania, such as the Lenape. As noted in chapter 2, the Lenape began having contacts with Europeans around 1630. By 1737, they were losing their land rights in eastern Pennsylvania, and by 1741 they were migrating westward. They were not literate cultures; as a result, they left no written records behind of their families or their communities. The only written accounts of them in the 17th and 18th centuries are by Europeans, and those accounts are few and seldom based on an effort to record the lives and genealogies of native peoples.

Natives and Europeans (as well as Africans) "intermarried" from the earliest contact periods—a trend that continues today. Nagel (1995) notes that 48% of Native Americans nationwide married non-Indians in 1980 and that by 1990 that number had grown to 59%. In a state like Pennsylvania, with a historically small native population, the rate of intermarriage is between 72% and 82%. As mentioned in earlier chapters, Native Americans have a long history of intermarriage among themselves and of adopting members of other nationalities into their midst. This only became a "problem" when European governments began to sort their populations by race and/or ethnicity, and identifying features like blood quantum became law. Nagel, in her survey of census records, also points out that between 1980 and 1990 parents in mixed-Indian/non-Indian marriages became somewhat less likely to identify their children as American Indian (47.4% vs. 46.7%), despite the growing population of Native Americans in that time period. Under those circumstances, it would be easy to lose one's native identity.

Several of our informants noted that when American Indians and non-Indians intermarried, it was usually an American Indian bride and a non-Indian groom. Given American cultural patterns, the children would most likely have their father's name. Before the 20th century, marriage records often did not record the woman's last name, especially if she was a Native American. Thus, a marriage from 1750 might record a wedding between "James Smith" and "Mary." Some of our informants took this as evidence that there was native heritage in their background. The U.S. Census in 1870 and 1880 counts many persons of native background without listing their full name or any name at all; words like "papoose" or "squaw" were sometimes used instead. The fact that many Native Americans adopted Christianity and therefore also adopted "Christian" names makes searching records for native background more difficult. For example, on the reservations today in New York State, almost every registered Iroquois has a European name.

One of our informants, a Lenape woman from Northampton County, said,

> I can show you the census reports that prove my grandmother existed, but they didn't say she was Indian. Back then, they didn't do that, even in the census reports. You had black, you had white, and the natives, many of them had married German farmers anyway, so they weren't pure, so they don't call them Indian.

Native Americans were not counted as a separate category in the U.S. Census from 1790 until 1860; rather, Native Americans were called "mulattos." The 1860 census was the first to establish a separate category for Native Americans (as a subheading under "color"). However, census takers were instructed to only count American Indians who paid taxes, which was certainly not the majority of Native Americans at that time. The 1860 census enumerated around 44,000 Native Americans nationwide, but this count also included "half-breeds"—the letters "HB" were placed next to people's names in census records to indicate this. Other records show that over 80% of Native Americans did not pay taxes in the middle or late 19th century; thus, their names do not appear on any federal document. The 1870 and 1880 censuses expanded the definition of American Indian somewhat, but, for example, American Indians living on reservations were not counted. The 1890 census was the first to try and list all Native Americans—taxed and not taxed—but those records were destroyed in a fire in 1892 and are not, therefore, available to modern Native Americans for research. One of our informants referred to this process as "documentary genocide," since thousands of people were not recorded because of various biases. The previously mentioned Dawes Rolls of 1906 listed several thousand Native Americans, most of who were Cherokees. The Cherokee Nation in Oklahoma will admit anyone to national membership who can show convincing linkage to one of those names, but, of course, this is of little use if a person is not Cherokee.

Thus, the time span involved, and the absence or spottiness of written documentation works against efforts by people today to definitively prove Native American heritage. But another important factor that works against recreating a native past has been the reluctance of past generations to admit to an American Indian background. Again and again, we heard comments like these: "My mother kept this from me my whole life," or "The old people, they were real nervous, like my grandfather wouldn't speak about it." Several told us about deliberate efforts their families took to conceal their native identity. A woman from Dauphin County said that her mother always told her to tell people she was a gypsy: "That was my nickname, Gypsy, until I graduated from high school." We met a young woman who, while growing up, was told that she was Italian. A Lenape woman from Sullivan County said the following:

> I'm native from my mom's side and my dad's side. I grew up with it, but a lot of things that were native, we were told that it was Pennsylvania Dutch. We always had fry bread, but my grandmother said it was a Pennsylvania Dutch kind of thing. They were raised to hide [their native background].

A Fox/Sauk woman from Monroe County told us,

> I didn't know about my Indian heritage until I was in my 30s. I had my suspicions as a child, but it wasn't a good thing. My mother would say to me, "Go comb your hair. You look like a wild Indian." My mother paid good money to have "white" marked down on the birth records.

A Lenape man from York County told us this:

> My family was in a state of denial. It was their tradition to pass information down to the eldest in each generation. My grandmother told her oldest daughter, my mom, and her son, who went off the deep end about it. "Oh my God, I don't want to be one of those Indians!" They knew a number of Indian kids in school at the time in Mechanicsburg, and they were treated quite badly by the other kids in school. So they didn't want to be known as an Indian. So [grandmother] made a joke of it. As she pushed them out the door Monday morning, she told them to forget what she had told them Friday night. "I was just teaching you a lesson about what it feels to be picked on, to be prejudiced against." So they felt it was just a game. Grandma just withdrew and never told anybody else in the family, until I came along.

Another woman in York County told a similar story: "And my grandmom, if we went away, she would warn us not to tell people we were Indian. I think because of a lot of the hardships they had faced. So that's how I grew up."

An idea we heard expressed often was that it was dangerous to be identified as an American Indian. A Lenape woman in Lancaster County said the following:

> In those days it was not cool to be an Indian. Matter of fact, it was dangerous to be Indian. You lost your job if you were Indian. You couldn't go to school if you were Indian. You certainly couldn't practice your religion because it was disallowed.

Many different reasons were given for why being an American Indian was dangerous. It was often pointed out to us that native people who were living peacefully among Europeans in the 18th century nonetheless became the targets in reprisals for American Indian warfare. Several people reminded us of what happened to the Susquehannocks at the hands of the Paxton Boys in 1763. Those natives were supposedly under the official protection of the authorities in Lancaster, but that didn't stop the Paxton Boys from murdering them.

We also occasionally heard about the massacre at Gnadenhutten in Ohio in 1782. This was a relocated Moravian community of Christian natives. The original Gnadenhutten settlement had been in present-day Lehighton. Founded by Moravian missionaries to convert the American Indians to Christianity in 1752, the original community was caught up in the conflict over the Wyoming Valley. In 1755, Lenapes attacked the community, burned the church, and killed several of the Moravian brethren. The converted natives, who were a mixed community of Lenapes and Mohegans, fled into the surrounding woods and hid; they eventually joined the general exodus of native people out of Pennsylvania into Ohio. During the Revolutionary War, Ohio became the focus of European-native warfare in the east, but the new town of Gnadenhutten was not involved. Rather, its members built log cabins, tended their crops, and did their best to remain at peace with their non-Indian neighbors. Nonetheless, a militia raised in western Pennsylvania under the command of Lt. Col. David Williamson, attacked the town and rounded up the inhabitants. Accused of harboring enemy natives, the Gnadenhutten Indians were sentenced to death. Weslager writes the following:

> March 8 was set as the day of execution, and while the Indians sang hymns taught them by their pastors, prayed, and pleaded for their lives, and protested their innocence, they were beaten to death with mallets and hatchets, and scalped. (1972, p. 316)

A total of 90 American Indians were killed: 29 men, 27 women, and 34 children.

Others pointed to the scalping bounties enacted by Pennsylvania officials in the 18th century. In 1756, Pennsylvania authorities offered cash for American Indian scalps—130 Spanish dollars for the scalp of a male and 50 Spanish dollars for a female's scalp. This bounty was reissued during the Revolutionary War, at which time the scalps of children were included in the offer. Several informants noted that these bounties remained on the books in Pennsylvania until the 1920s.

We were also told of stories involving the Trail of Tears. Though the focus of this incident was the Cherokees living in southern states, our informants also noted that many non-Cherokees were caught up in the indiscriminate round-up. Others told of family members fleeing and going into hiding for fear that they would be transported to Oklahoma, as well. There was also the fear that people could lose their children to boarding schools if they were identified as being American Indian. A Shawnee man said this:

> My grandmother told [my aunt] not to tell anyone they were Shawnee and the reason was they were sending all these kids off to school. She was afraid she was going to lose her children. In the Indian tradition—or any tradition—you can't lose your children.

Stories are told among Native Americans of U.S. marshals tearing Native American children from their parents' arms to take the children off to boarding schools.

Many of our informants also told stories of being discriminated against because they or their families were Native Americans. A Lenape man from Carbon County told us, "My grandmother remarried after my grandfather died, and her second husband refused to raise my mother. 'I'm not going to raise that Indian brat!' So my mother was raised by her aunt." The Lenape woman from Lancaster told of being refused service at a gas station in Tioga County because they "[didn't] allow sand niggers to use the bathrooms." A Lakota man from Wyoming County said, "We can be discriminated against and nobody says a word. I was actually shocked that that still exists today." He went on to say that he had been denied jobs because he was a Native American, and several others of our informants agreed. One told of having his job application torn up in front of him when he said he was an American Indian. Stories of refused service at restaurants or job discrimination were told by many—though not all—of our informants.

All in all, it made sense to older Native Americans to conceal their identities in the past and to not pass that information on to younger generations. A Mohawk man from Lycoming County said, "Most people who were Indian before it was cool hid it because if you were an Indian, you were savage." The Waccamaw woman from Allegheny County put it this way: "It wasn't kosher to be an Indian." Much of that began to change in the 1960s with the emergence of the Red Power movement among Native Americans. The civil rights movement for African Americans set precedents for other minorities within the United States. Native Americans became more assertive in protesting decades of mistreatment. At the same time, the general public began to develop new stereotypes of Native Americans as environmentally friendly, peaceful, noble people who had been wrongly abused by European contact; movies, such as *Dances With Wolves* (1990) gave Native Americans a more sympathetic audience. This ethnic renewal affected Native Americans in two ways: It reaffirmed pride for people who already saw themselves as Native Americans, and it led people who had not previously identified themselves as Native Americans to claim their heritage (see Nagel, 1995).

As noted in the first chapter, the average age of the Native Americans we interviewed was 53. About one third of our informants were 55 or older. That means that many of the people with whom we talked grew up during this period of native consciousness raising. Many had parents or grandparents who had been secretive about their heritage. A common story we heard was, "I didn't know about my native background until I was in my 30s." A Mohawk woman in Snyder County said this:

> There's a big blank space from the 1920s to people of my generation [she's 56]. My mother's generation—that's a big blank space where they were trained not to be Indian. You don't see a lot of Indian stuff when you're in their houses. It's my generation that tries to bring it back.

The period of discovery was filled with conflict and frustration for many of our informants. A woman from Lycoming County remembered learning about her native heritage this way:

> I didn't learn [I was Native American] until I was in 7th grade, and it was kind of by accident. It was kind of like a history class, but it had to do with wildlife. We were asked—we were studying Native American history, how Native Americans lived on the land, how they were with the animals. The class was asked to make a diagram showing how our families would have lived back then. I procrastinated. We had like two weeks to get this done, and I just really dragged my feet about it. So, finally, over the weekend before it was due, I made a little tipi village. And my mother went ballistic! When my parents met, my mom made my dad promise that we were to be raised in her religion and not his. When she saw that village, she went nuts. And she wanted to know why I did it. I didn't know. It was just what I felt. My dad finally told us that we did have Native American blood. I resented my mother over it for a long time because I felt I should have been able to make that choice. But we weren't given that choice.

Social scientists say that ethnic identity is often marked by a set of symbols and perceptions shared by an ethnic group that have different meanings or connotations for other populations (Jones, 1996, p. 450). The Tuscarora woman from Sullivan County remembered how a shared phrase helped her confirm her identity. She said that she always knew she had a native heritage through her grandmother, but her grandmother refused to reveal to which nation she belonged:

> There were clues to our identity, but I didn't know this when I was growing up. My mother would, at a certain time, when the winter was fading and the grass was starting to grow, she would look out the window and she would say "The grass is so green, it hurts your eyes." Nobody's else's mom said stuff like that. It was almost embarrassing to me. And I was talking to some Tuscarora women one day, and it was that time of year, and one said very casually, "The grass is so green, it hurts your eyes." And I said, "What did you say?" And she said, "That's Tuscarora for it's really spring now." And I said, "You've got to be kidding me." It was like, if I needed proof, that was the moment. When I was out in Western Pennsylvania, a fellow called up and said, "I hear you're Tuscarora." I said, "Well, by blood." He said, "I think I'm Tuscarora, too. My mom's in a nursing home, and I think she's gonna pass, and she won't confirm it." It was spring, and I said, "Go to her and look out her window and say this phrase." And I gave him the phrase. He called me up about three or four days later, and he was crying. He said, "How did you know? As soon as I said that, she confirmed [that we were Tuscarora]." Who would think a phrase like that would be so profoundly connected to your heritage?

As noted earlier in this chapter, the discovery of native identity gives individuals purpose and even a sense of redemption. It can also lead to reconciliation across the generations. A Shawnee man from York County told us how his father always refused to speak about his native background and that this was a source of conflict between them. He went on to say this:

> For us, it was a reconciliation with the past. My father still internalizes a lot of that shame. He's much more proud of me now. About six or seven years ago, I was home in Illinois, and I went to the garage. Everything happens at the garage in Illinois. When I was at the garage, my father introduced me to his friends. "This is my son," he said. "He's an ordained minister in the Methodist Church, but he's Shawnee and the Delaware accept him." For my

> father to say that—it went by pretty quickly, but I caught it. And that told me about how he had healed himself in the process.

His wife, who is Cherokee, added the following:

> And it was through the church, through spirituality and linking the spirituality of our Christian faith...we came out of it with two perspectives—one embracing the diversity of our blood, which for him had been secretive. That had actually saved his family. Without that secret, his family would have been called Indians and in the era of boarding schools, they would have been split up.

The Mohawk woman from Snyder County said,

> My grandmother was at Carlisle Indian School with several of her sisters...Our grand-dad—now we suspect that was where she met her husband, probably while she was in Pennsylvania, and he was from the coal regions and then they moved up to the reservation, up near Messina. That's where they had my mother along with a bunch of brothers and sisters—about six kids. And my mother was shuffled off to Indian School, too, so she kept it under her hat that we were at all Indian until one of her brothers showed up one day and she pretty much had to let us know. And since that time, she's 84 now, and now she's very concerned with meeting the relatives and finding out what happened. We're finding out that's more the rule than the exception for her generation. Now she's proud of her heritage, and she and her sisters sit and remember about how it used to be like.

RECLAIMING IDENTITY

So how does one assert Native American identity in a state that refuses to recognize that such an individual exists? In an article in 1998, Fogelson says that "Native American identity is central to the concerns of Native American study programs" (1998, p. 40). He goes on to argue that native identity is a product of three things: blood, land, and a sense of community. None of these criteria works well in Pennsylvania. One of our informants said, "There are no full-blood Lenapes in Pennsylvania today," a fact which the people with whom we spoke seemed to accept. As seen in the examples given previously, the connections to a Lenape ancestor may be generations in the past, and even those connections may be hard to pin down. Native organizations in the state place varying emphases on genealogical research. As mentioned, the Lenape Nation requires convincing genealogical proof for membership. The Eastern Delaware Nation has recently begun offering workshops on how to conduct genealogical research. Funding for this effort has been provided by the Pennsylvania Historical and Museum Commission, and additional grants are being sought.

Many of the people we met surrounded themselves with Native American symbols to bolster their claims of identity. These included wearing native jewelry, clothing items like headbands, or long hair. Tattoos featuring native themes were prominently on display on several of our informants. Homes were filled with paintings and sculptures with native images or symbols, sage was burned to scent homes, "Indian" blankets covered furniture and floors, and music by native artists played in the background. Bumper stickers saying "America, Love it or Give it Back" or "I'm proud to be a Native American" adorned cars and trucks, and T-shirts with slogans like "Homeland Security: Fighting Terrorism Since 1492" were proudly worn.

The availability of DNA testing raises the possibility of validating native status. The National Geographic Society (NGS) began its Genographic Program in 2004 with the express purpose of identifying indigenous strains of DNA worldwide. An article in the *National Geographic* in 2006 specifically pointed to native groups in the United States that needed verification of their genetic status for various kinds of recognition (Shreeve, 2006). For around US$100, an individual can obtain a DNA-testing kit from the society. Upon returning the kit, the individual receives a genetic profile some weeks later. These tests do not confirm anything as specific as being Lenape or Shawnee, but they do purport to identify how much of a person's genetic profile is Native American. Private companies provide a similar service for somewhat more money, but they promise more complete results, too. A few of the people with whom we talked had already obtained their DNA profiles when we spoke with them. (Recently, Native American groups have criticized the NGS for not having native representation on their governing boards or for not being clear about what the long-term consequences of collecting DNA samples will be [see Lutz, 2006a].)

But when we raised the idea of getting DNA testing with our informants, most expressed some ambivalence about it. Most indicated that they could not afford the tests, but others were concerned about the accuracy of the tests. One woman told us this:

> A woman who's a good friend of mine and a journeyman level beadworker said to me, "I went and had my DNA done." And I said, "Why?" And she said, "I just wanted to know." So I said, "What did you find out?" And she said, "I'm African! I'm not native. I'm African!" And she's whiter than me! And that's what her DNA showed. And I said, "You know what? That's so whacked! It doesn't matter." And she said, "I know, I know." But she went through this kind of psychological trauma for awhile. Now she can laugh about it. I said, "Didn't we all start in Africa?" You know, what's the difference?

A Lenape man said, "It really isn't that definitive. I don't know if the technology is really that advanced right now. I would wait down the road and see how it worked out better." A number of people echoed this man's comment: "What do I care what some organization or the government thinks? I know who I am. I'm a Native American."

Land and a sense of community are contentious issue in Pennsylvania, too. Opponents of state recognition for Pennsylvania's Native Americans often say that they fear that natives will demand the return of land now owned by non-Indians should recognition be granted (see chapter 6 for a more thorough discussion of this concern). Both the Lenape Nation and the Eastern Delaware Nation counter that argument by noting that they have already obtained land in the state on which they hope to build museums and cultural centers (see chapter 7). The Eastern Delaware

Nation already holds its periodic gatherings and council meetings on its land near Wyalusing; the Lenape Nation has moved its annual powwow to a community near its new land holdings. Both of these organizations point to other resources to claim a quasi-official claim on recognition. Both have 501(c)(3) tax-exempt status, which they both claim to mean they are legally recognized. The Eastern Delaware Nation proudly points to its listing on a federal document as an organization to be consulted in the repatriation of native remains as a sign that they are recognized. Both organizations claim stone cairns and structures in different parts of eastern Pennsylvania as proof that there is archaeological evidence for prehistoric native cultures in the state. They also claim their knowledge of these cairns as additional proof that they are legitimate Native American organizations. Similarly, the Council of Three Rivers in the Pittsburgh area notes that it is the legal recipient and administrator of federal monies for job training and educational opportunities for Native Americans in the state; this, too, is seen as proof of legitimacy as a native organization.

When we began our research, we were told by a cultural-heritage program manager in Delaware that Native Americans in Pennsylvania would never qualify as a recognized people since they had no tribe; "tribe" as defined by this person meant having a sense of community. Native Americans in Pennsylvania are surprised to hear this said. They agree that establishing community is more difficult for them because of the absence of a reservation around which they could rally as a people. One person told us the following:

> Living like we do in the community, we have to live a double life. You can be an Indian at home, but outside we need to earn a living, get along with our neighbors, so we need to act white. It would be easier on a reservation surrounded by your own people.

In the absence of reservations, Native Americans in Pennsylvania turn to their organizations and powwows. A Lakota man told us this:

> We sponsor two functions a year, and we work with a lot of the other ones, even if it's just showing up with a few van loads of customers to give the public something to see. Giving the public

> something to see is important because it's important to have a better light of what the Native Americans are. But that's not the biggest reason we show up. It's our way of having a chance to go to church. Five-six hundred years ago, our way of life was everyday, everywhere. We didn't need as many gatherings because it was something you did 24 hours a day. Nowadays it's not 24 hours a day because we have to live in a white man's world. We have to work in a white man's job. Getting together at these gatherings and functions, as I said before, it's a way of plugging in our batteries. Getting rejuiced for the next round.

Another person told us, "We go to Council because you get to be with your people. I can hardly wait to get to go and see people I haven't seen for awhile. It's like we're one big family again."

David Maybury-Lewis, in his book on ethnicity and identity, says this:

> Ethnicity is like kinship. When people recognize each other as belonging to the same ethnic group, they feel like distant kin, vaguely related to each other through common descent, but so far back that no one can trace the precise relationship. (2001, p. 47)

Fogelson (1998, p. 52) uses the word "peoplehood" to signify Native American identity—widely spread networks of differentially connected individuals having reciprocal rights and duties toward one another. He notes that while Europeans looked at native identity from outside inward (dark skin indicating native status), Native Americans looked inside out (how you felt being native). As one of our informants put it, "I know in my heart that we are a people."

CONCLUSION

Native Americans across the country have struggled with identity issues for generations. Since the first contacts, Europeans have ignored the cultural differences among native nations, while attempting to do away with American Indian ethnicity through genocide, assimilationist policies, and bureaucratic labels like blood quantum. Popular literature, movies, and television all associated Native Americans with stereotypes against which they still struggle. The reemergence of Native American pride that began in the 1960s has led many Native Americans to embrace their heritage and practice their customs and beliefs more openly, but more positive images of Native Americans also led to wannabes, non-Indians who identify with native culture and behaviors. In Pennsylvania specifically, the struggle for identity has been particularly difficult. The fact of early contact and removal, intermarriage and conversion, misleading and incomplete documentation practices in the past, and the fear of identifying oneself as Native American in the past have made asserting Native American identity in the state extremely problematical. But for Pennsylvania's Native Americans, being native is an increasing source of pride, reconciliation with earlier generations, and even personal redemption. What they seek now is reciprocity—recognition from the larger society that they exist.

CHAPTER 5

SPIRITUALITY

> They believe and from time immemorial have believed that there is an Almighty Being who has created heaven and earth and man and all things else.
>
> —David Zeisberger (as cited in P. Wallace, 1981, p. 68)

> If I'm driving to work early in the morning and the sun's coming up, it's beautiful sunrise, I'll say, "Eh, Wanishi! You did a hell of a good job today." That's a prayer.
>
> —Lenape woman

INTRODUCTION

Most of the conversations we had with Native Americans in Pennsylvania eventually turned to discussions of religion or spirituality. Among the standard questions we asked was, "Do you believe you have values different from those of other Americans?" Inevitably, this question led to comments about the person's view of the natural environment, practices of worship, or beliefs in supernatural beings or powers. Most had been raised in a Christian household, and many of them regarded themselves as practicing Christians. Most saw no contradiction in being a Christian while following Native American rituals or celebrations. Some rejected Christianity as incompatible with native beliefs, but most saw Christianity and native beliefs as being quite similar. A Cherokee woman in Armstrong County said this:

> We have so many things in common. Even our stories are quite alike. We have our flood story, we had our prophets. I just don't see the difference. The Creator, the rules are the same. If you can't accept those rules, if you can't respect your neighbor, regardless of color, then you can't say you're a Christian and you cannot say you walk the Red Path…I think the language would make you think there are a lot of differences, but there really aren't.

In this chapter, we will explore Native Americans' views of religion and spirituality as practiced in Pennsylvania today. The distinction between religion and spirituality is one that is often made. It was put best by a woman from Lancaster County: "What we have received from god is a spirituality—his essence is within us—and how we practice that spirituality is man-made. That's religion." She went on to say,

> Tecumseh, another great man, who was Shawnee, he said if you meet somebody of another religion, respect that religion, but honor your own. So you can have, you can live side by side, without giving up what you consider your principles to be. Nobody can take away your spirituality. You can give it away, but they can't take it away.

Thus, we take spirituality to refer to the beliefs and values by which one lives, while religion refers to the actual practice of one's beliefs. We will examine some of the traditional beliefs of the native peoples of Pennsylvania, while also focusing on the importance of spirituality for American Indians living in Pennsylvania in the 21st century.

NATIVE AMERICAN RELIGIOUS RIGHTS

The First Amendment to the U.S. Constitution begins "Congress shall make no law respecting an establishment of religion, or prohibiting the free exercise thereof." Despite this wording, Native Americans have had to struggle to defend and practice their religious beliefs since the beginnings of the United States. Early Native Americans who did not convert to Christianity were regarded as pagans—or as having no religion at all—and therefore were thought to be outside the guaranteed constitutional protections. In the 1880s as official U.S. government policy toward Native Americans turned to assimilation and detribalization, federal agencies began to actively discourage native religious practices. For example, as noted in chapter 2, American Indian children in government boarding schools were forced to abandon their indigenous practices and convert to Christianity. In 1921 the BIA authorized its agents to use force and imprisonment if necessary to repress native religious practice.

In 1978 as a reflection of changing national values with regard to Native Americans, Congress passed the American Indian Religious Freedom Act which seemed to grant the same constitutional protections to native religions as had long been given to other religions. While Native Americans celebrated the passage of this bill, it soon became clear that the Religious Freedom Act had no teeth. In a series of court cases in the late 1980s and early 1990s both individual states and private companies challenged the 1978 act and its provisions. In 1990 the Supreme Court ruled 6 to 3 that the 1978 act was advisory only in its nature and that it included no provisions for enforcement. This led in turn to the 1993 Religious Freedom Restoration Act in which Congress restated its intention that native religions be constitutionally protected and further decreed that local, state, and the federal government must prove a "compelling state interest" before intervening in a native religious practice. Subsequent bills have attempted to extend federal protection to Native American grave sites and to the right of Native American prisoners to practice their religions while in custody.

Nevertheless, Native Americans continue to find it a struggle to exert their religious freedoms. One man told us this:

> That is one of the problems we run across every single day. You can proclaim yourself a Muslim and have your holidays and

> no one will say one word to you. Run across it with the Native Americans and you literally have to threaten legal action just to get a day off for our religion. With most handbooks that they give you, company policies state that they recognize religious holidays—and they don't say what religion—but we always have to prove who we are and what we are. That shouldn't be. This is America. This is the Land of the Free.

A Lenape man who served as an advisor to Native American prisoners said, "Well, there's the spiritual rights of prisoners that we've been fighting for for years. And they keep Mickey Mousing us around on that. Prison wardens don't want to do anything that makes an extra effort." But a man claiming Susquehannock heritage told us the following:

> It's a lot better now than it used to be. Back when I was young, we weren't allowed to have sweat lodges. It was against the law. It wasn't until like 1978 that we were allowed to do a sweat lodge ceremony again. And that's like the Sun Dance, you know. We certainly weren't allowed to Ghost Dance. It's better now.

Stereotypes

As with other aspects of Native American life, views of native spirituality have become obscured by popular stereotypes. The oldest and perhaps most pervasive of these stereotypes is that Native Americans had no religion. This was clearly the view of the Europeans who first made contact with natives on the Eastern Seaboard. Natives were seen as pagans at best and devil-worshippers at worst; in the opinions of many Europeans, either perspective justified attempts to either convert or exterminate native people. This view was contradicted by 18th-century Moravian missionaries like David Zeisberger who lived among the Lenape for 62 years. As his quote at the beginning of this chapter shows, Zeisberger found the Lenape to have a deep and abiding faith in the supernatural. This view was confirmed by the Moravian minister John

Heckewelder who followed Zeisberger into Lenape territory. A Lenape man told us this:

> [Heckewelder] said, that after his 34 years of being with these people, he wrote a letter to a friend of his and he said "After all my time with these people, there's only two things I have been able to teach them" and that was about Christ and about the Devil and Hell. Other than that, they knew all about the Creator. And the more I started studying the Bible, I found what he said was true.

Another common stereotype is that there is one Native American religion shared by all the native nations of North America. One of our informants, a Lakota woman from Clarion County, told us, "It makes me so mad when someone comes up to me and says 'Do you speak Indian?' " Just as there are hundreds of Native American languages, there are hundreds of Native American religions. Some general themes run through native religions across the continent, but in the particulars, the religions of the Iroquois, the Lenape, the Shawnees, and others were unique to them. Even within a particular nation, there can be a great deal of variability from kin group to kin group as to how stories are told and ceremonies are carried out. Some themes such as vision quests and sweat lodges are being widely borrowed across the continent, but these Pan-Indian ideas are being adapted to fit each culture.

Other stereotypes are artifacts of Western movies and television. The expression "the happy hunting ground" as a label for a native afterlife is an invention of dime-store novels—it is not a phrase used by Native Americans except as a joke. Native peoples believed in an afterlife experience, which differed from nation to nation. In some, but not all of those traditions, the afterlife was seen as a paradise-like place in which a person's soul could spend eternity. But the phrase "happy hunting ground" is offensive. Another stereotype is that Native Americans singled out a monotheistic great spirit as the god of worship. Native religions do commonly feature a creator to whom they pray, but native religions feature many other supernatural beings that are also objects of worship.

NATIVE AMERICAN RELIGIONS: COMMON THEMES

In this section, we will examine several general themes found in Native American religions. Examples from the Lenape and the Iroquois will be used as illustrations of these themes. The first theme is the presumption of the unity of all life. This is the idea that a fundamental sameness runs through and connects both supernatural beings and all life on earth—plants, animals, and humans. A former chief of the Lenape Nation told us, "When Europeans first came here, they asked how many Lenape were there? And the Lenape couldn't answer that question. How do you count all the blades of grass or trees in the forest? They are all our brothers."

As one expression of a sacred unity, there are often universal symbols or numbers that are thought to link all things. Among the Lenape, 12 was a sacred number, and 12 objects or actions were a part of Lenape ceremonies and everyday life. It is not clear why 12 had this sacred property among the Lenape. One popular explanation is that there are 12 plates or scales that make up the shell of a turtle. Turtles were important animals to the Lenape. They believed that all life on earth began with the act of placing the earth on a turtle's back; Lenapes routinely referred to North America as "Turtle Island." The number 12 resonated throughout Lenape culture. There were 12 important supernatural beings, or gods, each living in a separate heaven superimposed upon one another. The Creator lived in the highest heaven, and lesser gods inhabited lower ones. The Lenape believed that humans had two souls and that when someone died, one of those souls remained on earth to become a ghost. The other soul stayed on earth for 11 days, but on the 12th day, the second soul left the earth to journey to be with the Creator in the 12th and highest heaven.

The most important ceremony for the Lenape was the Big House Ceremony—an annual ceremony to promote the health and well-being of a community; Big House ceremonies have not been held in Pennsylvania for decades. The Big House itself was a roofed area held upright by 12 poles, each carved with the face of one of the gods. The ceremony lasted for 12 nights. Twelve prayer sticks were set around the house, and tobacco was thrown 12 times into the central fire. On the last night of the ceremony, 12 songs were sung and 12 prayers were made.

Twelve appeared as a key number in many other aspects of Lenape life, as well. Twelve deer were sacrificed for the First Fruits Ceremony in summer. The sweat lodge was heated by 12 stones which had been heated in a fire made up of wood taken from 12 different kinds of trees. A cleansing bath had 12 different kinds of herbs added to it. And a young man who managed to fast and remain on his vision quest for 12 days was thought to be especially blessed. The repetition of the sacred number symbolically linked all supernatural and natural life.

Animals as Spiritual Beings

The Western world makes a distinction between human and nonhuman animals. Historically, the theological distinction was based on the belief that humans have souls—and thus are eligible for an afterlife—while animals do not. Native Americans did not make this distinction. Our informants often told us that the animals were their spiritual brothers, and this was a common theme in Native American religions. Animals were important in native religions in several ways. First, there was a belief in animal spirits—that is, on a supernatural level, the animals were represented as divine figures; capitalized names like Deer or Turtle often reflected this level of representation. When Lenapes went on vision quests, they were inviting these animal spirits to become their guardians and guides. Many stories are told of the role these animal spirits played in creating life as it is on earth.

There are also spirit animals—that is, some animals were seen as having special qualities when seen in the wild. An animal that was acting in an unusual way may have been perceived as being a spirit animal. These animals were often thought to be able to talk or at least communicate with humans in some fashion. Bears were thought of as being especially significant spirit animals because of their size and power. Birds were also considered significant spirit animals. Because they fly, birds were seen as creatures of the heavens. Closer than humans to the gods, birds could carry messages between this world and the heavens. The most important of the birds was the eagle, which was said to fly higher than any other bird and, thus, could contact the Creator in the highest heaven.

The actions of animals—and especially spirit animals—were thought to be of great significance for humans. They acted as omens, imparting important information to humans. One of our informants told us of a Lenape cemetery that had existed on a farm in Sullivan County for generations. Earlier owners of the farm had not bothered the cemetery, but when the land passed to a new owner, the new owner plowed over the cemetery to make a cornfield. This angered our informant, and he said that every time he drove past that farm, he thought about what a desecration this was. But once, as he drove past, an eagle glided overhead:

> And there was a bald eagle right over the barn, going round and round about fifty yards up. And I said, "Okay, I got the message. Leave it alone and try to channel that into something that's more positive for our people."

Another informant remembered that, when she was renewing her marriage vows with her husband in an outdoor ceremony, an eagle flew over them. This was seen as a blessing for the continuation of the marriage.

Not every animal is a supernatural being, a spirit animal, or an omen; some are animals to be hunted and eaten. But spirituality is significant here, too. Because of the belief that animals have souls, killing one, even for food, is seen as a kind of murder. Since animals have the same spiritual value as humans, the death of an animal takes on a significance not ordinarily seen in Western society. Native Americans believe taking an animal's life requires doing so with respect and care. Native hunters often ask the animal's forgiveness after taking its life, and the body must be processed appropriately. An animal killed for sport or a trophy is likely to take revenge on the hunter, as its soul will be offended by the lack of proper respect. One of our informants told this story to show the importance of properly handling a dead animal:

> The Lenape man was hungry. The animals were gone; he couldn't feed his family. He went out hunting, trying to find something

for his family. There were no animals around, and it's been a drought, so the beans didn't flourish, the corn didn't flourish, neither did the squash—the Three Sisters just sort of plopped away. And he's looking around and he sees Owl, and Owl talks to this Lenape man. Owl says to the man, "I will send you food. I will send the animals to you, but you have to make a commitment." And the Lenape says, "Certainly, what is it?" The commitment is to share some of the food with the other animals that I send you. The Lenape man said "Absolutely!" Well, he sees Deer, and Deer comes to him, and he shoots Deer and he gets Deer. He says his proper thank you's, and he picks up Deer to take it home with him because he was so excited about getting the animal, he forgot what he was supposed to do. But it was so heavy, he could hardly carry it. And Owl comes to him. And Owl says, "I'll never send you any more food. You forgot your commitment and you never break a commitment." The man says, "Oh, I forgot, I was so excited. Here, let me do it now." He cuts open Deer, and he guts it and leaves the insides for the other animals, and he lifts up Deer, and he finds it's a whole lot lighter to carry. Owl says, "Okay, I'll accept it this time, but remember, always keep your commitment." I guess you could say that's what it means to be Lenape.

Animatism

Animatism is a belief system in which objects, people, or places contain special supernatural powers which can be employed to important ends, such as healing. These powers may occur naturally—that is, as an intrinsic property of an object or place—or the objects may be endowed with their powers or qualities through ritual actions. The Iroquois, for example, believed in *orenda,* a spiritual power. Orenda was a natural part of some objects; Englebrecht (2003, p. 135) argues that some of the Iroquois' fascination with European trade goods stemmed from their belief that these glass or metal objects possessed orenda. The Iroquois at contact already presumed that natural copper and quartz possessed this spiritual power, and trade beads and metal implements may have been seen in this light by analogy. The Iroquois also believed that orenda could be obtained. A successful hunter had orenda, for example; if an animal managed to escape a hunter, the animal's orenda was greater than the hunter's. Ritual preparations, such as fasting or making tobacco ties, and visions or dreams could also create or reinforce orenda.

A common modern-day expression of animatism seen among Native Americans in Pennsylvania is what is commonly called a "medicine bag." Many of the people with whom we spoke wore small leather pouches suspended by leather throngs around their necks. These were typically tucked away out of sight, and we quickly learned not to ask about these bags or their contents. We were eventually given our own medicine bags by Native Americans, and in the process of receiving these gifts, we learned of their spiritual significance. We were told that medicine bags contained objects of special importance to the lives of individuals. These objects may have been picked up because they radiated a spiritual power the individuals recognized, or the objects may have been gifts from people important in the individuals' lives. Because of our perceived statuses as teachers, our medicine bags contain objects that symbolically represent our occupations. The medicine bag is thought to be extremely important to an individual's spiritual health and well-being, and the people we met were extremely reluctant to part with them or take them off.

We heard several stories of Native Americans being harassed because of their medicine bags. We were told one story of a Native American child who was repeatedly beaten up by other children because he would not let other children see what it contained. In that case, the child was eventually ordered to stop wearing the medicine bag to school because its presence was seen as disruptive. Our informant told us this:

> The boy went home to his mother who was an activist, and she wanted him to wear it anyway. But he said he didn't want to start fights and so he wouldn't wear it to school. And he got affirmation from our people because the warrior's first job is to promote the peace. So if the bag was going to cause a problem at school, it was his choice to make. If he's not going to wear it, that doesn't

> cause a problem. So he got a lot of affirmation from our people. He was a warrior, to promote peace. They could not stop him from being an Indian boy. They couldn't interfere with his prayers or anything like that. He does wear it now. He was younger then. He was a shy little boy, but he became a wonderful teacher for a lot of adults among our people, who get their feathers up, you know. A lot of them belong to the turkey clan, so they get their feathers up pretty quick.

Another woman told us that she experienced harassment at her work place in part because she wore a medicine bag: "They thought I had pot in there. I had to go to my supervisor and be questioned about possible drug use because this one co-worker was telling people that I stashed drugs in my medicine bag." Her husband added,

> They try to push you and bully you around. I wear a medicine bag at work. I keep things in my toolbox at work, things that are Native American. There are comments made, but it's none of their business what's there and what's in that stuff—my medicine bag.

We were told several times about Native American hospital patients who had their medicine bags removed in the hospital by medical staff against the patients' wishes. Since medicine bags are considered important to a person's health and spiritual well-being, having a bag removed in the hospital can seem counter-productive and discriminatory to a native person. Ken Hayden, a Methodist minister and hospital chaplain, told us the following:

> I had the hospital ask me, "We have this man from Massachusetts who needed surgery and he wears a medicine bag, what do we do?" And I said, "Do you have a sterile bag?" They said "Sure." So I said, "Have them put it in there or you ask permission for you to do it. You can seal it and tape it to the side of their arm or something or on the table so that when they wake up, it's right there." He called me back three hours later, "Hey, great, it worked. What's in the medicine bag?" So I e-mailed him some stuff about medicine bags.

THE IMPORTANCE OF VISIONS

Hultkrantz (1987) says that probably no body of religious belief puts more significance on visions or dreams as spiritual experience than Native American religions. Probably the most important example of this is the vision quest in which individuals subjected themselves to deprivations and rigorous physical activity in order to induce a vision. In these visions, a guardian spirit would bond with the individuals seeking the vision; through the bond, the persons received divine instruction and the promise of protection. Classically associated with the people of the Great Plains, the vision quest has become a standard part of the Pan-Indian movement. Sources on the Lenape seem to agree that the Lenape practiced a type of vision quest before contact with Europeans, though it is hard to tell whether this was, in fact, a precontact behavior. The Iroquois do not seem to have practiced the vision quest in the past, and not enough is known about the Susquehannocks to know what their religious practices were. Nevertheless, Native Americans throughout the Northeast today have embraced the vision quest as an important coming-of-age experience.

Visions are also an important part of group ceremonials and healing rituals. All over the Americas, native shamans enter trances in order to understand the supernatural origins of disease or misfortune. The Sun Dance, a ritual rapidly becoming a Pan-Indian ceremony, is built around dancers who subject themselves to fasting and pain to induce visions. Among the Mohawks, ill health or misfortune is combated through a group called the False Face Medicine Society. Members of the society are called upon to dance when someone in the community falls sick. They wear masks representing contorted faces which are carved from the trunks of living trees to give the masks greater orenda. One becomes a member of the False Faces when they have a dream that tells them that they should.

In addition, visions have also played an important role in the creation of new religious manifestations for Native Americans. The Handsome Lake religion among the Iroquois was based on a vision a Seneca named

Handsome Lake had in 1799 in which Four Spiritual Beings visited him and laid out a revitalizing religious movement for his people (A. Wallace, 1970). Another example of a vision-induced religion was the Ghost Dance religion which spread among Native Americans of the Great Plains in the 1880s—and which ended so tragically at the Battle at Wounded Knee Creek in 1890 (see Kehoe, 2006).

Many of the people with whom we talked have had vision-quest experiences. One man told us this:

> You were talking about traditional religions—when I was a young boy and I became of age, I had to go out on the hill. And then later in life, when I was a mid-teenager, I went on another vision quest. And I went on one when I was a young man. That one lasted three months. I went on one three years ago. I was out on the hill for four days because I needed to have a vision—to get in line and figure out what needed to be done for the people. That's why I'm here—for the people. I need to help the people pray. I need to give them hope. That's what my job is and my vision.

Another man told us the following:

> I met a man in the Seneca Nation—108 years old—and he spent three years with me and actually directed me in my vision quest. I did the vision quest in a state park. You're not supposed to do that. It was virgin forest. So I was dropped off there. They didn't know I was there; they never found me in there, and that's where I did my vision quest. I was 45 years old when I did that.

A Mohawk woman told us this about the importance of dreams in her culture:

> Do you know much about the Iroquois? They have a real strong dream tradition. They fully believe in what they call Dreaming True. You can have a dream that looks into the future or that sees something going on with someone to whom you have to deliver a message. We grew up with that, and we always knew it came from Mom, because Mom did it, too. And my mother knew it; we never lied to her. Sometimes you wake up in the morning and

> say "I had an interesting dream last night." Not all dreams are interesting, but sometimes you get one that seems special and everybody listens to it. Maybe one person would say, "I think that means…"—you know, and that was commonplace growing up. I had four sisters and two brothers, and that was commonplace growing up. We would all do that, and we all knew it came from Mom. And then when we found out we were Indian and then realized that was part of the whole tradition, that if you have an interesting dream, you tell somebody and that person will interpret it for you. And the interpretation would stand.

Later, this woman told us how she learned from a dream to tie a difficult knot for a craft item she made.

That dreams can be a source of meaningful information and that one needs to seek visions in order to embrace a native heritage were both taken for granted by most of our informants. The significance of obtaining land for some of the organizations in the state is in part to have a place of solitude in which individuals can seek visions without being disturbed.

Native Americans and the Environment

Given the significance of animals as spiritual beings and the emphasis on cosmic unity, it is not surprising that the people with whom we talked spoke often of the need to preserve the natural environment. One question we asked everyone we interviewed was "Do you believe you have values different from the rest of Americans?" Everyone with whom we spoke answered this question affirmatively, and over two thirds of them identified respect for the natural environment as the key difference between themselves and others. A Seneca man from Pittsburgh said this:

> We're not much different than any other spirituality as far as beliefs go except that we're brothers and sisters with everything that lives. That means insects, animals, everything! They're all our brothers and sisters, and we respect and honor them. And

> European culture seemed not to respect that. And for instance, we will not kill something unless we plan on eating it. And, of course, there's ceremonies involved in taking an animal or an insect as food. We don't just kill something because it's something that's there or we're disgusted by it or we fear it. We notice that other cultures seem to not have that kind of respect for nature.

His wife added, "We believe that everything is equal. And I've experienced that because many say that man is superior. I don't see that."

We asked a Lenape man in Lehigh County, "What do you find attractive about being a Native American?" He replied,

> Well, you know I always thought the Europeans were crazy. I thought their values were 180 degrees out of synch with reality. So when you go back to the traditional native way, it's like everything starts to make sense. I still think white people are crazy. I'm tolerant of them, but I think what they're doing is bizarre. They're destroying the environment; they're pissing in the water they drink out of. It's in every respect—they do the things that are worse for themselves as well as for the planet.

A Seneca man in Bradford County echoed those comments:

> Of course, you know how they've cleared out the trees, what they've done to the air, what they've done to the water, what they're doing to the deep sea animals out there, and everything depends on one another. If we weren't here, it wouldn't matter, because they would survive. Everything could survive without us, but we can't survive without them, and it's a shame that a lot of people don't know that and won't wake up to the fact that when you dirty the water, they're killing themselves. As they dirty the air, they're killing themselves.

Another man told us this story:

> We do things differently. I don't just go out with a gun and shoot things. I go out and pray, give some offerings, things like that. The Keeper of the Game is Mesing'w. Mesing'w is the Keeper of the Game. Way back when the people were first here and game

> was very plentiful, they started shooting animals and just taking a good piece of meat and leaving things set. And they would rot. The Creator didn't like that. That's not what he taught us to do. This was back in the Dark Times, when monsters were all over. So, the Creator told Mesing'w he had to do something. So Mesing'w took away all the game. Things went bad; people were starving. Until they finally started praying, doing what was right, saying what do we do? So Mesing'w went to men and told them, you can't be wasting these things. He taught them how to do it right. Then they started doing that, only taking what they needed and praying and offering it and thanking the animals for their sacrifices, and things got better. And that's how things are today. Mesing'w is not just Keeper of the Game; he's the protector of people, too. He kind of keeps us in line—lets us know when we're out of line—maybe getting a little too greedy or too careless. Look around and be a little more conscious of what we are doing—of our surroundings.

As we spoke with our informants about their views on the environment, several themes emerged. The first was that an appreciation for the environment and the need to preserve it was the first thing they associated with being a Native American. A Tuscarora woman said this:

> My mother never came out and said, "This is a Native American tradition or value." It was just our family. This is how we did things. And I knew that we did things a little differently than the neighbors. The neighbors' kids didn't have a heart attack if they threw their gum wrappers on the ground. It was just, you know, something you did. But if I threw my gum wrapper on the ground, it was like I committed a major sin. If I did it in front [of the other kids] for bravado, I had to sneak back later and pick it up, because I knew that Mother Earth couldn't deal with desecration. Before there was a conservation movement, our whole family had these values.

We asked a Nanticoke man, "What did you learn growing up about your native heritage?" He replied,

> I learned not to mess with any trees. My dad, if I put a nail in a tree, that was the same as if I gut shot a deer and let it run away.

> There wasn't any difference, you know what I mean? Between a live tree and doing something to an animal.

A second theme dealt with humans as caretakers for the natural world. A Lenape woman from Lancaster County said this:

> Ceremony is good because it reminds us what this whole world is about, what this life is about. Of why we were put here and that's what ceremony is for, to keep reminding us as to who we are. We were put here on this earth by the Creator to be caretakers of it. And that's the only reason we are here. Not to jump up and down with a bunch of feathers on our behinds, flopping in the breeze. Not the drumming or the dancing, but to be caretakers. And if you really look at Nature, Creation, the land—we're on Turtle Island—all the various beautiful animals we have here and the birds and the fish and all the beautiful clothing God has given them—and look at us! We're fairly ugly, aren't we? What do we have? Do we have colorful skins, stripes and stars, and shapes, waves? No! We're basically ugly. What has been given us, in my estimation anyhow, is the ability to remember yesterday and to plan ahead for tomorrow. And to walk upright to use our fingers—great tools for being caretakers! So we're here to be caretakers of His beauty. That's the only reason.

A Mohawk woman in Bradford County said something quite similar:

> The old, old people were put here by the Creator to protect this country. What we call Turtle Island, that goes from the Gulf of Mexico to the Arctic Circle—it was all one country. Of course, now it's Canada and all that jazz. We were put here to guard it. That's all we do. We guard the land. The white man couldn't understand that. All this beautiful land you could make a fortune off. They tried to buy it, right? They'd try to buy it from me, and I'd tell them, I can't sell it, it's not mine. I'm just protecting it.

A third theme had to do with preserving the environment for coming generations—what our informants called the "Seven Generations." We asked a Lakota man, "What do you mean when you refer to the Seven Generations?" He said this:

> What you plant today is going to affect your children seven generations from now. What you spray in the air. The fertilizers, the poisons you use on the ground, everything you flush down the toilet. It's going to affect, one way or another, the outcomes for our children, seven generations from now. You have to be mindful of what we're doing now, so they don't suffer for what we do.

Another man told us that this reflected traditional thinking:

> They made decisions in the Councils, even up in Canada, when they go to do anything that's gonna cause changes in the economy or the ecosystem. They'd think ahead seven generations—how would this affect them? You had to do that or you were going to ruin it for everybody. It's just the way our people are.

Yet another one of our informants said the following:

> Polluting the air we feel is wrong. We have to breathe the air. What we do today is going to pay on our children seven generations from now. The decisions we have to make today, we have to keep that in mind. That makes sense to me. You can see the truth of that everywhere you look.

A final common theme that emerged was that being out in the natural environment was a rewarding, spiritual experience. The same Lakota man quoted previously said this:

> I've always felt close to nature, but I never understood why until I rediscovered my native roots. It didn't make sense to my Christian friends and family. It was a way of getting away from what we see back to places men haven't touched yet. We were able to sense the Creator—His gifts to us.

Another said this to us:

> I've been in the woods since I was a child. I started hunting with my father when I was like eight years old. Not actually carrying

> a gun, but going along with him. My church has always been the outside. I could sit there and commune with God better in the woods than I could in church.

This man, who is a powwow organizer, told us that setting up a powwow was more time consuming than we might imagine: "A lot of work goes into clearing the grounds. People think you just drive a bunch of stakes into the ground. But every stake has to have an offering with it when you puncture Mother Earth." A Shawnee man from Tioga County said the following:

> There's always been a very spiritual connection for me, even as a kid. I always loved being in the woods. By myself for hours—that's when I felt more at home. Pine trees—I always had an affinity. Back then, I couldn't explain it, but I loved to be around pines, cedars, anything of that nature. Come to find out, later in life, I found out that my father's clan was the owl clan, and the cedars and pines were very special to them. Unfortunately I never met my father because he died before I had the chance, so that was a connection made at childbirth, but, of course, I didn't know that until later in life.

In the 1970s a popular view of Native Americans as conservation minded and environmentally friendly became entrenched in the minds of non-Indians. A popular television commercial of the period showed a native man dressed in buckskin observing the waste and pollution of a modern industrial society with a tear flowing down his cheek. This image seems to have left an indelible mark in the larger society with regard to Native Americans. Skeptics will point out that Native Americans were quite capable of destroying the environment (see Krech, 2000, but also Martin, 2000). The Iroquois, after all, hunted the eastern species of beaver into extinction in order to trade pelts to Europeans, and some archaeological sites seem to reveal large-scale slaughters of bison which would have gone way beyond the subsistence needs of the local people. It is believed that Native Americans set fires to clear underbrush in forests and prairies in order to insure that certain game animals, such as deer, proliferated; these fires certainly affected ecosystems. A more realistic view would be that Native Americans were pragmatically aware of the physical environment, and since they were dependent on it for their livelihood, they were careful to take only what they needed—at least most of the time. And there is no question but that traditional native life was more ecologically friendly than modern society.

This is not to question the sincerity of our informants with regard to their views of the environment. The different Native American organizations in the state all take some time to promote the preservation of the natural environment, and individuals give informational programs on Pennsylvania wildlife. For example, the Lenape Nation has reached out to a variety of environmental groups in southeastern and northeastern Pennsylvania and formed alliances with them to preserve the Delaware River drainage system. These efforts will be discussed in more detail in chapter 7.

THE WALAM OLUM

American Indians were preliterate cultures at the time of European contact—that is, they did not have indigenous systems of European-style reading and writing. Nonetheless, native groups had various ways of preserving past information and passing it down to future generations. In Pennsylvania, an important example of one of these traditions is the Walam Olum, a native history of the Lenape people purportedly preserved as a series of mnemonic pictures etched on pieces of tree bark which came into the possession of Europeans in the early 19th century. (One translation of Walam Olum is "ancient red engraved tally record," the pictures on it having been painted in red, a sacred color to the Lenape.) The Walam Olum is the story of the migration of the Lenape people from Asia, across the Bering Strait to Pennsylvania, in the centuries before European colonization (see Weslager, 1972, pp. 77–97; McCutchen, 1993). The Walam Olum is included in this chapter because of its contemporary use in ceremonial or spiritual contexts, such as a recitation as part of a vision quest.

The first historical mention of the Walam Olum dates from the early 19th century. Constantine Rafinesque, a professor of natural history at Transylvania College in Kentucky, claimed to have received the Walam Olum from a Dr. Ward who had been treating American Indians in Indiana, including some Lenapes who had fled Pennsylvania some decades before. In return for some medicines, Dr. Ward received a series of small wooden or bark tablets on which symbols had been painted. Professor Rafinesque did not indicate precisely when or how these tablets had come into his hands, but by 1822 he was claiming to possess them along with a transcript in Lenape that translated their meanings. Rafinesque subsequently moved to Philadelphia where he came in contact with Lenape dictionaries and grammars produced by Moravian missionaries. In 1836 he published his translation of the tablets as part of a two-volume text on Native American cultures. In subsequent decades, several other researchers added additional information or insights to Rafinesque's original work, most notably, Dr. Daniel Brinton, who obtained the tablets in 1885. It is Brinton's publication of the tablets that is used by Native Americans today in Pennsylvania.

Some researchers have questioned the authenticity of the Walam Olum, arguing that Rafinesque invented the text, the original tablets having long since disappeared. Weslager (1972, p. 86) accepts them as authentic Lenape documents based on his own research and comparisons with Lenape translations or ethnographies conducted by 19th-century scholars. The noted early 20th-century anthropologist, Frank Speck, an authority on the native peoples of the Northeast, also accepted the tablets' legitimacy, noting that there are other examples of Lenape stories stored on wooden tablets, as well as surviving Lenape pictographs consistent with the images on the Walam Olum (Speck, 1945, pp. 90–91).

If the Walam Olum is an ethnohistorical account, it is remarkable in that it describes the migration of Native Americans from Asia long before that became a popular scientific theory. It also seems to describe the cultural evolution of the Lenape from a predominately big-game hunting society to a horticultural society, again, long before these ideas became established anthropological dogma. It is on the Walam Olum that descendants of the Lenape make their claim to be the original inhabitants of the Northeast, the "Grandfather People," to whom all other native groups subsequently paid respect. Thus, the Walam Olum is an important narrative to the contemporary native people of Pennsylvania since it legitimizes their place in precontact times. The Walam Olum is seen as a sacred document today, and the periodic readings of it are conducted with reverence and respect.

Native American Beliefs and Christianity

Early in the contact period, missionaries from a variety of Christian denominations began proselytizing among Native Americans, and many native people converted to Christianity. Numerous communities of Christian Indians sprang up in colonial Pennsylvania, though they were eventually destroyed or displaced along with their non-Christian neighbors. Almost all of the people with whom we spoke had grown up in Christian households, and many were still devout Christians. The most common comment we received was that there was no problem in being both Native American and Christian; most of our informants found the two belief systems to be quite compatible. For example, a man from Wyoming County said this:

> Everybody's path to God is different. The Bible states, "Narrow is the way; few of you can find it." It does not say there's only one path and you must be on it to get here. God sees us for what we are, for what we do, for what's in our heart. If we are true to what He has placed there, then we can never go wrong. It's when we slide off that path that we make mistakes. That's what we try not to do. To help teach others. We are all brothers. I don't care what color the skin or what path you walk. We are all from the dust of the earth, created in His likeness, in His image, for His reasons. It is not for us to judge.

The Saponi woman in York County said the following:

> I have friends who are traditional. I have no problem with it. I think it's mostly Westerners who are hostile to Christianity, but I

> think people like that have to realize that other people had contact with Europeans 200 years before they did in the West. We became Christians. The church when I was younger was the focal point of the tribe. Because it was there, the building, they had school there. They worshipped there. They had tribal meetings there. It was the place where you did everything. I don't have any problems with it because I think when you read scripture, you see the connections between the two. A few years ago, I wanted to learn more about Christianity, so I took a class on Discipleship. It was almost like going back to school, but it was from the Old Testament. And as I went through it, I thought, "Wow! This is the same thing Indian people think!" I could connect to it. I think we have a Creator. We all do the same thing. We always believed that the Great Spirit was in the skies, and the eagle soared to the Great Spirit. We had prayers, and you used tobacco, and the smoke to your prayers to the Creator. That type of thing. It's all the same. The men have sweats, and they get back on their knees as they crawl back in. We have prayers. To me, it's all the same.

This woman had formed a Native American dance troupe which routinely performed at her church:

> We have a Native American Ministry Sunday...And we danced there this year. And all the money that people gave that Sunday goes to Indian communities and any Indian person who wants to go into a seminary. It helps to fund their ministry.

A Lenape woman in York County said this:

> As a Christian, [my husband] and I have both had this experience. We've had friends come up to us, talk to us about this, you know. "Aren't you getting off the track with this Indian stuff?" Obviously people who aren't involved don't understand our customs, but there's nothing in our beliefs that negate my fundamental religious faith in Christianity. I'd never do anything in any ceremonies, the activities that we participate in or in any of the beliefs I feel are native, if they were contrary to my basic Christian beliefs. Every once in awhile you have to reassure your friends and family—not so much family in my case, but friends—that you're

> not going off on some bizarre, New Age trip kind of thing with this native thing. Most people really don't understand.

As the quotation that began this chapter indicates, 18th-century missionaries understood the fundamental spirituality of the people among whom they were working. Differences certainly do exist between native beliefs and Christianity. The most fundamental of these is that while Christianity is a monotheistic religion, native beliefs were, and still are, polytheistic. The Lenape, for example, believed in a Creator God who lived in the 12th, or highest, heaven, but there were 11 lower heavens, each overseen by a particular god. The Lenape also believed in a variety of deities, like the aforementioned Mesing'w, Keeper of the Game, as well as in individual animal spirits. Traditionally, the Lenape, like other Native Americans, turned to the supernatural aspect that was required for the moment, offering, for example, a prayer or offering to the Earth Mother before planting a field or to the deer before a hunt. Less specific concerns or thanks were offered to the Creator. Some sources believe that the Creator became a more central figure in native spirituality once Christianity was introduced; the Christian God may have become merged with the Native American Creator to produce a monotheistic-like "Great Spirit." The people with whom we spoke did not dispute that possibility, preferring, however, to think that their traditional supernatural beings and the Christian God are all manifestations of the same supreme supernatural power. Other than that, only a few small differences are noted: "Christians bow their heads when they pray, but we look up because the Creator is in the sky."

Only a handful of our informants saw any significant contradictions between being a Native American and being a practicing Christian. A Seneca woman from Allegheny County said, "Native people say they are Christian. To us, they're not Native, because you cannot mix both. If you lose sight of your spirituality, your native spirituality, that's a major part of your being." A Navajo woman from Lancaster County said this:

> One of the hurdles [in reclaiming my native ancestry] was that I was an avid Christian for 18+ years. When I chose to raise my

> children the matriarchal way as I understood it from the people I talked to in my own nation, I was told that I can't have a mediator. In other words, it has to be between God and me, and I cannot detour my children to pray to somebody in the middle. I struggled for an additional two years because I was Sunday school superintendent, I did special music, I did Christian gospel tours—things like that. Four days a week I was involved in my church.

We asked, "By mediator, you mean Jesus?" She answered, "Yes, you can't be a Native and believe in praying to a mediator." However, she did go on to say that she had spoken with her elders about her children and their spiritual training:

> And this was what they told me—I should teach my children to find their own way of belief. But I can set an example by allowing them the freedom to go to many other churches and denominations and make sure that they see that I have one. So I could be traditional, and my kids could be Presbyterian, Lutheran, Hindu, Buddhist, whatever. So that was what I did.

A Christian Ministry

A good example of the blending of Christian and native beliefs can be seen in Ken Hayden, a Methodist minister from York County who was also a hospital chaplain. Ken was originally from Ohio and had Shawnee background. Because his own family tried to hide their native roots, he first began embracing his native heritage through his wife, Evelyn, and her family; they were of Cherokee background. He told us the following:

> I heard early that we were Shawnee, but it was always very hush-hush. Keep it quiet. Even though I knew it, when I would ask, I would get answers like "We don't know; we don't talk about that." There would be silence. So when I met Evelyn and eventually married into Evelyn's family, where they talked more openly about their tribal understandings of what to do, she

> provided some of the grounding that was necessary for me. That's consistent with what I call the Woodlands people—the Shawnee and the Delaware—where the women actually have a great deal of power. It's really kind of a matriarchal society where essentially women have the last word. If they say it doesn't go, guess what? It doesn't go! If they're not on your side, it wasn't meant to be.

When he went to seminary, his understanding of his native background broadened:

> But when I got to seminary, a faculty member who was Choctaw, was very helpful. That was the first time I met and saw someone in higher education who was an Indian. That was a very big part of the journey for me. He was very socially active, and he made his voice heard. And he was the guy who said, "You know, you may not like it, but I'm here. I'm not going to go away." So I spent a lot of time talking to him. He was very helpful, because up until that time, I had only been subjected to the fact that many of our people hid their heritage for fear of what might happen to them. You knew it intellectually, but you don't really know it until you embrace it. So at that point, I became more interested in my native heritage. I asked him more questions, and I began to do the family research.

After Ken graduated from seminary and was ordained, Evelyn and he were assigned to a ministry in Calgary, Canada. "There were more visible Indians there. At that point we began to have good Indian friends we would talk to." Ken was eventually introduced to a Native American lawyer who helped guide him to understand the relationship between his Christian background and his native background:

> So, here I was, around 35, with all this education, but I had these two parts of me that were still developing. I was introduced to Roy, and I asked him if he would be my teacher. He said he would. He really taught me in the Indian way, which is about experiencing. That's a significant difference in how Indian people understand themselves and how I as a

> Methodist minister understood myself. I expected to be taught what to do.

Instead, Ken's new guide took him on a journey of discovery, out into the Canadian woodlands in February:

> So he took me out and it was February and it was cold and he said "Go out into the woods." I was 36 or 37 years old then, and I was thinking in my usual logical way. What am I supposed to be doing here? What's my purpose? What's going on? I'm looking for all the data. He just looked at me and said, "Do you want to do this or not?" So I went out there, and I came back a couple of hours later because I'm cold. He said to me, "Okay, what did you learn out there?" Well, it's cold out there, and there's trees out there. There's snow. There's some birds occasionally, and I was cold. So he gave me some coffee and said "I want you to go back out again." So I did. This time I'm starting to get it, you know. Maybe I should be doing something else here. Something within as opposed to something outside, which is the typical Euro-American understanding of education. So this time, I go out and sit. I start listening within and without. I listened to the birds, and I asked them if they had a message for me. I built a little snow shelter, and I wasn't really cold anymore. I was actually warm. Later I went back in, and he said "What happened?" I said, "I'm sorry, I didn't hear you the last time. I opened my ears. I heard the birds talking to me and the trees and I was warm." And he said "Good! You're a good student." I continued to learn from him while I was in Calgary.

Ken and Evelyn's next position was in Yuma, Arizona, where Ken became the chaplain at a church near a reservation:

> When I went to Arizona, I sought out the same people. I sought out holy people, clan mothers, elders who would help me along the way, and Evelyn was along with me. We were in the right place at the right time. We were blessed.

While he was at the hospital, an incident occurred in which an ambulance driver refused to answer a call on the reservation where a native man was having a heart attack. Ken intervened with the hospital director and eventually went before the board of directors to ask them to open their facility to Native American patients:

> I asked them, "Do you receive any federal monies at the hospital?" And they said "Of course we do." So I said, "You won't go on a federal reservation with a federally recognized tribe, but you're accepting federal monies. That makes no sense at all. I'm wondering how the Medicare folks would feel about that." And they went into executive session. They came back and said, "We will do this, but we have one question for you. As Indians come to our hospital, who's going to give them care?" And I said, "I will." And lo and behold, one of them showed up in the next couple of days in the ICU. His name was Sanchez. He was frightened to death. He thought they were going to kill him. So I stayed with him for three or four days, just talking to him. This went very well. And a couple of days later, a man came by and said "You don't have an Indian name, do you? I had a spirit come to me and tell me your name." The naming ceremony was held a few days later in the local church. The name is "He whose words are stronger than the metal in their hand." Which is shortened to Iron Fist.

Following this experience, Ken was named chaplain at the Williamsport Hospital in Williamsport, Pennsylvania, where he encountered another conflict between a medical facility and native people. This time, the conflict was over whether the hospital would allow a pipe ceremony for dying Native American patients. Ken describes the conflict this way:

> At death, prior to death, there is a Sacred Pipe Ceremony. Briefly, let me tell you the story of how this came to be in Northeastern and Central Pennsylvania. Before I came to the Susquehanna Health System, our tribal chief had been refused admission to do the Pipe Ceremony for a dying tribal elder. This was very upsetting to our people and especially to the elders, clan mothers and chief. I was introduced by my tribal elder to the Nation sakima (tribal leader). He asked me to do a great deed for the people. He asked me to see that the implementation of the Sacred Pipe Ceremony be allowed

in the hospital—not only there but throughout Pennsylvania. I was frightened beyond words at this request but humbled by the trust of him and the people.

I contacted my tribal elder to initiate this request. Over the course of many months, we met with the officials of the health system. There were moments of despair and yet, it seemed that each small mountain was climbed. We learned that our sense of being victims was counterproductive to the overall trust of the people, the clan mothers, the tribal council and the Nation chief.

We were able to get a philosophical agreement that this Delaware (Lenape) ceremony was an essential and necessary spiritual aspect of our spirituality. Once this agreement was in place, we had to find a way to meet the fire and safety concerns of the hospital. These were legitimate concerns and we were wondering how to meet this issue. One of my management friends came up with a solution. He showed me an air evacuator. We began to see that it could remove the unnecessary smoke from an enclosed space yet allow the purification herbs to be present. All were satisfied with this arrangement.

My tribal elder and I collaborated with one of the system administrators to develop the hospital policy. It took nearly three years from the time we began until the first Sacred Pipe Ceremony was permitted in the hospital. When this was finalized, the accomplishment was met with shouts of "Wanishi" at our tribal council meeting. Many thanks were given to our Nation Chief, the tribal council, the clan mothers and our elders.

After this event, two tribal chiefs and I went to a number of hospitals or health care systems in Pennsylvania. There are a total of fifteen hospitals that have policies allowing the Sacred Pipe Ceremony for Indian people. In addition, they included other policies regarding medicine bags, birthing ceremonies and chanting. This event had much influence to other hospitals. We had numerous hospitals [in places] such as Massachusetts, Illinois, South Dakota, Virginia, and New York who used this process and the policy as a model of inclusion of American Indian spiritual practices.

Today, Ken is an active member of the Eastern Delaware Nation and a participant in Totem Rhythms, a Native American organization that creates totem poles for institutions and organizations both in Pennsylvania and elsewhere; Totem Rhythms is described in more detail in chapter 7. His story is both typical and unusual. It is typical in that he has been able to find a comfortable accommodation between his Christian faith and his native background; it is unusual in that he has been able to accomplish so much as a Native American living in Pennsylvania.

The Sun Dance

A final example of Native American spirituality in Pennsylvania is the increasing number of natives from the state who participate in the Sun Dance ceremony. The Sun Dance is originally a Plains custom. The Shoshone, according to Hultkrantz (1987, p. 67), may have learned the ritual through a Comanche, who had, in turn, learned it from the Kiowa. By the end of the 19th century, the Sun Dance had spread throughout the Great Plains. In its origin, the dance was held annually to thank the gods for good health and community well-being. Male dancers fasted and danced for 4 consecutive nights around a central pole or tree. The tree had been carefully selected and installed in the dance circle with great ceremony. At the top, an eagle's nest was created; the eagle was considered the most important of the birds because it soared so high—high enough, it was thought, to take prayers to the gods. A bison's head decorated the pole; the bison was considered the most important of the land animals, and in some origin tales, it was a spirit bison that brought the Sun Dance to the Plains people. Tobacco offerings were placed at the base of the pole. Rawhide ropes were extended from the pole. The dancers would insert pegs (or eagle claws) into their pectoral muscles. The ropes were attached to these pegs, and the men were lifted off their feet by others pulling on the ties. Suspended in the air until their pectoral muscles tore, the men would have visions. Their sacrifice was thought important in terms of guaranteeing good health for the next year.

Today, the Sun Dance is increasingly a symbol of both Pan-Indianism and the merger of Christian and native beliefs. A nationwide Sun Dance is held each year in June in Indiana, and Native Americans come from all over to participate. Participation in the Sun Dance requires years of commitment and participation after which individuals are invited into the dance circle. Today, the emphasis in the dance is more on individual spiritual health than on community well-being. We met a number of Pennsylvanians who had either participated in the Sun Dance or who were planning to do so in the next few years. The following conversation occurred between us and two native men, one an Abenaki and the other, a Blackfeet. The Abenaki was planning on participating; the Blackfeet had already been a participant at 82 years of age. We asked the Blackfeet how he made the decision to participate:

Blackfeet: I felt it was something I had to do. I had to see and I had to get the feeling for it. It was really a wonderful thing. I felt nothing. I gained a lot. It was just something that was there. I saw a lot of things. It was something I was proud to do.

Abenaki: It only took six months before his feet touched the ground again.

Blackfeet: Right! Well, we all put tobacco ties on the tree. We went into the woods, cut a tree down, carried the tree. Then we put ropes on it so we could hang off that tree when our turn came. I did this with two chiefs. They helped me do it so I wouldn't stumble. I did it right, and Sunday, when it was all over, we took the tree down, cleared up the ground where we were, and then we took the tree into the woods. We left everything on the tree that we put on it – all the feathers and all the tobacco ties. They were supposed to stay on it. It was a good thing.

Interviewer: Do they use eagle claws anymore?

Blackfeet: We used pegs, little pegs. Some had bone pegs, some had regular wood pegs. I carved my own pegs, so I would have the pegs. Of course, I've still got them for next time. Now next year, I committed to do double piercing, if I'm still alive. I guess I can make it. My partner here will be with me.

Abenaki: If you stopped chasing all those women, you'd make it [*laughs*].

Blackfeet: We'll make it. It's really something to be proud of.

We then asked him why he hadn't participated this year:

Abenaki: As with any political organization, there's something going on here. To have that happen here and to carry it out there with what was going on—he had to step down this year, which he's entitled to do.

Blackfeet: Yeah, I couldn't do it. It's not the place for it. I had to let it go. I'll make it up next year. I'll just add another year to it. You can't take hard feelings into the dance circle.

Some of our informants questioned whether it was appropriate for a Native American from the Northeast to participate in a Sun Dance. The Cherokee man from Allegheny County explained that it was wannabes who participated in Sun Dances:

> Wannabes take part in ceremonies that don't pertain to them. Like a Seneca taking part in a Sun Dance. We have our traditional longhouse ceremonies. Why would you participate in the Sun Dance? Or if you're claiming to be a Cherokee or a Seminole, and you do Lakota-style sweats, pipe ceremonies. You're mixing cultures. It's not right.

But the Abenaki man's response to this was the following:

> A lot of people question [the Blackfeet] going out there. Why do you as an Eastern Indian, why are you going out there? That's choice. That's the individual path I talked about. Now they don't ask you the first year when you go out there to dance. But they

> want you there. They want you to see what's going on. And then the challenge is made to you, if you want to. I've heard him say, "No pain, no gain." It's their interpretation of giving yourself for the betterment of all the people, not just the Indians, but for the rest of the world. And it's piercing and it's close contact with God. He knows it. He can tell it better than I can, but it's hard to get them to talk sometimes. I do know this—he gained a lot of respect out there last year. They claim he's the oldest one who's ever had it done.

The Blackfeet man said, "They said that, but it seemed like I was the youngest. I had to do my thing."

A Nanticoke man told us this:

> They have the Sun Dance where it is because that's where the people on the Trail of Tears spent their first winter. When they got there, the Mississippi was flooded. And so they had to camp there. There's over a hundred graves right there on the grounds where the Dance is. That's why they hold the Dance there, because a lot of people crossed over there—they were ill and stuff. My cousin was dancing quite a few years before I went. I'm not sure how many, maybe seven or eight years. He kept inviting me. I asked Grandfather [the founder of the Eastern Delaware Nation] about it. He said "It's not our way." Because the Sun Dance is done more in the Western areas. Then about seven years ago, I knew I was supposed to be there. So, I went, and I connected right with it. My brother went out with me, but he didn't really connect the same way I did. But there's reasons why I think I connected. I have a great-great grandmother who was on the Trail. She started coming to me in dreams before I danced the first year. The first few years out, I did Cedar. His job is to send the prayers. I spent the whole Sun Dance in the Sun Dance circle with the dancers. Then after two years of doing that, I learned the songs, so I had a better idea of what was going on. Then I started dancing. I made a commitment to dance. The commitment—it's always a four year commitment. I finished my commitment last year. But I was back out there again this year. I'm going to continue dancing as long as I can. Physically, it's a little taxing. When I can't dance anymore, I've been invited to the drums.

While the Sun Dance continues to be expanded to include native peoples from all over the continent, it is also taking on Christian connotations for many of the participants. In the converse of Ken Hayden's experience, who found his native roots through his Christian ministry, the Sun Dance retains traditional elements which are being reinterpreted as Christian practices. According to Bonvillain (2001, p. 307), the central tree in the dance circle is seen now by many as a symbol of the Christian cross with the bison head representing the Crucifixion. The traditional 12 poles set around the dance circle to contain the dancers are now seen as representing the 12 disciples of Jesus. Three black bands are sometimes painted on the central tree, which to Christian American Indians means the 3 days that Jesus lay in the tomb after the Crucifixion. And dancers increasingly see Jesus in their visions induced by the dance. Thus, the Sun Dance has become the ultimate syncretistic experience for Native Americans, as it accumulates and blends symbols from many native nations, as well as from Christianity.

CONCLUSION

As we noted as we began this chapter, most of the conversations we held with Native Americans in Pennsylvania turned ultimately to a discussion of native values, spirituality, and the need to protect the environment. These three topics were interwoven into many conversations, often in ways unique to each individual's interpretations. Native American religions do not appear to ever have been static, but rather they were constantly changing over time as new circumstances required and new visions emerged. The modern circumstances are no different. Native Americans select among the many spiritual elements available to them in American society and create their own personal meanings from them. As a Mohawk from Clinton County told us,

> I believe in one Creator. The ultimate Creator. I don't say I worship, but I give thanks to the trees, which give us fire and

wood. More or less, Mother Earth, here that we walk on. It's not that I pray to them, but I thank them. And if I take something from them, I thank them and offer them tobacco. The stone people, when we do sweats. I believe in one Creator, but I give thanks to the different animals and the trees, the stone people, but I don't necessarily pray to them. Other than that, it's a religion, but it's also how you treat people. It's treating people with the utmost respect. You respect them, and they respect you. And even if they don't respect you, it's a kind of turn the other cheek thing. I guess a lot of religions have that. But it's just living, day to day, knowing, well, you know the famous saying, "Today's a good day to die"? If today was my last day, how would I want to be known?

Illustration 4. Turtle, a sacred animal to the Lenape, rendered in traditional Lenape design.

Chapter 6

Issues in Conflict

Introduction

As we spoke to Native Americans around the state, certain issues repeatedly were introduced into our discussions. The first of these was the issue of casino gambling. Most of the people with whom we spoke had strong feelings, pro or con, about gambling. The idea of legalized gambling was very much in the air in Pennsylvania generally during this period of time, and as we began our research, legalized gambling was approved in the state for the first time. At the same time, politicians were outspoken in their opposition to recognizing Native Americans in the state, largely on the grounds that American Indians might open casinos. State recognition was a second issue about which most of our informants had an opinion, and recognition was being hotly debated within the Native American community, especially with regard to the question of which American Indians should be included. The third issue was the presentation of Native Americans in Pennsylvania schools. In our survey, 98% of the respondents agreed that not enough was taught in

Pennsylvania schools about American Indians and that what was taught was inaccurate. In this chapter, we focus on those three issues.

CASINO GAMBLING

> The big and only problem I have with Native casinos is the fact that all levels of government won't just let natives build and run their own; there always has to be white people.
>
> —Abenaki man

In 1988 Congress passed the Indian Gaming Regulatory Act legalizing gaming operations on reservations. Today, 224 of the 562 federally recognized tribes run casinos in 28 states. In 2004 tribal government gaming revenue was in excess of US$19 billion. In 2003 the American Gaming Association reported that American Indian casinos generated about 23% of the total gaming revenue in the United States; non-Indian casinos generate about 39% of revenues, and state lotteries raise 27%.

Benefits for Native Americans who open casinos include, on average, increased employment rates (about a 26% increase) and decreased mortality rates (about 2%) within the first 4 years of operations (Evans & Topoleski, 2001). However, crime rates climb about 10%, especially violent crimes such as auto theft and larceny. Fann says this:

> Indian gaming has been tremendously successful in helping tribes recover from unimaginable poverty, eliminating welfare, increasing employment and generating revenue, giving tribes the ability to be more self-determined by providing healthcare for their citizens, creating educational programs, and providing adequate housing emergency services, and civil infrastructure. Furthermore, Indian gaming is the only economic development tool available to many reservation communities, especially given that most reservations are located in remote locations where public and private sector economic development has not been successful. Tribal governments are using gaming proceeds to diversify and conduct other economic enterprises. (2005, p. 3)

One of the modern-day myths about Native Americans is that they are all recipients of gaming wealth. In fact, as can be seen by the numbers given previously, less than half of federally recognized tribes maintain casinos, and of those that have casino gambling, 55 casinos generated 69% of all gaming revenue. For the most part, the most successful casinos are the ones located near large metropolitan areas, such as the Mohegan Sun casino in Uncasville, Connecticut. Many American Indian casinos are small operations on reservations in geographically isolated locations. In general, only American Indians living on reservations share in casino revenues. Tribes that are not federally recognized do not have the right to run casinos.

Another myth is that American Indian casinos do not contribute to local economies—or, more specifically, that casinos rob non-Indian communities of potential income. This is a variation on the myth that American Indians do not pay taxes, a myth discussed in chapter 3. Studies conducted by a variety of organizations show that American Indian casinos provide employment to non-Indians, an increase in local incomes, and increased federal, state, and local tax revenues (see Darian-Smith, 2004; Light & Rand, 2005; Taylor, Krepps, & Wang, 2000). Reflecting the quote which begins this section, Gorman (2001, p. 1) says, "In many cases, most of the people employed by casinos are not Native Americans." A study conducted by the University of Connecticut in 2000 found that the Foxwoods Casino, owned by the Mashantucket Pequots, generates millions of dollars into the economy of Connecticut. And at the time of this writing, the first months of casino operations in Pennsylvania suggest that casinos will contribute US$1 billion in state taxes to the state economy. One of the three casinos in operation at the time of this projection is an American Indian owned casino, the Mohegan Sun at Pocono Downs (Shields, 2007). Riverwoods Casino (Pequot) in Philadelphia is in the process of construction.

In Pennsylvania, the issue of legalized gambling has been a contentious one, stretching back more than 20 years of public debate. Business interests, especially in tourist areas such as the Pocono Mountains, have argued for the tax benefits casino gambling would bring. They also point to the millions of dollars Pennsylvanians spend each year in Atlantic City, New Jersey; at reservation casinos in New York State; and on riverboat gambling on the Ohio River. Opponents have argued that gambling increases crime and destroys families when individuals become addicted to it (League of Women Voters, 2001, p. 1). Until 2004 state legislators had blocked every attempt to legalize gambling within the state. (Ironically, Pennsylvania has long had a state-sponsored lottery; Pennsylvania joined the Powerball consortium in 2002).

In 2002 former Philadelphia Mayor Edward Rendell was elected governor of Pennsylvania. Among his campaign issues was bringing about property tax relief—especially with regard to school taxes—by legalizing gambling. Rendell, a Democrat, was initially blocked by the Pennsylvania State Legislature, which was controlled by Republicans. In June 2004 Rendell and his supporters were finally able to win a slim majority for gambling by writing into the final bill a provision allowing state legislators to own gambling concessions (League of Women Voters, 2001). On July 5, 2004, Rendell signed a bill authorizing up to 61,000 slot machines at 14 sites around the state, mainly at racetracks and hotels. A racetrack was allowed up to 5,000 slot machines; a hotel could have a maximum of 500 machines (Campbell, 2004). Investors immediately began purchasing property in areas that were likely to receive permission to build casinos. Among the first to do so was the Mohegan Gaming Authority of Uncasville, Connecticut. The Mohegan own and operate a successful casino, the Mohegan Sun, in Connecticut. In October 2004 they purchased the Pocono Downs Race Track in Wilkes-Barre, Pennsylvania and announced plans to rebuild the aging facility and operate up to 3,000 slot machines, should they be able to obtain a license (Casino City Times, 2004). Developers like the Mohegan were themselves gambling on receiving the necessary legal approval for gambling on the properties they were buying. In the case of the Mohegans, the gamble was successful: They received the first license issued by the state in 2006.

While Governor Rendell was an advocate of legalized gambling coming into office, he was also outspoken in his opposition to Native

American casinos. An effort by a powerful Democratic state senator from Philadelphia to include casinos owned and run by Pennsylvania's American Indians in the final bill was undercut by the Rendell administration, and the provision was not included at final passage (Barnes, 2004). Rendell's opposition to this provision went unexplained; since American Indian casinos generate federal and state income taxes, there would not have been a significant loss of tax revenue to the state.

In January of 2004 the Oklahoma Delawares filed a suit in federal court to reclaim 315 acres of land in Northampton and Bucks Counties, based on a 1733 land grant from Thomas Penn (William Penn's son) to Chief Moses Tunda Tatamy in return for the chief's services as an interpreter (Duffy, 2004). In 1803 whites confiscated this land. The Oklahoma Delawares announced that if their suit was successful, they planned to open a casino on the reclaimed land. At that point, the Oklahoma Delawares were a federally recognized tribe and, therefore, presumably eligible to do so. Governor Rendell opposed this effort by the Oklahoma Delawares, and the suit was eventually dropped when a Federal Appeals Court removed the Delawares' federal recognition (see chapter 1) in October 2004. However, this effort did nothing to help the cause of Pennsylvania's Native Americans.

When we surveyed Native Americans in the state, we asked them what they thought about casino gambling. Two hundred and seventy-four (of 281) responded to this question. The results show that there was no consensus of opinion on this issue among Pennsylvania's Native Americans. In short, 92 indicated a positive response, 85 indicated a negative response, and 97 felt neither positively nor negatively about the issue. The respondents were also asked if they knew about the efforts by the Oklahoma Delawares to reclaim land in the state on which they planned to build a casino. Two hundred and eighty-one responded to this question, with 169 indicating that they had heard about this effort. They were then asked how they felt about what the Oklahoma Delawares were proposing. One hundred and seventy-two responded to this question, and those responses were mostly positive—111 positive responses, 44 indifferent, and only 17 negative.

Many of the respondents chose to clarify their answers with written comments. Several wrote that while they disapproved of gambling on moral grounds, they were pleased that Native Americans had made legal and economic gains in other states through casinos. Similarly, several wrote that they were pleased that the Oklahoma Delawares were pursuing land rights in Pennsylvania, since that might establish a precedent for other Native Americans to do the same. They were not necessarily supporting legalized gambling, but any land gain by any Native American was seen as a plus.

Several native organizations within the state have expressed publicly their opposition to casino gambling. The Nanticoke Lenni-Lenape Tribe of New Jersey had pledged their opposition to gambling in order to help win state recognition, and native groups within Pennsylvania seem ready to follow suit. The fear that Pennsylvania's American Indians will use state recognition to open casinos has been a barrier to that recognition, and this will be discussed in the next section of the chapter. However, since the law of 1988 restricts casino gambling to federally recognized tribes only, this would seem to be a meaningless objection.

State Recognition

> Many of us want recognition. How many other people, native born, need to have to carry a government issued card saying you are who you are. You can say you're black—no problem; Mexican—no problem; white—no problem! Say you're an Indian and they say, where's your card?
>
> —Lenape Man, Lycoming County, Pennsylvania

> I just don't get why they're so afraid to say, "Hey, we've got Indians in Pennsylvania." I've heard a lot of reasons why they think what they do. I have yet to find one person who can give me the reason why they won't say there's American Indians in Pennsylvania. I haven't figured that out yet.
>
> —Lakota Man, Wyoming County, Pennsylvania

Perhaps no other topic brought out stronger feelings among the majority of our informants than the question of state recognition. Almost every one of the people we interviewed had an opinion on this topic; very few people were indifferent. The effort to obtain state recognition for Pennsylvania's Native Americans has been going on for almost 20 years. Bills to recognize native people are introduced each year into the state legislature, but they have yet to have emerged from committee for a vote.

In chapter 1, we listed the current criteria, as of the time of this writing, that Native Americans have to meet to achieve federal recognition—that is, to be recognized by the U.S. government and the BIA. As stated in that chapter, it is unlikely that Native Americans in Pennsylvania will ever achieve federal recognition as the standards are currently written. In particular, because contact between Europeans and natives occurred in Pennsylvania so long ago and because American Indians were removed or chose to remove themselves from the state by the mid-18th century, two primary conditions of the federal standards cannot be met. These are that recipients of federal recognition must have lived in a specific area that is distinct from other populations and that they must have maintained a tribal political structure "throughout history until the present" (B. Miller, 2003, p. 79). None of the current native organizations in the state can lay claim to either of these conditions.

However, state recognition is separate and independent from federal recognition. Over 60 Native American groups in the United States have state recognition without federal recognition, and many of these are found in states like Ohio or Virginia which, like Pennsylvania, do not contain reservations. (See Koenig & Stein, 2007) Virginia is an interesting example: Eight native groups are recognized by the state, many of them like the Pamunkey and Rappahanocks whose circumstances are quite similar to groups in Pennsylvania like the Lenape—that is, the Virginia-recognized groups are often small, remnant populations of groups that had early contact with Europeans, were dispersed by them, and/or assimilated into European society. States are not required by the federal government to abide by the BIA standards; each state may enact its own standards. Many of the state-recognized groups received recognition in the 1970s and 1980s when states may have been more open to recognizing American Indians; after 1988 many states seemed to have become wary of Native American claims for recognition because of concerns that this might lead to casino gambling. But as the Abenaki case shows, state recognition does continue: As noted earlier, the Abenaki received recognition in Vermont in May 2006.

Those people with whom we spoke who favored recognition had many reasons for doing so. A Lenape woman from Lancaster County put it in this somewhat colorful fashion:

> Somebody once said, how will the state know that we recognize them? That's being facetious. State recognition to me is important for only a couple of reasons—and it has nothing to do with money. Let's get that dollar sign away—and it doesn't have to do with hunting or fishing without a license. Let's throw that away, too. I've heard those statements made, and I crack up every time I hear it. But, you have a child and you raise him in your culture. And he goes to school and in the school he hears that there's no such thing as the American Indian. Pennsylvania has no American Indians. How do you think that child must feel? That's one reason. To me, that's one of the important reasons.

In chapter 4, we discussed all of the difficulties associated with claiming Native American identity in Pennsylvania. No single criterion or set of criteria exists to definitively establish Native American identity, and the passage of time and a tendency toward assimilation have made it difficult to prove Native American heritage in the state. Should the state recognize the descendants of Lenapes, Susquehannocks, Shawnees, or other groups as Native Americans, many individuals would feel their sense of native identity to be validated. Thus, state recognition is critical to many in achieving a sense of identity.

A second issue has to do with the repatriation of Native American remains from archaeological sites and institutions such as museums. In 1990 Congress passed the Native American Graves Protection and Repatriation Act, also known as NAGPRA. This law allows for the return of Native American human remains, funerary objects, sacred objects, and objects of cultural patrimony to federally recognized American Indian nations (an object of cultural patrimony is defined as an object that is communally owned by a native nation; these objects may also be regarded as sacred objects).

Many of our informants believed that state recognition would give them the right to claim remains and sacred objects from state museums and other institutions, as well as to prevent developers and archaeologists from destroying burial sites. In reality, NAGPRA regulations are more restrictive than our informants believed. For one thing, only federally recognized tribes have the right under NAGPRA to claim remains. In addition, only excavations on reservations or federally-owned land fall under the terms of the law. State or local museums which receive federal funding are required to comply with NAGPRA rules, though the Smithsonian Institution in Washington, D.C. is specifically exempted from the law. We heard from our informants several accounts of developers or private landowners destroying Native American burial sites in Pennsylvania. Unfortunately, none of these sites would have been protected under NAGPRA.

At the time of this writing, the state of Pennsylvania has no law that specifically addresses the question of Native American remains. The Pennsylvania Historical and Museum Commission maintains an internal policy requiring compliance with NAGPRA on state-owned lands, but again there are no restrictions on privately owned properties. Should individuals carrying out excavations on state-owned land encounter human remains, they are required to halt their work and notify the local enforcement authorities. Penalties for not doing so include fines ranging from US$100 to US$2,500 and jail terms from 30 days to 1 year. If the remains are determined to be Native American, the state archaeologist must notify "lineal descendants of culturally affiliated groups" (Schamel, 1997, p. 1)—that is, the state archaeologist must determine if the remains are those of people descended from living indigenous peoples. Those determinations may be difficult to make. The acidic soils of Pennsylvania's woodlands mean that organic remains are poorly preserved; and the semi-nomadic lives of indigenous horticulturalists means that few objects were placed in graves. If, for example, remains can be clearly defined as Lenape, the question then becomes, "Which Lenape organization has the right to those remains?" If the remains are thought to be Susquehannock, there are no surviving Susquehannock organizations. And, of course, all of this depends on a developer actually notifying the authorities when doing so means a delay in the work.

In the course of our research, we were informed that the Native American Alliance of Bucks County, a Pan-Indian group in southeastern Pennsylvania, maintained a cemetery for the repatriation of Native American remains. An interview with the head of this organization revealed that the members were lobbying universities and museums for their collections of remains and funerary objects and that they had had some success in having remains turned over to the organization. Members of other organizations around the state expressed surprise that this was going on.

In short, it is not clear that being recognized by the state would automatically give Pennsylvania's American Indians more control over repatriation issues. Nonetheless, recognition would probably give Native Americans a legal basis on which to begin challenging developers in court over the destruction of burial sites.

Another potential advantage of state recognition is that it would give Native Americans in the state the legal right to label their arts and crafts as American Indian made. In 1990 Congress passed the Indian Arts and Crafts Act, which restricted the right of American Indians to label pottery, baskets, jewelry, and so forth as "Indian made." The trade in American Indians arts and crafts is a multibillion-dollar business, and some native arts, such as Southwest Indian pottery or Hopi kachina figurines, have become world-renowned art forms. Many of our informants made jewelry, baskets, or other crafts, but they believed that they may not label them as Indian made because they did not have state recognition; as one of our informants told us, "We could be arrested and thrown in jail if we call our things Indian-made." In reality, the Indian Arts and Crafts Act applies only to federally recognized tribes. Additionally, we have noticed in attending powwows and craft fairs that non-Indians seem to have no problems labeling their items as Indian made. However, state recognition might give American Indians in Pennsylvania some bargaining power in controlling their own arts and crafts businesses.

In its March 2007 issue, the *Lenape Nation Newsletter* summed up the issue of state recognition this way:

> The Lenape wish to be recognized by the state of Pennsylvania as its indigenous people so that our children and their descendants may take pride in their heritage. So that we may practice our religion freely. So that Pennsylvania and those that come to visit Pennsylvania may take pride in us in return: In the cultural center, libraries and archives we hope to build…in cultural and historical programs we conduct…in the goods, produced by our artists, musicians and craftspersons, that may be offered as "made by the Natives of Pennsylvania"…in the pow wows and other events we plan for them to attend…in the youth camps we will run for our children and all children…in the organic and Native gardening projects we will operate on our farm…in the knowledge that we hold Pennsylvania to be our sacred homeland and that we have always been and will forever be its caretakers, engaged in numerous projects to provide practical ways for all citizens to respect and protect our homeland and the health, welfare and future of the next seven generations of our children [ellipses in original]. (2007, p. 1)

In other words, the Lenapes and other American Indians of Pennsylvania see a host of advantages to recognition; these advantages are seen as accruing to both native people and nonnatives alike.

However, there have been significant barriers to recognition. The opposition to recognition has been so great that the bills introduced to the state legislature to grant recognition have not come up for a vote at the committee level, much less for discussion and action on the floors of the state Senate and state Assembly. Historically, the strongest opposition has come from those who thought that recognition would lead to casinos; on this, both native groups and legislators who support recognition agree. A Lenape woman who has been active in state government for years wrote us to say this:

> One central problem was Rep. X, who is anti-Indian and anti-gaming and equates the two as one despite the evidence…Rep X

> told several of us that he took his committee to Atlantic City to show them how the Indians ran their gaming there! There are of course no Indian casinos in Atlantic City. And this remark demonstrates both X's prejudice toward Native Americans and his lack of knowledge about "Indian Gaming." We gathered over 15,000 signatures on petitions, collected countless letters from individuals and organizations, and were supported by the Quakers, Episcopalians, Presbyterians and Lutherans; we were told none of this mattered.

Leaders of the native organizations with whom we spoke all expressed their opposition to casino gambling. We quote again from the *Lenape Nation Newsletter*:

> As caretakers of our homeland, it would be inconsistent with our beliefs to use land in Pennsylvania for gambling purposes. We have always stood against gambling, have continually expressed this to the state representatives, and have drafted legislation which clearly denounces any intention or privilege to do so. (2007, p. 1)

Since gambling became legal in Pennsylvania in 2004 and since the first gambling licenses were given to the Mohegans and the Pequots, this issue would seem moot. But both legislators and American Indians still see this as an obstacle. As one legislator told us, "If we recognize them, they'll want a reservation, and when they get a reservation, they'll get a casino and then the state won't be able to tax that revenue." This argument ignores the fact that only federally recognized tribes have the right to operate casinos.

A second source of opposition to recognition is captured in that legislator's comment—the concern that American Indians will use recognition as legal grounds to reclaim land. To date, none of the Native American associations in the state have indicated that they will make land claims should recognition be granted. Rather, two of the more prominent of these organizations, the Eastern Delaware Nation and the Lenape Nation, have each privately obtained parcels of land which they intend to use for meeting houses, cultural centers/museums, and educational programs. To be sure, some of the individuals with whom we spoke indicated an interest in claiming land, but not land that was already privately owned by non-Indians: "They've got plenty of state forest land out there that nobody's using," one individual said. Unfortunately, the failed effort by the Oklahoma Delawares to reclaim land in 2004 hangs over these denials; state officials remain suspicious of local denials, given the action taken by the Oklahoma Delawares.

In reality, Native Americans in Pennsylvania have few grounds on which to make claims for land repatriation. In other areas of the United States, some native groups have been successful in either reclaiming land or in being compensated for land lost. But in these cases, native groups have been able to successfully pursue their claims in court on the grounds that land ceded to them by the U.S. government in treaties had been illegally confiscated subsequently. An example of this would include the Penobscots of Maine who used a government settlement in 1980 to begin purchasing traditional lands (Prins, 1994, p. 442).

In Pennsylvania, the history of the removal of the native people was somewhat different. As noted in earlier chapters, William Penn was quite careful to extinguish Lenape land claims in southeastern Pennsylvania by purchasing land and obtaining legal title to it; Penn did not seize Lenape land as a right of conquest. Even the Walking Purchase of 1737, as fraudulent as this document appears to have been, seems to be a binding contract—at least that is the way state governments have viewed it since the early 18th century. Other native peoples of Pennsylvania were officially eradicated in the 17th and 18th centuries; for example, there appear to be no Eries left to make land claims. Furthermore, the areas where many Native Americans lived in precontact times, such as the Philadelphia area or the Wyoming Valley, are now among the most densely settled in the state. The Cornplanter Tract is under water and is located primarily in New York State. Realistically those areas are not going to be returned to American Indians. There seems to be little reason to deny Pennsylvania's native peoples recognition based on the fear they will be able to make successful claims on past homelands.

A Seneca woman from Allegheny County put it this way: "And I don't see the state of Pennsylvania giving any land up. They haven't honored the treaties so far, so they're not going to go back and change things."

A bigger problem for Native Americans seeking state recognition has been their inability to present a united front to state legislators. As will be seen in the next chapter, there are many groups in the state which represent different segments of the native population. Some are private organizations run by families or single individuals; others are prison-ministry groups. Some are affiliated with a specific native nation, such as the Southeastern Cherokee Confederacy of Pennsylvania. Others, like the Pittsburgh Indian Center, are regionally based and are composed of members from many nations. There are at least five organizations that purport to represent the Lenape/Delawares. While some individuals belong to two or more of these organizations, the organizations themselves are often hostile to one another. In many cases, the hostility is both personal and historical; in several cases, organizations split over the choice of officers ("chiefs"). In some cases, the hostility is based on other disagreements. For example, a member of one Lenape organization warned us in an e-mail about being too closely affiliated with another group:

> First I want to say that there is an inherent danger in only linking up with one small sect that does not represent more than its own members and has a history of sectarianism towards other Lenape groups in PA. I believe this group is only interested in self-promotion.

American Indians from other groups were frequently critical of the Eastern Delaware Nation because it has a category of membership for non-Indians. Others believed they needed to be more inclusive: "We need to reach out to everyone who has a good heart."

A Navajo woman in Lancaster County summed the issue up this way:

> You have to have a large percentage of people from the same descendancy in order to go to the state capital and petition for [recognition]. And that's not happening. What you have happening is that you have a so-called Lenape village over here and a so-called Lenape village over there and they absolutely don't like each other. I don't like to

> use the word "hate." But they greatly dislike one another to a point where they don't even communicate. If they would band together, you would have bigger numbers. So they shoot themselves in the foot. They're the biggest hurdle for these people.

The question of identity, discussed in chapter 4, permeates this debate, as well. Because Native Americans in Pennsylvania assimilated to survive and many do not have definitive legal proof of their ancestry, it is easy to question the legitimacy of people with whom one does not agree. Over and over again, we heard members of rival organizations dismissed with this phrase: "They're just a bunch of Wannabes."

As an example, we cohosted a luncheon in April 2006 to bring together Native Americans from around the state, as well as state university faculty interested in native issues. We were subsequently told that most of the Native Americans present had never before sat down together. As the luncheon began, we encouraged all of the participants to introduce themselves and to say a little about themselves. One man of Cherokee descent chose to use this opportunity to assert he was the only real American Indian in the room. Of course, this only angered the other participants who then had to assert their authenticity. The luncheon proceeded, and discussions followed on several issues, but afterward, several participants told us privately that they would not participate in discussions again "as long as X is involved" (who "X" was varied from person to person). An effort to recreate the luncheon in 2007 faltered because so few of 2006's participants wished to interact with each other again. We have been told by a state legislator who has sponsored a bill to recognize Native Americans in the state that the same thing happened in committee hearings: "You know, it's very sad," she said. "I don't think they will ever agree on anything."

Not having a single unified voice does not ultimately doom efforts to win state recognition. Blu (1980, p. 2), in writing about the Lumbee, says that the absence of unity worked to the advantage of these North Carolina natives. She argues that having several different spokespersons with differing points of view helped to keep Lumbee issues alive and in the news media for other non-Indians to see. But in Pennsylvania, native issues seldom become visible in the media, whether there is unity or disunity. Meanwhile, the prolonged debate and in-fighting takes a toll. The chief of the Southeastern Cherokee Confederacy told us that after years of traveling back and forth from Philadelphia to Harrisburg, she had given up:

> They're never going to give us recognition. Anyway, what do I need recognition for anyway? Everybody in Philadelphia knows me. If there's ever an event where they need some diversity, I get called. I'm so busy I don't know what to do. I don't need that frustration anymore [of going to Harrisburg].

CURRENT NEGOTIATIONS

The current (at the time of this writing) bill before committee would grant recognition to any group or individual who can prove that their ancestors were living in Pennsylvania before 1790. A board composed of political appointees and Native Americans would oversee applications for recognition. The documentation of claims will be based on historical records that will prove long-standing relationships between natives and colonial, state, or local governments. These documents must show that those relationships were based on the identification of a group of people as Native American. The proposed process is somewhat similar to that of the BAR in the BIA; the BAR evaluates applications for federal recognition. The BAR, however, does not have Native American representation, and its standards for recognition (as spelled out in chapter 1) are far more complicated and difficult to meet.

The author of the current bill sees it as a compromise intended to grant recognition to as many Native Americans in the state as is possible, while avoiding the issue of "urban Indians," most of whom come from groups that are recognized elsewhere. In other words, the bill would recognize not only native Lenapes, but also Shawnees, Nanticokes, and others who migrated into Pennsylvania in the 18th century, but it would not recognize resident Lakotas, Navajos, Apaches, and so on. The author believes that if the bill could be reported out of committee, it would win easy passage in the State Assembly.

This bill has not won widespread acceptance in the Native American community. In particular, the Lenape Nation has come out in strong opposition to the proposed bill, arguing that only the Lenape should receive state recognition. The former chief of the Lenape Nation told us this in reference to other organizations:

> They're a group that consists of all different tribes. They come together. They allow you to belong and you can promote the fact that you're Indian. The problem with that—they are social groups. They are not an indigenous tribe. They are not tied to the indigenous people of what is now considered the state of Pennsylvania. Their ancestors may or may not have treated with William Penn. Their ancestors may or may not have been involved in the Walking Purchase. Their ancestors may or may not have been involved in the Treaties of Easton. That's fine. But why would the state of Pennsylvania want to recognize an Apache person or a Lakota person or a Seminole person or a Cherokee person or any other person other than the ones that are indigenous to this state? That's the problem. I don't have a problem with anybody else living here. But I wouldn't dare go out to South Dakota, go up on Pine Ridge and demand that the state of South Dakota recognize me as an indigenous person of South Dakota.

The opposition of the Lenape Nation is significant because for years they have taken the lead in negotiating with state officials and in promoting the significance of recognition. They have written their own legislation which would restrict state recognition to those people with clear genealogical links to the Lenape. They now say they will refuse recognition if the current bill should be approved.

Other Opinions

As we talked to Native Americans around the state, we found that while most favored some form of recognition, there was a substantial minority that opposed the idea. Often, these people would say recognition was unnecessary. A Lenape man in York County put it succinctly: "I don't need recognition from the government. I have recognition from the Creator, and I have recognition from other natives. What else do I need?" A Tuscarora woman in Sullivan County said this:

> I'm not interested in seeing that for our people. I don't think it's gonna gain us anything. The kind of state recognition I would like to see happen doesn't have to do with benefits and casinos. It has to do with "We recognize you as a group of native people because that's who you are." I think that's beginning to happen in Pennsylvania, at least on some levels. And I guess I don't care whether legislators in Harrisburg recognize us as Indians, but if we get to tell our story, then the public is gonna see that and are gonna understand that we are Indian.

A Mohawk man in Clinton County took a different approach:

> If somebody wants to be state recognized, by the state of Pennsylvania, I don't have a problem with it. Do I? No. I don't want to be a poster child, because I know somehow or other, I could just see posters up of the Native Americans groups in Pennsylvania, sponsored by the Commonwealth of Pennsylvania, and I just don't like that. There's enough politics in our groups as it is. We don't need to get those politics into it.

Others saw the issue as impractical. When we asked a Cherokee man from Allegheny County what he thought about state recognition, he was quite blunt: "It'll never happen!" When we asked him why he said that, he answered, "There's too many tribes here. The state will never give them what they all want." The Navajo woman from Lancaster County saw it as a matter of having to pay your dues:

> The Indians in Pennsylvania want recognition on the fast track. They don't realize how long it takes to get recognition. They have been told by people like myself and heads from other nations and other important people like Ben Nighthorse Campbell—they have been explained to—the steps. But short cuts is what they take and as a result of the short cuts, they set themselves back. It may come about, but it will be a long time. They don't have a

> leader; they don't have advocates; they don't have that bulldog who will represent them and give them press.

(We note that both of these critics came from nations that are federally recognized.)

A Cherokee woman from Armstrong County reiterated the comment that it will take a long time to get what Pennsylvania American Indians want, but she put a more positive spin on it:

> I think there's hope, but it's gonna take a lotta, lotta work. Things need to be done, and you have to determine how you're gonna decide on who has native blood and who hasn't. Most of the people who want this think they're gonna get a reservation or they're gonna avoid paying taxes or they're gonna sell goods. Very few of them want what's really important—better medication, better medical treatments, getting a better education—things that are truly important, not just for themselves, but for their children and grandchildren. But it will take a lotta, lotta work to get this thing done and a lotta good minds to determine who is who.

But most of the people with whom we spoke seem to think the hard work is worth it. A Seneca man from Sullivan County put it this way:

> I can get state recognition. All I have to do is go up to New York State to my father's people and just move in, and I'd get state recognition. But I like Pennsylvania because my ancestors are buried here. And I need to be here. My vision is here.

Native Americans in the K–12 Curriculum

> Teach the true history of this country. Make students aware of the issues facing Native Americans in today's society. Teach that Native Americans are alive and not in history books only.
>
> —Lenape woman, Luzerne County, Pennsylvania

> What do I want to see taught in the public schools? The TRUTH!
>
> —Lenape woman, Lycoming County, Pennsylvania

As noted in the introduction of this chapter, the one thing that almost every one of the Native Americans with whom we spoke or who filled out a survey questionnaire agreed on was that Pennsylvania schools did not do a good job of teaching about native peoples. The Pennsylvania Department of Education has established a set of curricular guidelines that requires that instruction about Native Americans be undertaken in the 3rd, 6th, 9th and 12th grades as part of history lessons. There is typically a Native American day set up for sometime in November that may result in some material about Native Americans being discussed in the classroom. Both of these circumstances confirm what Native Americans told us during our research—that (1) very little is taught about American Indians in the Pennsylvania K–12 curriculum, and (2) what is taught fails to deal with Native American issues today.

As we interviewed Native Americans in the state, we consistently heard complaints about inaccuracies and stereotypes taught in the public schools. The inaccuracies began with the idea that no American Indians lived in Pennsylvania anymore. We heard several stories from Native American parents about their children being disciplined in school because the children challenged this inaccuracy. A Tuscarora man from Columbia County told us this:

> One day my daughter came home and said she'd been sent to the principal's office that day. That shocked me because she's always been a very good girl, very respectful. "What happened?" I said. "Well, my social studies teacher told us that all the Indians left Pennsylvania in the 1700s. I raised my hand and said that wasn't true. He got very upset and told me to go see the principal." I raised my daughter to take pride in her heritage. She's a fancy dancer at powwows—she designed and made her own costume and she wins prizes. So I got a call from the principal about my daughter being disrespectful to her teacher. I explained the situation to him, and he said "Okay, but I don't want your daughter challenging her teacher in class. We can't have that." She was only trying to tell the truth!

A Lenape women from York County who is herself an elementary school teacher told us this story about her daughter:

> My daughter came home from her fifth grade history class with this ridiculous concept of how the nations were separated by her social studies teacher. It made no sense at all. Of course, she knew that and so she did her own research, talked about the nations and where they should have been. He was totally unimpressed. But she felt better for doing it. She was upset because basically he said to her that there's only two Indian nations, one East and one West. She came home fussin' and fumin.' You can always tell when your kid is upset. I told her to handle it in a positive way. Sit down and write, not just to him, but write the truth. And carefully lay it on his desk one day. And that's what she did. Never got a reaction from him.

A Lenape/Seneca woman from Sullivan County said the following:

> And the education system is a problem, too. [Interviewer: What have you run into there?] There's no natives in Pennsylvania. They taught my son that—he was in the fourth grade this year. They tried to teach what some of the names around here meant. I know the teacher tried, but the names had the wrong meanings. She said Mehoopany means "Where the beans grow," but that's actually Meshoppen. It's supposed to be where the wild potatoes grow. Mehoopany means "wild potato." Mehoopany Creek had wild potatoes growing in the creek. So what they do teach is wrong.

Others focused on how poorly they felt teachers were trained. A Seneca man from Bradford County said this:

> I met this girl who was a sixth grade teacher. She told me that she did not know that there were Indians living this side of the Mississippi River. And she never knew that there were any in Pennsylvania or New Jersey. Well, it was loaded with the Nanticoke and the Lenape, everybody and their brother was down there. She said they didn't teach it in school. I said I went through the public school system in Philadelphia and about the only thing

> they ever said in there was we were savages, heathen savages at that, but the American Indian has more religion than 99% of the rest of America, unless you get up to priests, ministers and rabbis. The average population, compared to a Native American, can't even spell "Christian." But they didn't teach it in school. She said, "Yeah. But when I was in college studying to be a teacher, my major was history, and they didn't teach us anything there either." Well, I said, "That's par for the course."

Many felt that the public schools perpetuated myths and stereotypes about Native Americans. The Cherokee woman from Armstrong County said the following:

> When I used to do school programs, the biggest thing that the children thought was that we killed everybody. And we scalped everybody. No other thoughts about how we taught settlers, how we helped them to survive when they first came to this country. None of that! And just the stereotyped image of us. It would really be appreciated by a lot of us to see something done on that line. It's not just the students. The teachers aren't aware. The books that they receive that they're required to teach from aren't exactly truthful about what the natives contributed to the Europeans.

The Seneca woman from Allegheny County told us,

> And the teachers reinforce their students. We do school programs from K through college. Little eight year old kids—Where's your horse and do you have a tipi and why don't you do this and why don't you do that? Their teachers told them this. So we have to educate the teachers.

Her husband continued with the following:

> I've had teachers say to us that they weren't aware that there are Indians on the East Coast. I've been shocked because they're supposed to be teaching children and they say things like that to us. And you wonder how many children have passed through their teachings?

In his book, *Lies My Teacher Told Me*, James Loewen devotes two chapters to myths perpetrated about Native Americans in American school texts. He begins one of those chapters this way: "Historically, American Indians have been the most lied-about subset of our population. That's why Michael Dorris said that, in learning about Native Americans, 'One does not start from point zero, but from minus ten'" (1995, p. 99). Loewen shows how stereotypes are perpetuated in high-school history books through the use of incomplete thoughts or understated commentary. American Indian cultures at the time of contact are described as having a primitive technology, without noting how effective and well-adapted to the environment these technologies were or how similar the lives of the average European peasant would have been to those of the "savages." Europeans are called "settlers" rather than "invaders." Europeans are described as clearing the wilderness for farming, when many of the native groups already were farming people. Indeed, the Pilgrims built their first community where they did in 1620 because a native cornfield stood there. History texts gloss over the fact that thousands of American Indians were enslaved and even exported to other European colonies in the West Indies as laborers. The long history of warfare between Europeans and Native Americans is often reduced to a paragraph or two—and then the discussions are often limited to the Indian Wars in the West in the 19th century, with little mention of 17th- and 18th-century conflicts in the East. The old saying that "the victors write the histories" applies well to European-Native American interaction.

Loewen (1995) does say, however, that the situation has improved:

> Today's textbooks at least try to be accurate about Indian culture. All but two of the twelve textbooks I surveyed begin by devoting more than five pages to pre-contact Native societies. And to their credit most of the textbooks recognize diversity among Native societies. (p. 100)

The Native Americans with whom we spoke mostly echoed this sentiment. The Lenape school teacher from York County said this:

> It's going to have to come from the educators themselves. It will have to be an interest on their part. And I've seen a lot

> more of that. Not just knowing the surface information about Native Americans, but actually learning more the heritage and teaching the fact that we were not all the same. Just that very fact.

Her husband, who is also Lenape and an educator, said that he had sympathy for teachers today:

> When I think about teachers and educating the teachers—if you're a teacher, you have a limited time—eight and a half months or whatever—to actually give an education to kids, and you have so many things out there drawing their attention that you need to teach or that you think they should know. But even to lay the foundation—the groundwork—there's so many options what to teach kids—so many subjects. You don't know what to hit on. And of course, Native Americans are way back there, there's other stuff that's close by—you've got Gettysburg and all that other stuff—so if they do any historical teaching—it's things that kids recognize right now in their local backyards. So the native culture tends to get overlooked.

As we have traveled around Pennsylvania, we have been struck by the high level of interest people have in native cultures and lives. Over and over, we heard the same remarks repeated. First, there was the expression of surprise that Native Americans still existed in the state, closely followed by requests for more information about them: "How can I learn more?" Presentations we have given in classes, at conferences, or in venues like local historical societies invariably drew both surprise and sympathy for Native American issues. The Native Americans with whom we spoke agreed with us on this point. The Nanticoke man from Sullivan County told us, "Things have actually improved from what it was for our grandparents. We don't have to be hidden anymore. It's become more open; there's more interest." The Tuscarora woman from Sullivan County reinforced that idea:

> There is an enthusiasm now for native culture. And I can help feed that enthusiasm. Agencies like the Pennsylvania Historical and Museum Commission are now interested in helping us research.

> And it just gives us more ammunition and more information. It helps build the story.

And Native Americans in Pennsylvania are striving to build that story. In chapter 7, we will briefly describe the many Native American organizations in the state and the activities in which they are involved. American Indians in Pennsylvania are anything but insular and uninvolved. Outreach and informing the public are high on the agenda of all the groups we contacted. Powwows and gatherings are open to the public, and many of the American Indians to whom we spoke emphasized the importance of powwows as a way of teaching non-Indians about the indigenous people of Pennsylvania: "I invite the people I work with to come to our powwow. Bring your wives, bring your kids. Maybe you'll learn something. Who knows, maybe you'll like it." (Religious events such as vision quests and sweat lodges are not for non-Indians, however.) As noted earlier, as groups like the Eastern Delaware Nation acquire land, a first priority for them becomes building a cultural center/museum to help inform the non-Indian public. The Museum of Indian Culture in Allentown, Pennsylvania, sponsors dozens of exhibits or events to inform the public about native life in Pennsylvania. Over half of the people we interviewed had given programs about Native Americans in schools, and some maintain Web sites from which they volunteer their services to schools or community organizations.

The programs presented in schools are nonconfrontational and inclusive. As you may recall, a Lenape woman from Lancaster said this:

> When we go to schools, I first of all ask the kids, "Who's Native American here?" And you'll see one or two raise their hands. So I say, "Who here was born in the U.S.?" Ninety-nine per cent raise their hands. "Well, aren't you Native American, too? Aren't you a native of this country?" I'm against political correctness. Once you become an American, your history is America. Then, we're American. Your history doesn't start in 1776. Your history doesn't start in 1492. Your history starts

> when America started. So I tell the children that our history is your history, too.

A Cherokee woman from Lebanon County told us that this was the way she approached a non-Indian audience:

> I used to have a story I would tell. I would sing "Row, row, row your boat." I would pretend to go through the crowd. And I would say all of a sudden, "Oh, look, I see land. I think we'll call it Ireland." Then I would make those people move out of their seats. "Oh, this looks like good farm land. We need to move here—you go over there." I would literally move people from their seats. And the look on their faces because you've discomforted them, moving them from one seat to another! And I would say, "You think that's a discomfort, then how do you think it felt to have your homes taken from you?" And all of a sudden the light bulbs would go on and all the faces would go "Ah!" It's amazing to me.

In addition to the willingness of Native Americans themselves to put their cultures before the public and into the schools, there are resources easily available to help inform teachers and other interested people about Native American life—especially with regard to the past. A quick online search reveals several sites describing the history and traditional cultures of the Lenape/Delawares, the Susquehannocks, and people of the Six Nations. Some of these sites feature activities for children to help them learn a few Lenape words or some other aspect of indigenous lives. Lisa Mitten maintains a site which links students to hundreds of other sites by and about Native Americans. Mitten is a self-described mixed-blood Mohawk who was a librarian at the University of Pittsburgh for 14 years. The Pennsylvania Archaeological Council has created a middle-school curriculum in which students in grades five through eight can learn about Pennsylvania's past through reading, Internet searches, and archaeology. This curriculum is available to any classroom teacher who wishes to use it.

Josh Wilker (1992) has produced a colorful book for children that describes Lenape culture at the time of contact, as well as subsequent events in the 17th and 18th centuries. In addition, there are hundreds of books that describe Native American cultures and histories in general that would dispel the many stereotypes about American Indian life. For example, Weatherford's 1989 book, *Indian Givers: How the Indians of the Americas Transformed the World*, is an inexpensive and readable book that is still widely available; it describes the many contributions of Native American cultures to the Western world.

The problem is a disconnect between Native Americans in Pennsylvania today and teachers, government institutions, and the non-Indian public. Native Americans are eager to tell their stories and share their cultures with those who want to learn. Many non-Indians seem equally interested in learning, judging by attendance at powwows and museum events. At the time of this writing, we currently have projects underway to create Web sites for teachers to make available to them source materials about Native Americans in Pennsylvania. We hope to create in-service programs for teachers to help them learn about indigenous cultures in the state. Another project in which we are involved is to create a speaker's bureau of Native Americans to make available to interested teachers and program developers of all sorts. The key is to inform the relevant audiences of the availability of these materials.

Of course, not everyone will be interested in listening or learning. The Seneca man from Bradford County told us this:

> We try to explain [our culture] to Europeans (my wife doesn't like it when I say "white people.") at a powwow. And this happened at two or three different powwows. I like to talk and talk to these people and explain about our people. I don't make up stories. I tell them just the way it was. I've had young men—and some my age—standing in the back, listening, who pipe up and say, "If you don't like it here, why don't you go back where you came from?" Well, where does the Native American go, if he goes back to where he came from? I told this one guy, I am where I came from. He walked away. It was no great loss, but it's hard.

Native Americans know that there are those who will walk away; as noted in earlier chapters, many of our informants directly experienced some form of discrimination because they were American Indians.

But they continue to tell their stories to prevent things like this:

> I had a child at the nursery room at church run from the room screaming at the top of his lungs, he "didn't want to die," he "didn't want to die." Four years old! Now where did he hear that from? He heard the term "scalped." He was going to be scalped by an Indian at church today. Mother or Dad had to have said that, or an older brother or older sister. The point is that it put a seed that frightened that little man. I had to go get out of my traditional clothes, put street clothes on, before I could get down on one knee and talk with him. He was deathly afraid of me.

We look forward to the day when myths such as those are dispelled.

Chapter 7

Native Organizations and Events

The native organizations in Pennsylvania—they all have their hearts in the right place. Everybody is trying to do their part.

—Lakota man, Wyoming County, Pennsylvania

Here in Pennsylvania, I don't go to the powwows down here. I don't hang out with people who call themselves Indians.

—Mohawk woman, Snyder County, Pennsylvania

I go to the powwows faithfully, but I don't feel that I'm showing off or anything. I'm just me, doing it for myself.

—Lakota woman, Columbia County, Pennsylvania

Introduction

In this chapter, we will briefly describe some of the Native American organizations in Pennsylvania with which we became familiar during our research. We begin with a look at powwows, an event that many of these organizations sponsor and have in common.

POWWOWS AND GATHERINGS

Few weekends go by in Pennsylvania without a powwow or a gathering being held somewhere. All of the organizations we highlight in this chapter sponsor one or more powwows during the year, as does the Museum of Indian Culture in Allentown, Pennsylvania. In addition, there are many communities or individuals that sponsor powwows. Several of the people we interviewed travel the "powwow circuit" as vendors, booksellers, dancers, or members of drum groups. In fact, it was difficult to schedule some interviews because people were either preparing for powwows or participating in them. Most of the people with whom we spoke had strong opinions about powwows; in short, they either loved them or despised them.

The word "powwow" is derived from the Algonquian *pauau,* which meant a gathering of people. "Powwow" was one of many words borrowed by Europeans in the 17th century from Native Americans living along the northern Atlantic Coast. Europeans used the word to refer to a get-together or, especially, a meeting for discussion; it is, of course, still used that way by non-Indians today. Social scientists, historians and Native Americans alike agree that the celebratory occasion featuring Native American dance and music originated among American Indians on the western plains in the 19th century. More specifically, sources agree that the modern powwow started as a religious ceremony among the Pawnees, who lived in what are today Kansas and Nebraska, until they were removed to their current reservation in Oklahoma in the 1850s (see Powers, 1994, p. 476). Several of our informants suggested that the 19th-century rendezvous—a gathering of mountain men, trappers, and Native Americans—contributed to the concept. Powers also suggests that the Wild-West shows of the 19th century played a part in popularizing American Indian dances and costumes among non-Indians. At any rate, by the 1950s the modern powwow was well-entrenched among reservation communities in the West. With the rise of native consciousness in the 1960s and 1970s powwows spread east of the Mississippi. Powwows are now big business in every state (including Hawaii), and numerous Web sites advertise their schedules of events, featured dancers, contest prizes, and so on.

The events we attended were sometimes called "powwows" and sometimes called "gatherings," and a question we often asked was, "What's the difference?" Our informants did not agree on the answer. Some distinguished between the two based on how commercial the event was. A Cherokee man from Westmoreland County who organized an annual event called his event a "gathering" because he said,

> It's not really for non-Indians, and we don't have any outside vendors. It's just for our people to get together and enjoy each other's company. I mean, we won't turn white people away; they can come if they want. But our focus is the native community.

A woman who sponsors an annual event at a state university told us, "I call ours a gathering because it's really about educating the public; it's not about selling things." A Lakota man who handles security for some events in northeastern Pennsylvania told us that "a powwow is what we're doing now—just sitting and talking. A gathering is for our community to get together and have a good time." But the most common response we received was this one: "There's not really a difference; it's just what you want to call it."

Powwows have certain elements in common. The spatial focus point is the dance circle. This is a space marked off and separated from the rest of the grounds by some barrier, though the barrier is usually a rope or ribbon suspended from stakes in the ground. In chapter 5, we quoted an Abenaki man talking about the significance of setting the stakes into the ground with offerings to the Earth Mother for piercing the soil. In an indoor space such as a gymnasium, chairs or tables serve this purpose. A Master of Ceremonies announces each dance before it is performed and informs the audience of events associated with the powwow. The dances are accompanied by drum music and singing; an important advertised aspect of a powwow is the drum group or groups that will perform. A fire was lit in the middle of the circle at outdoor powwows we attended. An important office in some of the organizations with which we made contact is that of the "firekeeper"—a person who keeps coals from the ceremonial fire going throughout the year. New fires at powwows or tribal meetings are kindled from these coals.

A feature we observed at every powwow we attended was the Veterans' Dance. This dance was always the first dance featured on the program. Native Americans who were armed-services veterans would dance in their regalia while presenting the U.S. flag, as well as service banners and tribal colors. All attendees who were service veterans were generally invited to participate in this dance. The Nanticoke man from Sullivan County told us this:

> There are no more patriotic people than the Native Americans. Despite all the government has done to us over the years, we volunteer for the services in greater numbers than any other American group, and we are proud of our veterans. We are proud to honor them at the powwow.

As noted before, non-Indian visitors are welcome at powwows. Powwows are seen by most native participants as educational events, as well as important ceremonies and family get-togethers. Native Americans want non-Indians to attend and see how interesting and real American Indians are. Powwows usually charge an admission fee, and this fee is important in helping the organization pay the rent on the facility they are using or in funding other organizational activities. Nonetheless, natives expect non-Indians to be courteous and respectful and to follow a few basic rules. These are usually announced at the beginning of the dances. Visitors are asked to refrain from taking pictures during the opening dances or the prayers or ceremonial invocations that precede them. Visitors are also asked to request permission to take pictures of the native people in regalia. It was emphasized to us that what American Indians wear on these occasions are regalia—not costumes. As one Lenape woman stressed to us, "Clowns wear costumes. We honor our past with our regalia." In our experience, participants have carefully researched and constructed their regalia to be authentic representations of native clothing at some point in their history. If asked, they are happy to explain the significance of their regalia and why they choose to wear what they are wearing. Often, they have gone to great expense and effort to recreate a particular time period.

For example, the Navajo woman from Lancaster County told us the following:

> My mother was Navajo, and because we are matrilineal that makes me a Navajo. But at powwows I wear a 19th century Cherokee dress in order to honor my father who was Eastern Band Cherokee. It's called a "tear" dress, not because it tears easily but because Cherokee women wore dresses like this on the Trail of Tears. You will notice that the dress completely covers my body except for my hands and face. The Cherokee women were modest; only your husband could see you with your hair down. Our powwows are in the summer, and people will say to me, "Aren't you hot in that dress?" And I am, but it is very important to wear the dress properly and to act properly in it so that people get the right ideas. When I wear this dress, I am honoring my father's people.

An important feature of most powwows is the vendors who sell a wide variety of crafts, native-related paraphernalia, and food. When we were trying to organize a powwow on our campus, the first thing we were asked by the American Indians who agreed to help us was, "Where will you get your vendors?" A man who organizes several powwows in northeastern Pennsylvania told us that he had the names of over 400 different vendors he could call upon. Some of the vendors are local natives, many of whom sell crafts or food they have made; others are from other states and make their living by traveling to powwows all over the country. A potential problem we had in our research was finding a place at a powwow to set up our table to distribute surveys and to display posters about our work; there often simply wasn't room for one more table among all the vendors present. Some powwows ban any political content; others invite participants to engage in political programs.

As we noted in the introduction, powwows can bring out strong feelings among Native Americans. We encountered a number of informants who chose to not attend powwows because they did not see them as authentic. As noted in chapter 4, there are Native Americans in Pennsylvania who see powwows as the province of wannabes; "that's a Wannabe powwow" was a comment we occasionally heard. A question we regularly asked our informants was whether there were any powwows they regularly attended or which they would recommend. And there was almost always one that stood out as "a good one"—that is, one that seemed closer to traditional native practice than others. We found no consensus as to which powwows were "the good ones;" rather, there were many that seemed to satisfy at least some of our informants.

Whatever a particular Native American might feel about powwows, it is nonetheless the case that they are well-entrenched institutions in Pennsylvania, and the calendar of most native organizations revolved around these events. Anyone who wonders what Native Americans are like in Pennsylvania today might look into visiting one and talking to the people in regalia about their lives. As the Lakota man from Wyoming County told us, "Come and see what we're like. You'll like what you see. I guarantee it."

The Council of Three Rivers American Indian Center

Founded in 1969 the Council of Three Rivers American Indian Center in Pittsburgh, Pennsylvania, was created to help Native Americans in the Pittsburgh area maintain their native identities and become more conscious of their rights as American Indians. The Council of Three Rivers is classified by the U.S. government as an urban American Indian center—one of the many that began in the 1950s and 1960s as a result of federal efforts to move American Indians from reservations into urban areas. The Saponi woman from York County told us the following:

> When I moved to Pennsylvania in the 1960s there were three Indian Centers here, one in Pittsburgh, one in Harrisburg and

> one in Philadelphia. I worked for the one in Harrisburg for many years. The Council of Three Rivers in Pittsburgh is the only one left.

Over the years, the Council of Three Rivers has expanded its base to provide services not only to Native Americans, but also to people of other ethnicities. For example, the council runs a free Head Start program for preschool children from any federally eligible family background. The council also offers adoption and foster-family services. Families interested in adoptions are advised and trained by the council in the procedures involved in the placing of an adopted child. Support groups and other services for adoptive parents are also provided. The council also trains families to serve as foster homes and helps place children in these homes. While the council advertises special consideration to Native American children and families, the programs the council offers are open to anyone who meets federal or state guidelines for these services.

The council also maintains a work-training program for Native Americans (as well as Alaskan natives and native Hawaiians). Funded through the U.S. Department of Labor, these programs assess applicants' skills and provide vocational training, job placement, and counseling services, such as assistance with job interviewing. The Abenaki man from Sullivan County said, "Yeah, I've heard of the Three Rivers Council. They helped my nephew train as a mechanic. He's got a good job now because of them." In addition, the council sponsors an annual powwow in September in the Pittsburgh area.

We found that there were many strong opinions about the council among our informants, as well as a general lack of knowledge about what the council does or what services it provides. Since most of our informants were from central or eastern Pennsylvania, this was not surprising, since the council provides its services to people primarily in the Pittsburgh area. However, our informants from western Pennsylvania similarly did not seem to know much about the council. Throughout our period of research, we made repeated attempts to contact the council or individuals employed by the council via telephone, e-mails, or letters, but none of our efforts were acknowledged. The Seneca woman from Allegheny County laughed when we told her that: "That's no surprise. They don't talk to anybody," she said. A Lakota woman from Westmoreland County who once worked for the council said, "They're just like that—they're very insular."

The Eastern Delaware Nation

The Eastern Delaware Nation, or EDN, was founded in 1984 by Carl Pierce, also known as Chief Wayandaga. A Nanticoke originally from New Jersey, Wayandaga was also instrumental in organizing the United American Indians of the Delaware Valley—an organization that is now defunct. Wayandaga's vision was to unite all the native people of northeastern and central Pennsylvania into a single organization to help promote a sense of native pride and identity. Wayandaga seemed to have been a widely respected figure, at least among native people in eastern Pennsylvania, but after his death in 1992, controversies arose over the succession of chiefs in the organization, and other groups subsequently splintered off from the EDN. Nonetheless, the EDN remains a vital and robust organization.

The EDN sponsors two powwows each year—one in Lovelton in May, and a larger event in Forksville over the Father's Day weekend in June. In 1999, the EDN purchased 1,500 acres near Wyalusing at a place known as Prayer Rocks. The EDN maintains that the Prayer Rocks site, a scenic rock outcropping overlooking the Susquehanna River, was a sacred place to the native people of the area. What was probably the first powwow held in Pennsylvania occurred at this site in 1963. A pamphlet advertising the 1963 event states that the powwow was organized by:

> Chief Lightfoot Talking Eagle and the Princess Fleet Deer (Susquehannocks) of Tamaqua, PA, as a "memorial to the Ancient of Ancients of the Americas…" The Chief and Princess were assisted by Chiefs Loud Voice and Fighting Bear from the Tuscarora Reserve in New York State. (Grand Spiritual & Temporal Council of North American Indians, 1963, p. 2)

A few of our informants fondly remember attending this event as children and first sensing their identities as Native Americans at that time.

Today, the EDN holds its quarterly tribal council meetings at a small facility maintained on the Wyalusing site. Sweat lodges are located at the site, and vision quests are carried out on the property. As part of the council meetings, the EDN recites the Walam Olum (described in chapter 5) in a nighttime ritual celebration. In the future, the EDN plans to build a larger facility at the site which will house a council house and a cultural museum. The EDN has been quite successful in obtaining grants from organizations, such as the Pennsylvania Council on the Arts and the Pennsylvania Historical and Museum Commission, either to fund programs to train members in new dances or to help members conduct their own genealogical research. The EDN also publishes a periodic newsletter for its members and interested parties.

At the time of this writing, the EDN claims approximately 600 members, though privately, EDN officers suggest that only about 400 of those are active dues-paying members. The EDN maintains two types of membership: one for people with known American Indian ancestry and one for "social" members (i.e., people who are interested in Native Americans but who have no genealogical connections to them). Those interested in joining the EDN are asked to fill out a membership questionnaire on which they document, if possible, their native heritage. Officers of the EDN told us that approximately two thirds of their active members have native backgrounds. Membership applications are submitted to the tribal council, and council members vote on their acceptability. A waiting period of 6 months is required before membership applications are finally approved.

We found that members of other native organizations in the state were critical of the EDN for its willingness to accept members from native nations not indigenous to Pennsylvania or members who had no genealogical connections to a native heritage. Several of our informants dismissed the EDN as "just a bunch of Wannabes." We found EDN members to be proud of their ecumenical membership criteria, and some asserted that the EDN was the only officially recognized native organization in the state because of their 501(c)(3) nonprofit status (in reality, several native organizations in the state have nonprofit status, and the EDN 1 Web site states that it is "not recognized by the Commonwealth of Pennsylvania or the federal government") (Eastern Delaware Nation, 2006, p. 7). As one of the EDN's officers told us, "If you're going to restrict native status to only those people with pure Indian blood, you're not going to have any members pretty soon."

Totem Rhythms, an organization affiliated with the EDN, will be described in a separate section that follows.

THE LENAPE NATION

Unlike the EDN, the Lenape Nation of Pennsylvania restricts its membership to those individuals who can lay claim to Lenape ancestry. The chief of the Lenape Nation traced the origins of the Nation to Chief Sam Gray Wolf, a Lenape/Seneca man who was active in Native American issues both in Pennsylvania and in the United States generally during the 1940s and 1950s. Others suggested a more recent origin for the Nation, suggesting that it was about 15 years old. The Lenape Nation maintains a Web site and publishes a periodic newsletter. Current council members estimated its membership at about 200 persons at the time of this writing.

Like the EDN, the Lenape Nation has been able to obtain a piece of land on which it plans to build a cultural center/museum. In this case, the land is a former farm in Pike County, Pennsylvania. In addition to the cultural center, the Nation plans to grow traditional Native American crops on its land and to hold demonstrations about Lenape customs for the general public. The Nation also sponsors a powwow each year in September at a park in Hawley, Pennsylvania.

Though the Nation restricts its membership, the organization actively seeks to involve and inform the non-Indian public about Lenape culture. In 2002 the Nation created the Rising Nation River Journey, a 330-mile canoe trip down the Delaware River from Hancock, New York, to Pennsbury Manor—William Penn's historic estate near Morrisville, Pennsylvania. In a ceremony held at Pennsbury Manor, the Nation presented the Treaty of Renewed Brotherhood, built around Penn's letter to the American Indians in 1681 (see chapter 1). The Nation invited organizations from around the state to join the Lenape Nation's members in reaffirming Penn's words. Specifically the treaty reads as the following:

> In the spirit of Chief Tamamend, and in the spirit of William Penn, we the undersigned do openly recognize the Lenape Indian Tribe as the original inhabitants of eastern Pennsylvania. We acknowledge the Lenape people as the indigenous stewards of their homelands and also as the spiritual keepers of the Lena'pe Sippu, or Delaware River.
>
> And we hereby commit to actively support our Lenape sisters and brothers in whatever way we are able to, for a term of four years, helping to maintain the cultural identity of Pennsylvania, Delaware, New Jersey and Southern New York.
>
> We will support the Lenape people in one or more of the following ways:
>
> - Hosting cultural/educational programs;
> - Creating support for a Lenape cultural center;
> - Assisting in Lenape language revival projects;
> - Assisting in displays/exhibits of Lenape culture;
> - Helping the Lenape people to obtain and/or protect sacred land sites;
> - Encouraging updated curriculum in public schools;
> - Attending Lenape functions;
> - Volunteering service and support;
> - Distributing information;
> - Financial assistance.
>
> We also recognize that this treaty is good for a term of four years, August 24th 2002 until August 24th 2006, at which time a new treaty may be entered into.
>
> May these partnerships serve to heal the past, give direction for today, and brighten the future as we move forward, learning from the mistakes of some of our local forefathers, and may we together bring to light the cultural and geographical significance of Pennsylvania, preserving this natural history for all of our children.

> May the creator of all things embrace us as we move ahead. ("Lenape Nation," 2006, p. 4)

A variety of historical, environmental, and educational groups signed the Treaty of Renewed Brotherhood in 2002. In August 2006 the Nation repeated the Rising Nation River Journey, and the treaty was reaffirmed and signed again at Pennsbury Manor.

The Lenape Nation has taken the lead in pressing the state legislature for legal recognition. However, as described in chapter 6, the Nation has created controversy in this effort by insisting the state recognize only the Lenape. Their viewpoint is that only the Lenape represent the truly indigenous people of Pennsylvania from the time of European contact and that other nations should seek recognition elsewhere.

The Southeastern Cherokee Confederacy of Pennsylvania

The Southeastern Cherokee Confederacy of Pennsylvania is an organization based in the Philadelphia area, though people of native heritage from Delaware, New Jersey, Maryland, and the District of Columbia belong to the group and attend its meetings. The organization came into existence in 1988 according to the confederacy's chief, Buffy Red Feather Brown. The confederacy holds monthly meetings which focus on teaching the Cherokee language and making authentic native crafts, such as beadwork and finger weaving. The confederacy sponsors an annual Cherokee festival at the Ambler campus of Temple University over the Memorial Day weekend; it also maintains a speaker's bureau. In addition, the confederacy sponsors a female drum group called the Cherokee Sisters.

Chief Brown told us this:

> People are surprised we are still here. That doesn't bother me; I know who I am and what my heritage is. I know I'm doing something positive by educating people about the native people. Through our efforts, people are constantly learning, and we try

> to make sure they understand what the dances mean, what our regalia means, and so on.

The confederacy seems to be the organization that Philadelphia-area organizations, companies, and educational groups turn to when they are looking for Native American participation or educational programs. Chief Brown told us, "The demand is overwhelming. I am on so many boards; it seems like all I do is attend meetings. And the city keeps wanting us to do more."

Other native organizations in the state tended to dismiss the Cherokee Confederacy, arguing that wannabes are more likely to claim Cherokee affiliation than any other. Since the Cherokee Nation accepts anyone who can claim ancestry to a name on the Dawes Rolls of 1898–1914, its numbers have steadily grown over the years until it is now the largest Native American group nationally. Chief Brown said the following:

> I meet people all the time who believe they are part Cherokee. What we try to do is help these people establish their heritage and teach them the authentic traditions. It's an insult to put on false regalia and pretend that you're something you're not. It damages the Indian image. You can step in and help—that's okay—but you don't want to create a false image.

The Pittsburgh American Indian Center

The Pittsburgh American Indian Center was created in 1986 as a result of the work of the Edward Hale family of McKeesport, Pennsylvania. The Hales had been active in the Pittsburgh area for many years, working with the Council of Three Rivers and the Allegheny County Head Start program. The president of the center, Mrs. Lydia Hale, told us,

> Every time an Indian came in, other government offices would call us. If Indians came into town, they went to federal offices, who would send them to us. If they were in jail, we would get called. If they were transients, we would get them up and going, find them housing, welfare, so on. We decided we needed to be

> incorporated, to be more organized, so that we could help these people better.

Today the center continues to meet those needs, providing services or arranging services for Native Americans in western Pennsylvania.

In addition to its role as a service provider, the center also strives to preserve and promote Native American culture through educational programs. The original populations with which the center worked were "urban Indians"—people who had left reservations in other parts of the country and had migrated to western Pennsylvania for economic opportunities. The center served as a bridge between the individuals' reservation communities and their lives in urban America, helping to preserve those individuals' native cultures.

At the same time, the following quote can be found on the center's Web site:

> The Center stands for racial justice for Indians in the McKeesport, PA community that had previously not had a voice or a leader. By eliminating the prevailing stereotype of all Indians "living out West" or on reservations, the Center promotes the idea of a better understanding of the cultural, spiritual and religious values of Native Americans in the Greater Pittsburgh area.

Mrs. Hales told us that she hopes to see the center create a cultural center along the Monongahela River some day, but "funding is always a problem." The center continues to work in congress with the Council of Three Rivers. To quote Mrs. Hales, "We can help each other out. We don't take over from each other. We stand together."

TOTEM RHYTHMS

Totem Rhythms is the result of the vision of Marietta Dantonio-Fryer, a woman of Lenape heritage and a professor of art at Cheyney University of Pennsylvania. Ms. Dantonio-Fryer said this:

> In 1998 I had a Vision. This was a common thing for me. Since I was a young child, my art work was created from dreams and

> visions. In this vision I saw thousands of wood story poles, similar to the totem poles of the Pacific Northwest, standing tall, proud—beautifully painted, some carved, all saying the same thing: We are survivors! I also heard sounds—many drums beating, the sounds of melodic voices in harmony and the sounds of the earth. The harmony of dancers' footsteps vibrated deep within me. My new vision was to be called Totem Rhythms.
>
> As I prayed for more guidance, I was shown the story was to be about the beautiful people who are the indigenous people of this great land called America. These totems were to be used as story poles, illustrating the wisdom and stories of each nation, tribe, clan and family. I saw the poles as a symbol of strength, knowledge, hope, and wisdom, representing a torch to pass on to the next seven generations of children. These poles are meant to educate the world about what it truly is to be Native American. They are Honoring poles.

Today, Totem Rhythms is an internationally known organization which has displayed poles at the United Nations building in New York City and the International Conference of Indigenous Peoples in Durban, South Africa. Totem Rhythms makes available a variety of programs, but its signature program is an experiential workshop where Totem Rhythms members design and construct a totem pole on-site at a host organization; examples can be seen, for instance, at Lycoming College in Williamsport and at Lock Haven University of Pennsylvania. Usually, the pole is designed to be locally meaningful to the host institution. Members of the host institution are invited to join in the design and building of a pole, and Totem Rhythms members also conduct workshops and other educational programs in concert with the building to help inform people about Native American cultures.

We were fortunate to be included in the early design stages of one of these poles in July 2006. Totem Rhythms members got together at a member's home to dedicate the wood for a pole and to brainstorm design elements. The pole was to be made of two trunks from an eastern red cedar tree (*Juniperus virginiana*) which had been harvested a number of years before and allowed to cure in storage. Both the trunks and the participants were purified by a sage smudging, and participants asked for supernatural guidance in the design. Many months later, the finished pole was displayed in a juried show at the United Nations as part of the International Indigenous People's Day Celebration. The two poles were designed to represent a paired native man and woman, each decorated with Native American design elements (e.g., the base of the poles was set in a tree trunk base that was made to look like a drum).

Totem Rhythms is occasionally criticized for its use of a Northwest-Coast cultural element in a Northeastern-native context. As noted in chapter 3, this mixing of Pan-Indian cultural items is common in Native American life today. A Totem Rhythms member told us,

> We are deliberately embracing a stereotype—the totem pole—that non-Indians have of Native Americans generally. We want people to confront their stereotypes and to learn from them. As they come to see our poles, that gives us the opportunity to tell them the real story of Native American cultures.

Totem Rhythms also invites native people from outside of Pennsylvania to join in the creation of these story poles; to date, Navajos, Cherokees, and Shinnecocks have joined their efforts.

THE MUSEUM OF INDIAN CULTURE

The Museum of Indian Culture is located in Allentown, Pennsylvania, in a historic stone building on Fish Hatchery Road. The museum consists of two rooms: one dedicated to cultural artifacts from Eastern Woodlands cultures and the other dedicated to artifacts from native cultures nationwide. The museum is a nonprofit charitable organization dedicated to presenting and preserving authentic information about native cultures. The museum sponsors three festivals/powwows each year and a wide variety of workshops and educational programs. Workshops on such topics as flint knapping, pottery making, and beadwork are hands-on programs for the general public. The museum also maintains a Web site and a resource library. The museum prides itself on the presentation of authentic native culture. Run by volunteers, the museum has limited hours on weekends for visitors, but group tours and programs are made available.

Native Nations Dance Theater

The Native Nations Dance Theater of Philadelphia performs Native American dances state wide as well as nationally and internationally; when we first contacted the theater, they were leaving for an 8-week tour of Great Britain. The founder, Vaughnda Hilton, is of Blackfeet and Seminole/Creek background. The theater was created in 1992, and it provides a wide variety of programs for schools, universities, powwows, and other groups. Programs range from a trio performance to a full-company performance designed for a theater or auditorium. In addition to dancing, the theater provides drum groups and singers—all in traditional regalia. Audience participation is encouraged.

The theater also provides historical lectures or seminars about Native American cultures; these may be presented in conjunction with dance performances. The theater has created a program called Express Your Dreams, which focuses on the history of African American–Native American interactions. Craft demonstrations can also be arranged, as well as a 2- to 4-week Artists in Residency program.

Included on the theater's Web site is a description of the various dances the group performs and which can usually be seen at a powwow. Examples include the Women's and Men's Traditional Dances, the Grass Dance, and the Fancy Shawl Dance. People who have not been to a powwow before might want to take a look at the descriptions the Native Nations Dance Theater provides of these dances in order to better understand what they will be seeing at a powwow.

A Final Word

In addition to the organizations previously described, there are many other groups in Pennsylvania that sponsor powwows or programs and serve as social gatherings for Native Americans. We found that it was not unusual for individuals to belong to more than one of these organizations, even when the organizations to which they belonged were rivals of one another. As we attended events around the state, we often met the same people over and over. A Cherokee man from Centre County summed up the significance of these organizations this way:

> You know, we don't have a reservation in this state. We're scattered around. We have no physical community, like they do in other states. You can lose your sense of being an Indian. That's why the powwows and belonging to an organization are so important. It's an opportunity to get together with our people, with like-minded people. We believe powwows are an important way to inform the non-Indian public about our ways, but they are also important to us, the Indian people. They give us a sense of community.

Appendix A

Survey Questionnaire

Age:

18–30 31–43 44–56 57–69 70–82 Over 82

Gender:

Male Female Other

Are you a resident of Pennsylvania?

Yes No

In which <u>county</u> do you reside? ______________________________

Do you identify yourself as:

a) Native American
b) Indian
c) Tribal/ethnic name (please specify) ______________________________
d) Other (please specify) ______________________________

In your opinion, what is the most important issue Native Americans face today?

a) Jobs
b) Self-determination on reservations
c) Better representation in Washington, D.C.
d) More federal assistance
e) Return of lands to Native Americans
f) Other (please specify) ______________________________

Is there reservation land in Pennsylvania today?

Yes No Don't Know

Were there reservations in Pennsylvania in the past?

Yes No Don't Know

Does the state of Pennsylvania legally recognize any Native American groups?

Yes No Don't Know

If so, which group(s)? ______________________

Does the U.S. government (federal government) officially recognize any Native American groups from Pennsylvania?

Yes No Don't Know

In your opinion, how good a job has the state of Pennsylvania done with regards to meeting the needs of Native Americans?

Very Positive Positive Neither Positive nor negative

Negative Very Negative

Do Native Americans have any game rights (hunting & fishing) in Pennsylvania not granted to other citizens of the state?

Yes No Don't Know

Are you aware of the new National Museum of the American Indian in Washington, D.C.?

Yes No

If so, how do you feel about it?

Very Positive Positive Indifferent

Negative Very Negative

Who do you think does the best job of helping Native Americans?

a) The Republican Party
b) The Democratic Party
c) Neither national political party

How do you feel about Native American casinos?

Very Positive Positive Indifferent
Negative Very Negative

Are you aware that the Oklahoma Delaware are trying to build a casino in Pennsylvania on land that they believe was wrongly taken from them?

Yes No

If so, how do you feel about this?

Very Positive Positive Indifferent
Negative Very Negative

How do you feel about teams using Native Americans and/or Native American symbols as team logos (e.g., Washington Redskins, Cleveland Indians)?

Very Positive Positive Indifferent
Negative Very Negative

Do you think enough is taught in American schools about Native Americans?

Yes No

Do you feel that what is taught in American schools about Native Americans is accurate (based on your experience)?

Yes No Indifferent

What would you especially like to see taught about Native Americans in Pennsylvania public schools?

Do you have any comments or wish to address any issues that were not brought up in this survey? If so, please share your opinions:

____

____

Appendix B

Interview Format

*Please feel free to answer any and all questions as you see fit. If at any time you do not understand a question do not hesitate to say so—the question can be rephrased or explained further. If there are any questions that you feel uncomfortable answering, please feel free to skip those questions. Please know that the researchers will keep your anonymity by using pseudonyms for your protection, unless otherwise requested. You are entitled to any and all compiled data—articles, films, books—upon request.

Name: Date of Interview:
By:

Native Name: Date of Birth:
Age:

Tribal Affiliation:

Gender: M F I

__ Married # of Children:
__ Single Age Range of Children:
__ Divorced/Separated

Household Income Range:
less than 30,000 30,000–50,000 50,000+

Do you give your consent to be tape recorded for this interview: Yes No

Do you give your consent to be filmed for this interview: Yes No

Do you give your consent to be photographed for this interview: Yes No

County in which you reside now: ______________________

How long have you lived in Pennsylvania:

Were you raised on a reservation: Yes—where: ____________
No—where: ____________

Do you have legal recognition of *any* kind regarding your indigenous background:

Yes
Benefits ______________________
____
____

No
Explain ______________________
____
____

What makes you Indian? Or: How do you legitimate your Native American identity (i.e., blood quantum, tribal affiliation, etc.)?

How do you know this?

If Native American ancestry: how far back can you trace your descent?

Have you recently discovered your Native American identity? If so, when? How?

Where did you learn your Native American values? From whom (parents, grandparents, elders)?

What was taught?

Do you openly share information about your cultural identity, do you prefer to keep that to yourself, or restricted to certain kinds of situations? Explain.

Have you ever experienced a sense of illegitimacy, even if this idea came from an outside source (i.e., "Kmart" Indians)? If so, what is your reaction to this?

What cultural values do you hold as a Native American? What values or beliefs make you different than other non–Native American residents of Pennsylvania?

In which types of Native American–related activities do you participate (i.e., ceremonies, powwows, etc.)?

Do you feel that you are politically active? Why and how? Or, why not?

Do you belong to any tribal organizations: Yes—which: ________
No

How did you become associated with this group?

Would you say that there are other organizations like yours in Pennsylvania?

How do you feel about other Native American–based organizations in Pennsylvania?

Is it important to you to have legal federal and state recognition?

How do you feel about recognition of Native Americans in Pennsylvania, generally?

Which groups do you feel should be recognized, if any?

Why do you feel that only these groups should be recognized?

Do you feel that legal recognition is as, or more, important than simply your cultural identity?

In your opinion, what has been the biggest stumbling block(s) in gaining recognition for Native Americans in Pennsylvania?

Why do you believe this?

How can this problem be overcome?

If recognition was achieved for Native Americans, generally, in Pennsylvania, what types of services or benefits would you like to see provided? Why?

Would you like to name any other Native Americans who would like to take part in this project?

References

Barnes, T. (2004, November 23). Legislature votes reform of slot machine measure. *Pittsburgh Post-Gazette.*, p. A1.

Beatty, E. (1975). *William Penn as social philosopher.* New York: Octogan Books.

Becker, M. J. (1989). Lenape populations at the time of European contact: estimating numbers in the lower Delaware Valley. *Proceedings of the American Philosophical Society, 133*, 112–122.

Berger, T. (1964). *Little big man*. New York: Fawcett Books.

Blu, K. (1980). *The Lumbee problem: The making of an American Indian people.* Lincoln, NE: University of Nebraska Press.

Bonvillain, N. (2001). *Native nations: Cultures and histories of native North America.* Upper Saddle River, NJ: Prentice-Hall.

Burke, J. (1969). The Cherokee cases: A study in law, politics and morality. *Stanford Law Review, 21*, 500–531.

Caffrey, M. (2000). Complementary power: men and women of the Lenni Lenape. *American Indian Quarterly, 24*(1), 44–63.

Campbell. J. (2004). *Pennsylvania approves slot machines at tracks, casinos.* Retrieved November 2004, from http://www.umc.org/interior.asp.asp?ptid=2&mid=5233

Carlson, L. (1994). *Indians, bureaucrats and land: The Dawes Act and the decline of Indian farming.* Portsmouth, NH: Greenwood Press.

Casino City Times (2004). *Mohegan authority names new president, CEO for tracks.* Retrieved November 2004, from http://casinocitytimes.com

Churchill, W. (1994). *Indians are us? Culture and genocide in native North America.* Monroe, ME: Common Courage Press.

Clifton, J. (1989). *Being and becoming Indian.* Homewood, IL: Dorsey Press.

Cornel, S. (1988). *The return of the native: American Indian political resurgence.* New York: Oxford University Press.

Darian-Smith, E. (2004). *New capitalists: Law, politics and identity surrounding casino gaming on Native American land.* Case Studies on Contemporary Social Issues. Belmont, CA: Thompson/Wadsworth.

Deloria, P. (1998). *Playing Indian.* New Haven, CT: Yale University Press.

Deloria, V. (1969). *Custer died for your sins: An Indian manifesto.* New York: Macmillan.

Deloria, V. (1981). Native Americans: The American Indian today. *Annals of the American Academy, 454*, 139–149.

Deloria, V. (1995). *Red earth, white lies.* Golden, CO: Fulcrum Publishing.

Duffy, S. (2004). *Indian tribes sue over Pennsylvania land.* Retrieved November 2004, from http://www.law.com/jsp/article.jsp?id=1074259221938

Eastern Delaware Nation. (2006). *History*. Retrieved July 2006, from http://www.easterndelawarenations.com/history.html

Ellis, E. (1903). *True stories about Indians.* Chicago: John Winston Co.

Englebrecht, W. (2003). *Iroquoia: The development of a native world.* Syracuse, NY: Syracuse University Press.

Ember, C., Ember, M., & Peregrine, P. (2002). *Anthropology*. Upper Saddle River, NJ: Prentice-Hall.

Evans, W., & Topoleski, J. (2001) *Social and economic impact of Native American casinos* (NBR Working Paper #9198). National Bureau of Economic Research.

Fair, R. (2000). Becoming the white man's Indian: An examination of Native American tribal Web sites. *Plains Anthropologist, 45*(172), 203–213.

Fann, A. (2005). Native American gaming and tribal economic development: Myths and realities. *Center for Entrepreneurial Leadership Digest, 05–11*, 2–12. Retrieved April 2007, from http://www.celcee.edu/publications/digest/Dig05–11.html

Fogelson, R. (1998). Perspectives on Native American identity. In R. Thornton (Ed), *Studying native America: Problems and prospects* (pp. 40–59). Madison, WI: University of Wisconsin Press.

Forbes, J. (2000, November 27). Blood quantum: A relic of racism and termination. *The People's Voice*, pp. 1–2.

Fried, M. (1967). *The evolution of political society: an essay in political anthropology*. New York: McGraw-Hill.

Garbarino, M., & Sasso, R. (1994). *Native American heritage* (3rd ed.). Long Grove, IL: Waveland Press.

Giago, T. (2005, October 10). One thing Columbus didn't do. *Philadelphia Inquirer*, p. A25.

Gorman, L. (2001). *The social and economic impact of Native American casinos.* Retrieved November 2005, from http://www.nber.org/digest/feb03/29198

Grand Spiritual & Temporal Council of North American Indians. (1963). *Wyalusing Prayer Rocks: Land of peace, enchantment and mystery* [Brochure]. Wyalusing, PA: Author.

Greenbaum, S. D. (2002). *More than black: Afro-Cubans in Tampa.* Gainesville, FL: University Press of Florida.

Grobsmith, E., & Ritter, B. (1992). The Ponca Tribe of Nebraska: The process of restoration of a federally terminated tribe. *Human Organization, 51*(1), 1–16.

Gupta, A, & Ferguson, J. (1992). Beyond "culture": Space, identity and the politics of difference. *Cultural Anthropology, 7*(1), 6–23.

Harjo, S. (2006). *Cherokee wannabe:...Clues about not only what, but who Ward Churchill is.* Retrieved September 2006, from http://www.americandigest.orgmt-archives/005070.php

Harris, M. (1988). *Culture, people, nature: An introduction to general anthropology* (5th ed.). New York: Harper & Row.

Hauptman, L., & Wherry, J. (Eds.). (1990). *The Pequots in southern New England: The fall and rise of an American Indian nation.* Norman, OK: University of Oklahoma Press.

Hoxie, F. (1986). [Review of the video *Contrary Warriors: A Story of the Crow Tribe*]. *The Journal of American History, 73*(3), 838–839.

Hoxie, F. (Ed.) (1996). *Encyclopedia of North American Indians*. Boston: Houghton Mifflin.

Hultkrantz, A. (1987). *Native religions of North America: The power of visions and fertility.* Long Grove, IL: Waveland Press.

Indianz.Com. (2004). *Court rejects federal recognition for Delaware Tribe.* Retrieved February 2007, from http://www.indianz.com/News/2004/005383.asp

Jennings, F. (1993). *The founders of America: From the earliest migrations to the present.* New York: W.W. Norton.

Jones, S. (1996). Discourses of identity in the interpretation of the past. In P. Grave-Brown, S. Jones, & C. Gamble (Eds.), *Cultural identity and archaeology: The construction of European communities* (pp. 1–24). London: Routledge.

Kehoe, A. (2006). *The ghost dance: Ethnohistory and revitalization.* Long Grove, IL: Waveland.

Kennedy, J. F. (1963). Introduction. In A. T. White, *The American Indian* (p. 1). New York: Random House.

Kent, B. (1984). *Susquehanna's Indians* (Anthropological Series #6). Harrisburg, PA: Pennsylvania Historical and Museum Commission.

Knack, M. (2004). Women and men. In T. Biolsi (Ed.), *A companion to the anthropology of American Indians* (pp. 51–68). Malden, MA: Blackwell Publishers.

Koenig, A., & Stein, J. (2007). Federalism and the state recognition of Native American tribes: A survey of state-recognized tribes and state recognition processes across the United States. *Santa Clara Law Review, 48*(1), 79–154.

Kraft, H. (1986). *The Lenape: Archaeology, history and ethnography.* Newark, NJ: New Jersey Historical Society.

Krech, S. (2000). *The ecological Indian: Myth and history.* New York: W.W. Norton.

League of Women Voters of Pennsylvania. (2001). *Gambling.* Retrieved November 2005, from http://pa.lwv.org/issues/gambling

Lenape Nation—A tribal community. (2006). *Treaty of Renewed Brotherhood.* Retrieved April 2006, from http://lenapenation.org/txt/treaty signing.html

Lenape Nation. (2007, March). The Lenape Nation seeks state recognition. *Lenape Nation Newsletter,* 1–2.

Light, S., & Rand, K. (2005). *Indian gaming and tribal sovereignty: The casino compromise.* Lawrence, KS: University of Kansas Press.

Linnaeus, C. (2005). An early racial taxonomy from "Systema naturae." In M. Park (Ed.), *Biological anthropology: An introductory reader* (4th ed., pp. 156–157). New York: McGraw-Hill. (Original work published 1758)

Loewen, J. (1995). *Lies my teacher told me: Everything your American history textbook got wrong.* New York: Simon & Schuster.

Loth, D. (1949). *Chief justice: John Marshall and the growth of the Republic.* New York: Greenwood Press.

Lutz, E. (2006a). Cultural Survival calls for genographics moratorium. *Cultural Survival, 30*(3), 9.

Lutz, E. (2006b). Restoring the Abenaki. *Cultural Survival, 30*(3), 13–14.

Madison Archives. (2007). *The Madison era: Native Americans: Remarks by Ben Franklin*. Retrieved January 2007, from http://www.jmu.edu/madison/center/main_pages/madison_archives/era/native/franklin.htm

Martin, C. (2000). *The way of the human being.* New Haven, CT: Yale University Press.

Maybury-Lewis, D. (2001). *Indigenous peoples, ethnic groups and the state*. New York: Allyn & Bacon.

McBeth, S. (1984). The primer and the hoe. *Natural History, 93*(8), 4–12.

McCutchen, D. (1993). *The red road: The Wallam Olum.* New York: Avery Publishing Group.

Mieder, W. (1993). "The only good Indian is a dead Indian": History and meaning of a proverbial stereotype. *Journal of American Folklore, 106*(419), 38–60.

Miller, B. (2003). *Invisible indigenes: The politics of nonrecognition.* Lincoln, NE: University of Nebraska Press.

Miller, R. (2006). *Native America, discovered and conquered: Thomas Jefferson, Lewis & Clark and Manifest Destiny.* New York: Praeger.

Mio, J. (2003). On teaching multiculturalism: history, models and context. In G. Bernal, J. Trimble, A. K. Burlew, & F. Long (Eds.), *Handbook of racial and ethnic minority psychology* (pp. 119–146). Thousand Oaks, CA: Sage Publications.

Mitten, L. (2005). *Native American sites.* Retrieved November 2005, from http://www.nativeculturelinks.com/Indians

Nagel, J. (1995). American Indian ethnic renewal: politics and the resurgence of identity. *American Sociological Review, 60*, 947–967.

Nagel, J. (1998). *American Indian ethnic renewal: Red power and the resurgence of identity and culture.* New York: Oxford University Press.

Nanticoke Lenni-Lenape. (2006). *Our history.* Retrieved November 2007, from www.nanticokelenape.info

Navajo Central. (2007). *American Indian or Native American?* Retrieved June 2007, from http://www.navajocentral.org/indian.htm

Nietschmann, B. (1984). *Fourth world nations: Conflicts and alternatives.* Retrieved November 2006, from http://www.tamilnation.org/selfdetermination/fourthworld/bernard.htm

Oswalt, W. (1998). *This land was theirs: A study of Native Americans* (7th ed.). Mountain View, CA: Mayfield Publishing.

Pennsylvania Archaeological Council. (2001). *Project archaeology.* Retrieved September 2004, from http://www.pennarchaeologymonth.org/workshops

Porter, F. (1987). *The Nanticoke.* New York: Chelsea House Publishers.

Powers, W. (1994). Powwow. In M. Davies (Ed.), *Native America in the twentieth century* (pp. 476–480). New York: Garland Publishing Co.

Prins, H. (1994). Penobscot. In M. Davies (Ed.) *Native America in the twentieth century* (pp. 441–442). New York: Garland Publishing Co.

Richter, D. (2005). *Native Americans' Pennsylvania* (Pennsylvania History Studies Series, No. 28). University Park, PA: Pennsylvania Historical Association.

Schamel, K. (1997, July). *Update of compilation of state repatriation reburial and grave protection laws.* Retrieved November 2007, from http://www.arrowheads.com/burials.htm

Schlegel, A. (1977). Male and female in Hopi thought and action. In A. Schlegel (Ed.), *Sexual stratification* (pp. 170–178). New York: Columbia University Press.

Service, E. (1962). *Primitive social organization*. New York: Random House.

Shelton, B., & Marks, J. (2001, September). Genetic markers not a valid test of native identity. *GeneWatch, 14*(5). Retrieved October 2004, from http://www.genewatch.org/genewatch/articles/14–5nativeidentiy.html

Shields, J. (2007, February 28). The reels of fortune: Pennsylvania gamble pays off. *Philadelphia Inquirer*, p. A1.

Shively, J. (1992). Cowboys and Indians: Perceptions of Western films among American Indians and Anglos. *American Sociological Review, 57*, 725–734.

Shreeve, J. (2006, March). Reading secrets of the blood. *National Geographic, 209*(3), 70–73.

Sipe, C. H. (1927). *The Indian chiefs of Pennsylvania.* Lewisburg, PA: Wennawoods.

Speck, F. (1945). *The celestial bear comes down to earth.* Reading, PA: Reading Public Museum.

Spicer, E. (1962). *Cycles of conquest: The impact of Spain, Mexico and the United States on the Indians of the Southwest, 1553–1960*. Tucson, AZ: University of Arizona Press.

Taylor, J., M. Krepps, & P. Wang. (2000). *The national evidence on the socioeconomic impacts of American Indian gaming on non-Indian communities.* The Harvard Project on American Indian Development. Cambridge, MA: Harvard University Press.

Trimble, J., Helms, J., & Root, M. (2003). Social and psychological perspectives on ethnic and racial identity. In G. Bernal, J. Trimble, A. Burlew, & F. Long (Eds.), *Handbook of racial and ethnic minority psychology* (pp. 239–275). Thousand Oaks, CA: Sage Publications.

Ullmann, M. (2006). Vermont finally recognizes the Abenaki. *Cultural Survival, 30*(3), p. 8.

U.S. Census Bureau. (2004). *The American Indian and Alaska native population: 2000.* Washington, DC: U.S. Department of Commerce.

U.S. Const., amend. XIV, § 2.

U.S. Const., art. I, § 8.

Wallace, A. (1970). *The death and rebirth of the Seneca.* New York: Knopf.

Wallace, P. (1981). *Indians in Pennsylvania* (Anthropological Series #5). Harrisburg, PA: Pennsylvania Historical and Museum Commission.

Watts, D. (1987). *The West Indies: Patterns of development, culture and environmental change since 1492.* New York: Cambridge University Press.

Weatherford, J. (1989). *Indian givers: How the Indians of the Americas transformed the world.* New York: Ballantine Books.

Weinstein, L. (1989). *The Wampanoag.* New York: Chelsea House.

Weslager, C. (1972). *The Delaware Indians: A history.* New Brunswick, NJ: Rutgers University Press.

Whyte, M. (1978). *The status of women in preindustrial societies.* Princeton, NJ: Princeton University Press.

Wilker, J. (1992). *The Lenape Indians.* The Junior Library of American Indians. New York: Chelsea House.

Williams, R. A. (1994). Law. In M. B. Davis (Ed.), *Native America in the twentieth century* (pp. 312–316). New York: Garland Publishing.

Wilson, J. (Producer), Costner, K. (Producer/Director), & Blake, M. (Writer). (1990). *Dances with wolves*. [Motion picture]. United States: Orion Pictures.

Witmer, L. (1992). *The Indian Industrial School: Carlisle, Pennsylvania 1879–1918.* Carlisle, PA: Cumberland County Historical Society.

Wolkomir, R. (1995). Bringing ancient ways to our farmers' fields. *Smithsonian, 26*(8), 99–109.

Index